Thirty Tons a Day

Bill Veeck (1914–1986) grew up in Hinsdale, Illinois, and learned about the business of baseball when his father, William Veeck Sr., became president of the Chicago Cubs. After schooling at Phillips Academy and Kenyon College, young Veeck worked as club treasurer for the Cubs before purchasing the American Association Milwaukee Brewers. There and later as owner of the Cleveland Indians, the St. Louis Browns, and the Chicago White Sox, he brought a flamboyant, fan-oriented entrepreneurship to the game. He is best remembered for his innovative promotion of baseball and for his publicity stunts that brought fans to the ball park. He also wrote, with Ed Linn, *Veeck as in Wreck* and *Thirty Tons a Day*.

THIRTY TONS A DAY

BILL VEECK

with Ed Linn

Ivan R. Dee   *Chicago*

www.ivanrdee.com

The Viking Press edition of this book was previously catalogued by the Library of Congress as follows:

Library of Congress catalog card number: 72-76838

ISBN: 978-1-56663-828-9 (pbk : alk. paper)

To Mike,
who can tell you all about the Thirty Tons
and tell you
and tell you
and tell you . . .

Contents

viii /

Thirty Tons a Day

Introduction

Being of sound mind and in reasonable possession of my faculties, I marshaled my forces, at the tender age of fifty-four, and marched upon the city of Boston, Massachusetts, like a latter-day Ben Franklin, to seek my fame and fortune as the operator of a racetrack. Two years later, fortune having taken one look at my weathered features and shaken its hoary locks, I retreated, smiling gamely. And bravely. And winsomely.

I grew up on the Chicago West Side in the Big Bill Thompson–Al Capone era, and I always had a lively interest—precocious, my daddy thought—in chicanery, the uses and abuses of power, the flashing arc of the knife into the underbelly and the dull thump of a body in the alley. As Leo Durocher says (the baseball background does stick, doesn't it?), the Boston pols weren't getting a maiden when they got me. That's what I thought! My education was just about to begin, courtesy of—but by no means tuition-free—the Great Commonwealth.

What I got for my money was an inside look at a system that had gone corrupt. Because what is more corrupt than to pay homage to free enterprise, demanding the booty thereof, while all the time you are operating within a series of interlocking agreements that encompass not only all the alleged competitors but also all the presumed watchdogs. When we came aboard and began to rock the boat, the Attorney General took such a lively interest in our affairs, great and small, that we were never out of court. We beat him every time. I have come out of this with great faith in the American judicial system. If virtue and a bright young lawyer are on your side, you will win every time.

Virtue is optional.

It wasn't the politicians who did us in, then. The second part of my education took the form of a two-year seminar in big business, conglomerate-style. Everything didn't suddenly turn black, Judge; it slowly turned to ashes. The money poured in, like a great green sea, and poured right out again. It was like trying to operate a powerful motor boat with a hole ripped in the bottom. Down we went, with the motor roaring and the bow still straining forward.

"How sharper than a serpent's tooth it is to have a thankless child," King Lear cried out in his travail. Well, Shakespeare was a good man when he had it, but he didn't know the half of it. "More poisonous than a scorpion's tongue to have a wastrel parent"; that's more like it. For the second year of our existence, we were like a child supporting his parent's drug habit—not because we were so dutiful but because Papa controlled the bank account.We were drained dry, so we foundered.

And yet, I have to issue a small warning here. The pitfall in writing a book like this is that by the very act of compressing a four-month battle with the Attorney General into a few pages, you are creating the impression that it was a period of constant tension, vexation, and harassment. That simply isn't true. On a day-by-day basis, I was operating a racetrack, and that was always a lot of fun. So much fun that we frequently had a group of customers and waitresses hanging on, still laughing it up long after the races were over.

From beginning to end, every day was hectic, too hectic to brood upon the kind of problems that other people were being paid to handle. I was always on the go. A couple of days a week I'd have to rush back from a lunchtime speaking engagement to make the first race. Scarcely a night came around when I wasn't off somewhere, speaking. Nick Del Ninno, our incomparable publicity man, would say, "We'd better get started, Bill," and we'd be off and running. After I gave my talk we'd sit around with the people who wanted to stay, having a great time, and then we'd be off into the night and end up in some joint, tossing ideas for future promotions back and forth while the beer bottles piled up, and taking on all comers in between. Until, suddenly—and it never failed to happen—there was nobody left except me and Nick and one dim light and one last weary waitress.

In sum, the legal and financial difficulties were dark threads running through a lighter and brighter tapestry.

One other thing. I have always said that in everything I've ever ventured into, I've had the luck to run across exactly the men I needed. In addition to Rudie Schaffer, without whom I cannot function, in Boston I ran across two more: Joel Kozol, our undefeated lawyer, and Nick Del Ninno. Both of them were towers of competence when things were going good, and both of them were rocks of strength when things began to go bad. And one lady, Miss Bea Furlong.

To come out of any experience with a lot of happy memories and three such firm friends—that's not so bad a scorecard.

1

Dr. Frankenstein, I Presume

"Look for me under the arc-lights, boys. I'll be back," I wrote in what was then thought to be the last line of my autobiography. I was talking about baseball. I had departed the scene in 1961, having sold the Chicago White Sox in order to—and here comes that most ominous of all phrases—put my affairs in order. For though the medical men were in some disagreement about what was wrong with me, they were in total agreement that it was fatal. I had my choice, it seemed, between dying from cancer, from a tumor of the brain, or from the somewhat more leisurely debilitations of a stroke. Either way, I couldn't see what was to be gained by stopping smoking.

A year or so later, having persisted in staying alive and undebilitated, I returned to the Mayo Clinic for another go-around. Sonofagun, it was an aneurism alongside the brain. More rest, good food, don't aggravate yourself—and, for heaven's sake, stop smoking. Those cigarettes are going to kill you one of these days.

That's what it's like to be reprieved. I had started *Veeck—as in Wreck* in the hope of getting it all on tape before I shuffled off. And now I was going to be able to hold the finished product in my hand.

In subsequent years, I made a few passes at ball clubs, partly because that's what I had done since I was fifteen, and partly because I had

7

discovered over the years that an intimate association with the Lords of Baseball was the best therapy known to man—laughter being the medicine of the gods.

Even as an outsider, I had the contacts to feed me enough information to keep me functioning as a useful, productive member of society. There was, for instance, the hiring of General William D. Eckert as the new Commissioner, an announcement which was followed by one of the great impromptu lines of all time: "Omigod, they've hired the Unknown Soldier."

That line, uttered by Larry Fox, a previously unsung New York sportswriter, seemed to clear the typewriters of every other sportswriter in the country almost as it was clearing Fox's throat. They didn't know how right they were. The truly glorious part of the whole story is that Eckert was just as unknown to the men who hired him. He was, in a manner of speaking, the wrong man.

It came to pass, boys and girls, that in the winter of 1965 the Lords of Baseball were searching for a man to fill the shoes of Ford Frick, an admittedly difficult task in that Frick had padded discreetly through the Commissioner's office for thirteen years without leaving a single footprint.

No, that isn't altogether fair. Baseball wasn't looking for an empty pair of shoes this time around. Troublemakers, malcontents, and other enemies of the commonweal had been trying to chip away at the special exemption baseball enjoys from the antitrust laws, and the owners were looking for somebody with lots and lots of influence in Washington. John Galbreath, the owner of the Pittsburgh Pirates and everything else on his side of the horizon, was the power on the screening committee, and his candidate was General Curtis LeMay, that being back in the days when generals were still riding high in the halls of Congress. General LeMay wasn't interested, but he received the members of the screening committee in order to extol the virtues of General Eckert, a man whom, he could assure the committee, he had worked with for years and could recommend wholeheartedly. And Galbreath and his committee jumped. They jumped for him because, although they had presumably heard the name right, they had confused it in their minds with that of General Eugene Zuckert, who had only recently retired as Secretary of the Air Force.

It was, let us concede, an honest mistake. LeMay and Zuckert had been associated together for years. They had come to their high offices as military and civilian heads of the Air Force at the same time, had run the Air Force together for four years, and had retired at approximately the same time. Zuckert was a man of considerable weight within the ruling circles. Exactly the kind of man they were looking for.

Eckert was something else again. The stark truth is that LeMay was pushing Eckert precisely because Eckert didn't have enough prestige or influence to do himself, let alone baseball, any good. Eckert had been the Chief Supply Officer under General LeMay in Europe and had continued to serve under him, as his chief procurement officer, in the postwar years. He had retired, five years earlier, after suffering a heart attack, and was scuffling around as a lobbyist in Washington. LeMay was simply doing what he could for an old Army buddy who needed a job.

The screening committee went to see Eckert thinking he was somebody else, and when they found out their mistake they decided, what the heck, they had set out to get themselves a general who had influence in Washington, and this guy qualified—he was a lobbyist, wasn't he?—on both counts. Besides, he had captured their hearts right off the bat by admitting that he didn't know a thing about baseball. That qualified him on three counts.

Eckert had also told them, quite frankly, that he was nothing but a rather colorless administrator. "If you're looking for a personality kid," he said, "I'm not your man."

Wow! A general who knew his place. The worrisome thing about Curtis LeMay was that he had a reputation for chewing down on his cigar and telling people what they had to do. This new guy, however he was, had fallen to them like a gift from heaven. This Eckert, whoever he was, was so perfect that nobody had ever heard of him.

They hired him at $75,000 a year.

If Frick didn't leave any footprints, Eckert didn't even cast a shadow. Three years later they paid him off and hired Bowie Kuhn, a Wall Street lawyer. Kuhn treats the Commissionership as if he were still a lawyer and the owners were his clients. He is, in short, out to protect them, not to police them.

Leave it to the Lords of Baseball to find just the kind of man baseball doesn't need at the time. A strong administrator might have forced the owners to smarten up and get their labor relations in order. A lawyer for the defense won't.

As far as my own club-hunting was concerned, I had beamed my not necessarily welcome attention upon the Washington Senators. The original expansion franchise had ended up in the hands of a nine-man syndicate that had placed it under the command of former Air Force General Elwood Quesada, and he was running it about as effectively as I would have run his Air Force. I wanted to operate in Washington for many reasons. The ball club was so bad it had to improve. The city was so ripe for anything that would provide fun, excitement, and maybe even hope, that it would be practically impossible to make a mistake. Washington hasn't had a pennant-winner since 1933, and the longer a city has been without a pennant, the more valuable it becomes, to my way of thinking.

And oh, yes. The best reason of all. In 1963, I got the word that the club was up for grabs. My partner in the pursuit was Nate Dolin, the man who had put together the syndicate that had bought the Cleveland Indians from me, thirteen years earlier.

Now, I am going to tell you something about both Nate Dolin and that sale, and I want you to take my word that this is essential background for the explanation of how I ended up in racing instead of baseball. Nate was the box-office manager, and later treasurer, of the Cleveland Arena while I was operating the Indians. He is unschooled. He comes off the streets. Which only means that he doesn't have any degree to confirm the fact that he is a financial wizard. It might even be said that Nate and I have always got along so well because he has as naïve a mind as I do when it comes to bookkeeping. *Note:* Don't ever, ever sneer at bookkeeping; that's where the fortunes are made.

When I found it necessary, for good and sufficient personal reasons, to sell the Cleveland Indians, Nate and I figured out a way to make the club worth more money to his syndicate and thereby, from where I was sitting, increase the selling price. Actually, it was Nate who came up with the basic concept. I just did a little of the filigree work on it. But if you're a promoter you've got to take credit for other people's ideas. I've taken credit for this one for so long that not only am I firmly convinced that I dreamed it up, but I suspect that Nate may have come around to my way of thinking.

It is a tax gimmick that has doubled the worth of all ball clubs.

Keeping it simple, it went like this. Instead of selling the corporation, I would, in effect, sell the players' contracts to a newly organized corporation, individually or in one big package. The difference is this. When you buy a corporation, you are buying a stock. When you buy players you are buying assets which can be depreciated—along with the new typewriter and new furniture—over a period of five years. The corporation tax at the time was 50 per cent. And that means that if you paid $5 million for the club, you would be saving about $2.5 million that would otherwise have been paid in taxes.

To put it boldly and unblushingly, the government is paying half the purchase for you. *If you have been able to earn the $5 million to apply it against.*

All right. Store all this business about the depreciation allowance in the back of your mind, because it is going to come back to haunt both of us. A direct line can be drawn between that day in 1949 when Nate sat across my desk and spelled the thing out to me, and the day, nineteen years later, when we walked into Suffolk Downs together to inform the gathered press that I was the new president of the track.

There is a Hand, my friends, which guides our destinies toward other ends than we planned. And I wish He'd cut it out!

Now that I have established my credentials in high finance and in sophomore philosophy, we will turn our eyes back to the financial and philosophical situation in Washington.

Unlike every other club in baseball, the Quesada group had been set up not as a corporation but as a small-business partnership with ten shares split up among nine partners. That was a tax gimmick too. Each of the shares had gone for $300,000, and by setting it up as a partnership, the investors, wealthy sportsmen all, would be able to write their anticipated losses off against personal income. As simple as that.

The only flaw in the arrangement was that the losses had come faster and surer than any of them had anticipated. After two years, the original stake had been completely wiped out, and each of the partners was faced with a choice between getting up some fresh money or accepting our offer of $5 million and getting out with a $200,000 profit per share. Being intelligent men, they voted 8 to 2 to sell.

The strong men in the old set-up were two Washington investment bankers, James M. Johnston, the man who had taken the two shares, and his business partner, Jim Lemon—who is not, to clear up any misunderstanding, the ballplayer of the same name. They were so anxious to sell that they even helped Nate arrange a $3,750,000 loan at their Washington bank, the American Security & Trust Co.

Now we're back to the wonderful world of finance again. When you're buying anything with a short bankroll, the idea is to find a way to come out with the most possible ownership for the least possible amount of money. This time it was Nate who did some filigree work on a debenture-stock gimmick which I had invented for the benefit of myself and my backers when I bought the Indians.

The D. C. financing was set up this way: We were paying $5 million for the club, and putting out only $350,000 for stock, a leverage of over 14 to 1. The bank loan of $3,750,000 was, of course, being made not to us but to the club. That left us with the necessity of taking our $350,000 worth of stock and cranking $1,250,000 out of it. It was done in two steps:

1. Nate and I were going to buy 30 per cent of the stock for $105,000.

2. The remaining 70 per cent of the stock ($245,000) was to be sold as a part of a debenture-stock offering, in a 4-to-1 ratio. A debenture is nothing but a loan. Money to be paid back. We (meaning the corporation) were therefore borrowing $980,000 from the other stockholders. For those of you who have followed the arithmetic, the additional $80,000 over the purchase price was for working capital.

Nate and I were also going to take 10 per cent of the debenture-stock issue, which would cost us another $122,500. That gave us 37-per-cent ownership for $227,500.

Part of the agreement with Johnston and Lemon was that after we reorganized we would sell each of them back one-seventh of the combination stock and debenture, at a cost of $175,000, which would result in their still owning 10 per cent of the company. In other words, they were going to get back their 10-per-cent ownership as a now fully financed operation, plus a $25,000 profit, plus another $140,000 that would be owed to them on their debentures. Johnston would also be realizing a flat $200,000 profit on his extra share. Pretty good deal, huh?

A couple of days later, we got the word that Johnston didn't want it any more. Johnston now wanted to buy the 10 per cent in straight stock (i.e., without any debentures), which would have cost them $35,000 each, instead of $175,000 each, and forced us to dig up another $280,000 somewhere else.

Well, we weren't going to accept a deal like that. And Johnston knew we weren't going to accept a deal like that.

What had happened was this. After the loan had been arranged, Johnston and Lemon had driven Nate to the airport, and in the course of that ride Nate had outlined our entire financial structure for the benefit of our new partners. The way we figured it, Johnston had decided that what was good enough for us was good enough for him. The original partnership contract had contained right of first refusal which gave any of the partners the right to match any outside offer. Johnston decided that he would match ours.

I had never met Johnston up to that point, but I knew enough about him to be able to work up a pretty firm psychological portrait. People buy ball clubs for many different reasons these days, none of them having a thing to do with the love of the game. They buy them to sell insurance, to grab the TV-radio rights, to pitch their beer. The one common denominator is visibility. The moment a man becomes the owner of a big-league franchise he becomes an instant celebrity. Automatically newsworthy. Eminently quotable. For all his material success, Johnston had never been looked upon as anything more than the guy who paid the bills. It was only with his emergence as the power in the Senators' operation that he had finally won a public identity. On the other hand, leading investment bankers do not like to lose money; it flies against their image of themselves. The beauty of latching on to Nate's debenture-stock plan was that it would allow him to cut his losses and congratulate himself for doing it so cleverly, without ever having to admit to himself that he was on an ego trip.

Sooner or later, if I read my man right, the thrill would be gone. In the meantime I could let my continuing interest in the Senators be known to the press. Whenever I wandered into Washington, I passed the word on to people who could be counted upon to carry the message back to Johnston.

For two years I sat back and waited. And then, early one summer afternoon, Lemon called from Chicago to ask Nate if we could be at the Johnston building at eight o'clock that evening to meet with them. "I've got to take it all back, Bill," Nate said. "You were right. It looks like we've got it."

You're darn right we had it. Johnston was so anxious to unload that he was rushing back from New York. Secret meeting and all. Did I know my man or didn't I?

Nate caught the next plane out of Cleveland. I drove in from Easton, sixty miles away, and we had dinner together. A dinner that was punctuated by frequent laughter and triumphant smiles.

Johnston and Lemon were waiting for us by the elevators. The building was empty. Lemon motioned to us, and we followed them through the high, deserted corridor. The tiled floor was so clean and smooth that you had the feeling your shoes would squeak if you stepped down too hard, a grievous social error.

Into the darkened brokerage office we went. Into Johnston's lighted office. Johnston slipped behind the desk. We remained standing on the other side. Lemon stationed himself more or less between us.

At last, Lemon spoke. "We don't want to sell," he said.

Of course. They didn't want to sell. THEY DIDN'T WANT TO SELL????

"Well, okay," I said. "But what is the meeting for? What did you want to see us about?"

Well, they had wanted to talk to me, Lemon said. "You've never met Mr. Johnston."

I said, "No, I have never met Mr. Johnston."

He said, "We thought it would be nice if you did."

I said, "Nice to meet you, Mr. Johnston."

He seemed equally happy to meet me.

We chatted for five or ten uncomfortable minutes more, but I was in such a whirl of confusion that I couldn't for the life of me have told you what it was about three minutes after we left.

Obviously something had happened between the time the call was made and the time we met. What it was, I never did find out. I'm not going to ask Lemon what happened, either, although if he ever wants to tell me he will find a most attentive listener.

Some time later Roger Kahn, an old friend, was interviewing one of baseball's most eminent citizens, in the course of putting together one of his *Esquire* columns, when he casually asked, "What about Bill Veeck?" The baseball man shook his head. "Uh-uh, never. From what I hear, never." Not long afterward Roger repeated that conversation to another bright, knowledgeable operator. "Jesus Christ, never quote me," the operator said. "But you can take my word for it. He'll never get back in the game."

That would put a new light on what had happened between Chicago and Washington. It would put a new light on a lot of things. Even to the reneging on the first deal back in 1963. Maybe it wasn't Nate Dolin's financial fandango that had done us in, after all. Nobody can own any part of a big-league club until he has been certified as acceptable by the league office. One does have to consider the possibility that I may have been stamped "Unacceptable" and that Johnston was advised to get out of the deal with the least possible embarrassment to anyone.

But, you know, it's hard to believe. I have a lot of friends in baseball, and it seems likely that somewhere along the line somebody would have told me. But, then . . . suppose I sued, and they were called to testify. They'd be in the terribly uncomfortable position of turning their backs on their colleagues or turning their backs on me. The way I feel right now, I'd prefer to believe that it isn't true. To have tried and failed is one thing. To have labored to no purpose is quite another. It is the difference, I suppose, between losing honorably and being cheated out of a few good years of life.

Washington still beckoned. As the 1967 season came to an end, I received word from a most reliable source that Johnston was so ill that he had set his attorneys to clearing up his estate. The executor was Norman Frost, who had been the lawyer for the Washington club since the days of the Griffiths. Taking inflation and the general feel of the situation into account, I upped my offer to $6.5 million. Frost's attitude was so encouraging that I invited Elston Howard and his wife to breakfast on the opening day of the World Series to find out whether Ellie would be interested in managing the club if I got it.

After the World Series, however, Frost took a wait-and-see attitude, and this time I could understand it. The American League had met in Chicago, in more or less solemn conclave, immediately following the World Series, to consider the request of Charles O. Finley, that lovable madcap, to move his club to Oakland—or, I suppose, anywhere that would have him. (This would make them the Philadelphia–Kansas City–Oakland Athletics and allow them to ride shotgun in the gypsy caravan that had previously been occupied only by the Boston–Milwaukee–Atlanta Braves.) Following a good-grief-they're-doing-it-again fandango of illegal meetings, broken promises, and double dealings they voted to (1) permit Finley to move and (2) put expansion clubs into Kansas City and Seattle in 1971 "or as soon as is practicable." That won them a threatened Congressional investigation by Senator Symington, and so they met in a hastily called rump session at 1:30 a.m. and voted—illegally, since they needed seven votes and only six clubs were represented—to expand immediately.

Frost, who is a good lawyer, was bright enough to realize that although the prices that are charged for expansion franchises are purely artificial—i.e., the cost for admission into a very exclusive club—a psychological phenomenon would come into play which would automatically escalate the prices of the established clubs, even so deplorable a club as the Senators. And he was right. The American League set their initiation fee at $8 million, and the National League at $10 million.

The following October, Johnston died, and the Washington Senators were up for grabs. Nate and I came in with an initial offer of $6 million. We were prepared to go up to $6.5 million.

A year earlier, it had been too little, too soon. This time, it was too little, too late. Now that the club was officially on the market, there were other entries, other bids. Bob Hope, whom I had invited into the Cleveland Indians as a small stockholder, had always had a yen for the Senators. We had talked about getting into it together from time to time— just chatter, you know—and I had intended to let him in for a piece of the debenture-stock deal if he was still interested. Bob Short had been shopping for a ball club from the time he sold the Los Angeles Lakers, and he came popping out of the weeds too. Short came in with a bid of $9 million, and Hope matched it. To break the deadlock Short went higher.

We had figured the top dollar the club was worth to us, and maybe a little more. And we were 3 million short.

How could that be? Simple. Remember, I told you to hold on to the business about the depreciation of the players. Nate and I were calculating on the basis of what the club was worth to an independent operator. Bob Hope has a vast financial and real-estate empire; Bob Short has a private conglomerate that includes his trucking companies and his hotels. When you can absorb a ball club into a vast and profitable operation, you don't have to worry about showing a profit with the ball club in order to take advantage of the depreciation write-off. You know, up front, that you will be able to write it off against the guaranteed profits of your other holdings. You also know, conversely, that, under the worst of conditions, the club can be supported by the rest of the empire.

So what happened to Bob Short? The same thing, for those of you who enjoy black humor, that happened to Suffolk Downs. Short bought the club almost entirely with borrowed money, perhaps counting upon using the depreciation allowance to take care of interest. What happened was that the collapsing economy bathed his hitherto thriving conglomerate in red ink and forced him to run back to the bank for more money.

Mickey Weil, who was representing Hope, talked to me about combining forces, with Hope putting up the money and me running the club for a piece of the action. But to run a club is a full-time job for me. I don't just work at it, I live it. If I'm doing all the work, I want a commensurate share of the profits.

What the Washington bidding did accomplish was to confirm, once and for all, that an independent operator like myself had been eliminated from the baseball scene. The fact that Nate and I had created the means of our own destruction was only a wry historical footnote, a final irony. Hi there, Dr. Frankenstein. . . .

"Well," Nate said. "What about Suffolk Downs?"

Nate had been throwing Suffolk Downs at me, on and off, for about a year on behalf of a New York company named Realty Equities. Nate had become involved in a couple of deals with them and had ended up with a considerable amount of their stock. As a matter of fact, the subject had first come up immediately after the unsuccessful sortie in 1967.

Realty Equities is a publicly owned corporation which had done wondrously well in real estate. Its president, Morris Karp, was described to me as a financial genius, and it was hardly worth being a financial genius in those days if you didn't diversify and become a full-fledged conglomerate. Realty's primary interest in Suffolk, as Nate explained it to me, wasn't in the racetrack itself, it was in the two hundred acres of land the track stood upon. Still, if they closed the deal, they were going to have a track on their hands, and they were willing to let us in on a piece of the ownership to run it for them.

The collapse of the Senator deal had left me feeling at loose ends. I was aching to get back into action. Not that I had been vegetating for seven years. Not with six kids at home and a monster of a mansion to keep up. We had written a couple of books. I had written a syndicated column for four years, I had conducted a TV show out of Chicago for a year and a half, and I still had a syndicated radio show. I had also been writing a great many book reviews and an occasional magazine article.

For steady income, I was a consultant for the National Brewery Company (National Bohemian Beer), which is owned by Jerry Hoffberger, who also owns The Baltimore Orioles. It always pleased me to say that I was paid $25,000 for working one day a month, and if anyone wanted to leap to the conclusion that I was the highest-paid consultant, by the hour, in captivity, who was I to disabuse them? The truth, of course, is that we had a monthly meeting to talk over the ideas that had been fermenting in my sometimes overheated brain during the previous twenty-nine days.

And I had been on the lecture circuit for about six years. My agreement with the agency was that they would hold down my engagements to three or four a month and do their best to bunch them within roughly the same period of time and if possible in the same section of the country. My interests are primarily inquisitive and acquisitive, and the lecture circuit took care of both of those needs quite adequately. My fee was roughly $1000 a shot and, though the agency cut came out of that, you can see that you don't have to go out more than four or five times a month to end up with something around $50,000 for the year. Beyond that, it satisfied my need to get around the country, exchange views with a wide variety of people, and—yes—to catch a corner of the limelight. A man is what he is, and I'm a publicity hound. Why should I deny it? I find few things quite so delightful in life as to have my opinion solicited by the new crop of newspapermen and to swap a few yarns with the old ones. Publicity hounds never die; they keep right on talking away.

Not a completely unsatisfactory life, then. But not a completely satisfactory one, either. "I don't know, Nate," I said. "I'm guess I'm kind of interested. Why don't you go see your friends again. Get me the details, and we'll see what happens."

Well, to begin with, it entailed no money, and that's the most interesting kind of deal you can make. I was to become president of the track at a salary of $50,000 plus an unlimited expense account. Nate and I would each get 10 per cent of any profits over a million dollars and—here comes the really attractive part of the proposition—we would both be given a five-year option to buy 15 per cent of the track. If you've come this far, I don't have to tell you that we were not lacking in confidence that we could devise a way to use the anticipated bonanza from our 10-per-cent override to pay for the option.

There was one other thing. The irreducible part of the deal as far as I was concerned was that I would have absolute control over every phase of the operation. I had never run anything for anybody else before, and I know myself well enough to understand that I am probably constitutionally incapable of accepting suggestions, let alone direction, from some money men sitting in an ivory tower in New York. To keep our relationship at a healthy distance, it was understood that all dealings between us would continue to take place through Nate. Not only in working out the mechanics of the contract, but in any other matter that might ever come up.

Through the full year of the negotiations, I met with Karp only twice.

He turned out to be a tall fellow, just beginning to show a bit of a pot belly but otherwise rather nice-looking and obviously bright. He endorsed my view of a proper working relationship enthusiastically. He and his associates had all they could do to take care of their rapidly burgeoning empire. The less they had to be involved with Suffolk Downs, the better they would like it.

Obviously I did not leap at the offer. Hank Greenberg, who is doing every bit as well in the investment business as he did in baseball, checked the company out for me, and so did a neighbor of mine from across the Creek, Steve Bremer, who is a broker. They both reported back that Realty's stock, which was listed on the American Exchange, had been going up steadily, and that from everything they had been able to gather from their financial statements the company looked to be in good shape. Both suggested caution, however.

And, finally, I did what any man of minimal intelligence would do. I took the deal to Louie Jacobs. You've probably never heard of Louie Jacobs. Well, Louie was the owner of Emprise, the largest racetrack and ballpark concessionaire in the country. He had owned more racetracks, in part or in whole, and knew more about racetracks, than anyone else in the country.

Louie always had the reputation of being a tough, hardheaded businessman. Well, there are hardheaded businessmen and there are hardheaded businessmen. If you put it to Louie that you wanted to sit down with him, with your respective lawyers at your side, and work out a deal with all the *whereases, what ifs* and thirty-day escape clauses, Louie Jacobs would not rise from his chair. If you went to him, in all sincerity, with both hands above the table and let's keep the lawyers out of this, Louie would break his back for you. Oh, he'd probably do it with a gruff ill grace because, like many other men who have had their essential nature crusted over early in life, he was embarrassed by an act of generosity.

All I ever had to know about Louie Jacobs I learned in my first real contact with him. I had become the poor but proud owner of a debt-ridden minor-league ball club in Milwaukee, at the age of twenty-eight, for the excellent reason that no one else wanted any part of it. The largest debt—something like $20,000— was owed to Sportservice, and the president of the American Association informed me that Louie had not only agreed to wipe the slate clean but, knowing that I had been running the concessions for the Cubs at Wrigley Field, had volunteered to help me out even further by turning the contract back to me.

Immediately, I got Louie on the phone to ask whether he really wanted to cancel out the debt and waive his rights.

"Of course I don't want to," he growled. "What kind of a fool do you take me for! I'll put it this way: I'm *willing* to. I'd like to see you make a go of this thing, and if you want to know the truth, your chances of pulling it off are so remote that you need every bit of help you can get."

"Well," I said, "that's nice of you but it's also a little silly. I'm not looking to run out on any debts. All I really need is a little time. If you're willing to give me the time, I want to reinstate the debt and extend the contract."

"Do whatever you want," he told me gruffly. "Draw up any kind of contract you want and I'll sign without reading it."

For twenty-five years Louie had remained my friend, my confidant, and my benefactor. When I went into the Marines I gave him my power of attorney, and my affairs were in much better shape when I returned than when I left. Later, when I went out in search of a big-league club, it was Louie who tipped me off that the majority of the stock in the Cleveland Indians was owned not by the president of the club, as everyone seemed to think, but by a couple of middle-aging brothers who were, insofar as baseball was concerned, virtual recluses and would probably be receptive to any decent offer.

The night before my option ran out, the league notified me that one of my investors was unacceptable. The banks would open at nine. The option would run out at eleven. Somewhere within those two hours, I had to come up with a cashier's check for $150,000. Guess who I called? Louie sent me to the Shaker Heights mansion of Sammy Haas, Cleveland's leading criminal lawyer. Haas was willing to lend me the money, at no interest, for an indeterminate time, on nothing more than Louie's recommendation.

I could go on and on and on, but I think you've got the idea. So I went to Buffalo and sat down with Louie at the 41 Club, the spot where I always met him and which I would suppose he had a piece of. It turned out that Louie had been involved in an attempt to purchase Suffolk Downs himself at one time, and he knew everything that was to be known about the place. After the deal had been laid out before him, he said, "You can't afford to turn it down, Bill. Fifteen per cent ownership on a $12-million property. That's too good a deal to blow."

We spent the whole day together. We had lunch, and we drank some beer, and pretty soon it was time for dinner; when they were ready to close the joint down, we were still drinking beer.

In between the guzzling, I told him that if the thing worked out I'd be wanting him to come in as the concessionaire. Public bids would have to be asked for, as he very well knew, but I somehow had all the confidence in the world that we could arrange to have him match any other offer.

"I'll tell you what," he said. And then he began to smile. "You draw up any kind of contract you want, and I'll sign without reading it. . . ."

We looked across the table, and we were looking back across twenty-five years. "Oh no you don't!" I roared. "Then you're going to expect me to lean over backward not to write too onerous a contract. You suckered me into that kind of a deal once, and you're not going to sucker me into it again."

Would that I could have. Before I took over as president of Suffolk Downs, I was flying into Buffalo again to serve as a pallbearer at Louie Jacobs' funeral. It was an unbelievably hot day for Buffalo. On sudden impulse I told the taxi driver to take me to the 41 Club. I went in, sat at the same table, and ordered a couple of beers. One for Louie and one for me. A foolish and sentimental gesture, I suppose, but it had a meaning for me. As the years go by, I find myself burying more and more old friends. I was in no hurry at all to get to the funeral home.

If Louie had been alive, the adventure at Suffolk Downs would have had a far different ending.

I should explain here that months and months had intervened between those two trips to Buffalo. Well over a year. After the first trip, I had given Nate the go-ahead to have the agreement drawn up. It sat on my desk for ten months. Even with Louie's seal of approval, I hadn't been able to shake a nagging, overhanging sense of misgiving that had nothing at all to do with the possibility that we still might get a shot at the Washington Senators. There were nights when I sat over that contract until two o'clock in the morning, giving myself every possible reason why it was ridiculous not to put my signature to it. And then I'd put down the pen and go to bed.

I was fifty-four years old, you understand, and I knew that whatever I turned my hand to next was probably going to be the last throw of the dice. I wanted it to be right. I wanted to be sure.

At last, in November of 1968, Nate told me that I had to make up my mind. The negotiations for the purchase of the track had been spluttering along through those entire ten months, and Realty had run out of excuses. The point had been reached where they were going to have to submit a proxy statement to the Securities and Exchange Commission. If I was coming in, Realty would have to make full disclosure on the details of our contract. If I weren't, they'd have to decide whether they wanted to go ahead without me.

Well . . . It was no more than two weeks after we had failed to enchant anybody with our $6-million offer for the Senators. Baseball was definitely out, and yet the latest chase after the Senators had triggered something in me. I had come to feel that I had been living in bits and pieces. The time had come, I felt, to do something that could be described in a word rather than a paragraph.

Racetrack operator was good enough.

"Okay, Nate," I said. "Tell them to go ahead."

2

Dream and I'll Dream with You

The Paddock Club is a glass-enclosed membership restaurant which sits atop the clubhouse. Shortly before the gates were to be thrown open on our first day, I found myself gazing out upon the ten thousand empty grandstand seats down below. Ten thousand seats, freshly painted in royal blue. That's what my life has been, putting people into just those kind of seats. And for the first time in my life I was at a loss.

Way off behind me, at the other end of the room, a team of carpet men were taking the final tucks out of the two tons of green carpeting that had been laid two days earlier. Two tons of freshly laid carpet cover an awful lot of floor and also give off an awful odor of burning glue. Closer behind me, where the concession people were setting up a buffet table, the steam was just beginning to rise. The reason they were setting up a buffet table in our plush, glass-enclosed membership restaurant was that they had not been able to get the kitchen ready in time.

Through a freak of lighting in this dark and overcast day, my reflection came swimming back at me from the glass in broken, disjointed pieces, like the reflection of a face in a pool. On such a day as this, I thought, Narcissus himself would have been overcome by modesty at the sight of himself, and the whole body of psychiatric literature would have been the poorer.

We had set our sights on an attendance of 30,000 and a record handle of $2.5 million. Everything that could be done had been done, and still I didn't know. In a ball park, you can take your advance sale, put it into an equation with the attraction and the weather, and estimate within a thousand of what your attendance is going to be. Sure, you'll get trapped once in a while with a flash crowd. Like the first time Satchel Paige pitched in Cleveland. We thought we'd get 55,000, and we ended up with 78,000.

On a racetrack there is no advance sale except for the membership in the Paddock Club (which doesn't guarantee they are going to be there on any given day) and a relative handful—768—of box seats. And that leaves you with very little to go by except the day of the week and the seat of your pants.

Understand one thing. This is not just a guessing game you are playing for your own amusement. Decisions are made on the basis of your day-to-day estimates that are going to be reflected in your end-of-the-year profit-and-loss statement. How many mutuel clerks are you going to put on? How many ushers should you hire? What kind of parking facilities must be opened up?

If you've estimated 21,000 and you get 19,000, you are 10-per-cent overstaffed. Turn the figures the other way, and you are not providing the services to which the customers are entitled.

In baseball, the equation is set up so scientifically that you can sit down and figure out what happened to those 2000 people. Or, as in the case of Satchel Paige, why we got that extra 23,000. I can assure you that we didn't underestimate Satch's drawing power again. On a racetrack, you can come up with a thousand explanations, none of them valid. For the benefit of connoisseurs, "It was such a nice day that everyone went to the Cape," is the all-time favorite.

A week later, under equivalent circumstances, you estimate 19,000 and get 23,000. "It was such a nice day that everyone decided to come out to the track."

I'm not only talking about myself, I'm talking about everybody. Rockingham Park's Lou Smith, the patriarch of New England racing, was so sure he was going to shatter all records on the first running of the New Hampshire lottery—not just an all-time record, but 50 per cent above the all-time record—that he called for helicopters to handle the traffic and set up special concession stands in the infield. All he got for his trouble was peace and quiet. Less than an average Saturday crowd showed up.

I had admittedly complicated whatever equation there might have been by cutting off all the passes. If all the people who had made it a point of honor to tell me they were never going to set foot inside Suffolk could be counted upon to keep their word, we were in for the greatest nonattendance in the history of American sports.

The weather wasn't going to do us a world of good, either. It had been raining when I got up at 5:30 A.M. and hadn't seemed to be letting up a bit when I dove back under the covers at 5:31. Off and on, it had been raining all morning.

On the more positive side, our opening attraction, the Lady Godiva Handicap—eight girl jockeys on eight three-year-old fillies—had caught on so well that we had a flock of out-of-town writers gracing the grounds. But that could be misleading. Writers like Dave Condon (Chicago *Tribune*), Barney Nagler *(Morning Telegraph)*, and Stan Isaacs (Long Island *Newsday*) were old friends. Whether they had been drawn to Suffolk by the quality of the event or out of friendship for the Old Operator was impossible to tell.

In the interest of full disclosure and accuracy, I did have to admit that I seemed to be coming back into style. For three months, I had been speaking all around the Boston area, and night after night I had been greeted by a heady mixture of kindness and enthusiasm.

I looked down at all those empty seats and, whatever my sense of uncertainty, I couldn't see where anything would be gained by lowering my sights.

One thing I did know. I had tried to do too much, too fast.

And yet, thinking back on the deep depression that had settled over me after I had inspected the track for the first time, we had come a long, long way.

Arthur McCue picked me up at the airport motel the morning after I had been introduced to the press. I had been to the track the day before—in the door and up in the elevator—and now I wanted to see it. Early in the morning, before anybody else was there.

To get to Suffolk Downs, you drive out of the airport onto Route C-1, a workhorse two-lane highway which runs along the back section of East Boston. A couple of miles at most, and you come upon a huge sign that directs you into the track. Once you have turned into the access road, you become aware that the sign had been obscuring a large oil farm. Oil farms are blights upon the landscape and all that, but they carry a rich and powerful cargo. Rich land. Money everywhere. Down toward the end, the access road curves around to the left and the plant, set back behind the parking area, comes into view. Like a factory, I thought. That was my first thought upon seeing Suffolk Downs. It was a dismal November morning anyway, dark and dreary and drizzling. The joint looked like a factory, I thought. A dirty, dingy factory.

As we turned into the curve, I could see that they had built a fence around it. Topped by barbed wire, yet. "What's the fence for?" I asked Arthur. "To keep the people in or out?"

From that close up, I could also see that the exterior had been painted —once upon a time—in a sleazy green and dirty gray. It didn't look so much like a factory to me any more. It looked like a concentration camp.

Well, at least I knew what the first item on the agenda was going to be. I was going to tear that miserable fence down.

The inside was even grimmer. And grayer. Under anything approaching normal conditions, a certain airy, structural beauty is imparted to the most functional of stadiums by the open latticework of ramps and staircases. Somebody had sealed this place tight by constructing a false ceiling underneath the upper staircases. By then painting the ceiling over in the always popular prison gray, they had given the place all the charm and grace of the county jail.

The first thing I do in any new operation is inspect the lavatories. I expect that they will be unfit for human beings, and I have never been disappointed. These lavatories had an abomination all their own. Pay toilets. Holy smoke. You charge them to get in, you charge them for food and drink, and then you clip them for another dime to do what comes naturally.

"That's the second thing," I told Arthur. "Those obscenities are going to be knocked out of here."

There was still one last little delicacy to delight us. Between the grandstand and the clubhouse, we found a lavatory that could be entered from either area. The door on the grandstand side said: MEN. On the clubhouse side, it said: GENTLEMEN.

"The caste system strikes again," Arthur said. "I'm beginning to get an awful feeling that we're back in the Corps, Bill."

I had met Arthur in the Marines. On Bougainville. He would have been a kid of nineteen then—everybody was a kid of nineteen then—and I was an ancient twenty-nine. When you're a twenty-nine-year-old Marine, you're ancient enough to be known as Pops. I was not only ancient, I was ridiculous. But certainly no more ridiculous than Arthur McCue. Arthur was a small kid with a tendency toward pudginess, and he had this wonderfully strange and interesting voice that made it inevitable that he was going to be called "Squeaky."

Even more than his voice, though, it was his personality that miscast him. Arthur was a gentle man, the most gentle man I have ever known. Not that he wasn't courageous in battle. He was. But basically he always left you with the feeling that he thought this whole business of shooting at people was—well, ridiculous.

Arthur didn't want to hurt anybody. All in the world Arthur ever wanted to be was a second baseman. He had been an All-Scholastic second baseman around Boston, and his consuming ambition was to play in the major leagues. Unfortunately, desire and dedication aren't enough to do the trick; it takes a very special and unique talent. Either it's there or it isn't there. With Arthur, it was almost, but not quite. He couldn't hit quite well enough or run quite fast enough, and his arm wasn't quite strong enough.

When we were brought back to Guadalcanal, Arthur—with perhaps some minimal help from the colonel—organized a division ball team. I had been carted back with one leg in a cast and the other rotting away from jungle fungus. That didn't stop me from becoming his manager. Arthur would come breezing into the barracks, pick me up and put me into a wheelchair, and deliver me to the ball field, where he and I—the two permanent Pfcs—would have ourselves a marvelous time putting the captains and the majors through their paces. "Hey, you bum," he'd squeak at a twenty-three-year-old captain. "Get your butt in gear. I catch you dogging it one more time, Mister, and you can turn in your uniform." And then he'd throw me a broad wink, and, Squeaky being Squeaky, we'd all throw back our heads and roar.

In the worst of times he was the best of friends. When at last I was about to be flown back to the States in a hospital plane, it was Squeaky who came down on a terribly stormy day with—well, it looked like the whole darn regiment to see old Pops off.

We never lost touch. Arthur got married and went to work for the telephone company. Any time I landed a ball club I'd give him a call and hire him to bird-dog high-school kids for us in his spare time. When the Cleveland Indians pulled into Boston in 1948, for the playoff game against the Red Sox, who was standing there on the platform, grinning from ear to ear, but our local bird dog. He hadn't been able to make it, but I had, see, and he took such pride in my success that if I'd had the slightest spark of decency I'd have been ashamed of myself.

What could have been more natural, then, than that I should have picked up the phone to tell Arthur that we were back in business? "I'm coming into your back yard this time," I said. "And I'm going to need your help."

"What do I know about racing?" He protested. "All I'd do would be to get in your way."

Good! We'd be starting out even. "Hey, Arthur!" I chuckled. "Think of all the fun we're gonna have learning."

I knew what I wanted Arthur to do. I wanted him to be there. This was going to be the last roll of the dice, and I wanted him to have the pleasure of enjoying my success with me. Not from outside. Not even from inside. From right alongside.

Six weeks later, when I officially took over the reins, we unfurled a banner across the top of the plant.

OPENS APRIL 19 FOR RACING UNDER NEW MANAGEMENT

A week before that immodestly advertised opening, I had some placards painted to be spread around the racetrack;

WE'RE SORRY
TOO MUCH SNOW
TOO MUCH INDECISION
—Bill Veeck

A winsome and winning confession of fallibility, no? Now that I have a somewhat larger canvas to work on, I am changing my plea to guilty, with an explanation:

A racetrack is more than a racetrack. It is a plant. With its three large dining rooms and the spacious upper and lower concourses which house the concession and betting areas, Suffolk Downs has more floor space, in terms of total square footage, than any auditorium or exhibition hall in New England. It can also provide more parking space. What that means is that the premises can be rented out between the harness season and the Thoroughbred season. They had, in fact, been rented out to the Trailer and Camping Show, Boat Show, and Flower Show, and that had cut our three-month preparation period in half. Nor, as I quickly discovered, is it wise to discount the sheer perversity of New England weather. Ten minutes after I had sat down, it seemed, we were hit by three snowstorms, two of them so bad that we were completely snowed in.

To get the plant dressed up to greet our customers, we spent $1 million in forty-five days. Or, anyway, we tried to. The trick was to dress the place up fastidiously, as it were, with a bulldozer. To tear it down and build it up again. The whole place was aswarm with workmen. If a carpenter left his hammer on a nail too long, he ran the risk of getting it painted. If a painter lingered too long over a panel, he stood to get himself flanged to the floor.

The track superintendent, Joe Tomasello, lived in his trailer at the far turn of the racetrack. We spent more money than we should reconditioning the grass course. Ultimately we spent $80,000, $50,000 of it widening and improving one turn.

The fence came down. The false ceiling came down (to the delight of the sponsors of the Boat Show, who were able to accommodate high-masted ships for the first time.) The pay toilets were disposed of, though not quite so arbitrarily. The guy who had the concession threatened to sue us for breach of contract. But, as I always say, if you act in a mature and responsible manner it is always possible to work these things out. The way we worked it out was that I took a sledgehammer and knocked a couple of the locks over the left-field wall. I'm still not sure, to be honest, whether that was enough to convince him I was serious about it, or whether he just couldn't bear to see me enjoying myself so much. At any rate, he agreed to take a small settlement, and I agreed to leave one pay toilet in every lavatory. A rather handsome gesture on my part, I thought, especially since I always try to do that anyway. From time to time you will find somebody rushing in, in obvious trouble, and complete privacy is exactly what he wants.

Once those original goals were realized, the party was over and we got down to the hard work. The boxes were solid concrete sweat chambers, reaching almost up to the chin. We ripped them out, put in pipe railings, and ordered new upholstered seats.

The ladies' rooms were completely renovated at a cost of $250,000. We lined the walls with gleaming tile and installed indirect lighting, full-length mirrors, vanity tables, and rugs. Lest you jump to an unkind and wholly unwarranted conclusion that something went wrong with my toilet training, please be advised that my hangups are far more spectacular than that. What may seem to be a fixation about toilets is, in reality, a firm conviction that any establishment, and particularly an establishment where food is served, is judged—consciously or unconsciously—by the condition of its lavatories.

We let out the largest painting contract in New England in something like twenty years. My instructions to the contractor were to paint anything that had ever been painted before or looked as if it wouldn't object too strenuously to being painted now. "When the last painter picks up the last dropcloth," I told him, "I want him to walk out of a plant that looks as if it had just been built."

Wow! It took a hundred tons of sand to blast all the paint off the exterior. Fifteen coats were burned off the grandstand railings. A hundred and fifty painters were put to work. Night and day.

When they were able to work, that is. The Flower Show was coming in around the middle of March, and our work schedules had been drawn right up to the moment when the doors were to be opened to the mad rush of the flower-lovers. No chance. One sniff, and the flower people let out a wail that the paint fumes were going to wilt their plants. The painters had to be restricted to outside work even while the flowers were still coming in. For all the other workers, it was a race to get as much as possible accomplished before the show closed them out too. The night before the opening, the sponsors threw a champagne party and seated me at the head table so that I could make a gracious speech welcoming them to our disheveled and dishabille premises. I was seated next to the Governor's wife, and neither of us ever got to finish a sentence. Superintendents, foremen, independents—they were literally lining up to get at me. Finally I said to the Governor's lady, "Look, the only thing for us to do is get half stoned. It's not going to discourage them, but it will make it a lot more pleasant for us."

In the rush to get on with the work after the Flower Show closed, one poor guy, carrying a five-gallon can across each shoulder, tripped as he was stepping onto the escalator and came skidding straight down, head first, trailing two perfect yellow and white stripes behind him. Gee, it was funny. Unless, of course, you happened to be the poor guy sprawled out there at the foot of the escalator. "You do good work," I told him, trying to keep a straight face. "But our colors are yellow, white, and *red.* Go back and try again. And keep on trying until you get it right."

The painting schedule wouldn't have been quite so tight, I must confess, if I hadn't spent so much time hunting for an architect who would bring a fresh mind and unfettered eye to the job. I found them, in the veriest nick of time, in a young married couple, Larry and Sherry Cutler. "Dream and I'll dream with you," was the inspirational message I imparted to them, and they came right back with some lively, provocative ideas. The entire decor was based upon sound psychological theory, and if much of the theory was their own, so much the better. Sherry had developed some of her most ingenious ideas while redecorating the zoo, a training ground deemed by many to have been fortunate.

The red, yellow, and white motif had been chosen to give the place a bouncing, carnival air. Red is supposed to impel people to keep moving, and so we painted the betting windows, concession stands, and traffic doors red. Black repels them, which was why any door that led to an off-limit area was painted black. Dark blue was the color for our grandstand seats, because blue is supposed to encourage people to take a deep breath, scratch themselves, and perhaps even meditate. We couldn't promise to make them millionaires overnight, but there was nothing to stop us from soothing their heated brows while they were trying. And what was the devious reasoning behind the green, green carpets in the dining rooms? Only to establish a fresh, outdoorsy atmosphere.

The Flower Show moved out on March 25, which left us with twenty-five carefree, unallotted days before opening day. The only thing that could keep us from getting the job finished within that time was that it was clearly impossible. So what did I do? I did what I have always done when things get tough. I went hollering for Rudie Schaffer. Rudie has been at my side, smiling knowingly, from the day I walked into the Milwaukee office and found him sitting there as a volunteer accountant. He hadn't intended to be a volunteer, you understand, it had just happened to work out that way. Rudie and I complement each other perfectly. I'm the one who takes the bows, and he's the one who does the work. Although he was still the business manager for the White Sox, Rudie had assured me that he was ready to rejoin the old established floating firm any time I needed him. I was never going to need him more than right now. Without him, we'd never have had the place in shape to open.

Those three months were as kaleidoscopic as the colors were variegated. All the while we were fixing up the track, I was also making the hundred administrative decisions and attending to the thousand administrative details, great and small, that are part and parcel of starting up any new operation.

Like: Attending to the insurance and hiring an advertising agency. Working out a very difficult and most complex concession situation, and trying to make the best possible deal with a beer company and a soft-drink company, the only concessions that would remain under our control. Negotiating with various concerns for the uniforms for our mutuel clerks and ushers, and working out a deal for jitney buses to shuttle the customers between the track and the parking lots. Finding a radio station that would carry our races and hiring a track announcer to replace the old one, who had retired.

There were policy decisions to be put in force, like cutting out the passes and overhauling the security program. There were Racing Commission hearings to be attended, plus legislative hearings and council meetings. There was an existing contract to be reworked with the horsemen, and an ugly union jurisdictional dispute which had already spilled over to the National Labor Relations Board.

The union dispute had arisen because the Teamsters had tried to come in earlier, with no objection from Dave Haber, my predecessor, and take over part of the operation from Joe Arena of the Mutuel Clerks' Guild. Arena, who moves very well in the clinches, had beaten them back. Since the dissidents hadn't paid their dues, Arena had thrown them out of the union, and the Teamsters were suing on their behalf. Everybody warned me to keep out of it because Arena was impossible to deal with; that's why Haber had presumably wanted to get rid of him. Everybody described for me how he ranted and raved and screamed. Well, I didn't want a suit hanging over the place for five years, I didn't want to see anybody lose his job, and I was going to have to deal with Arena sooner or later anyway. They were right about one thing. Arena was a screamer, all right. On the other hand, I could see that each recognized the other on sight as the kind of guy he was used to getting along with. On the second or third meeting I got sick of his yelling and said, "Hey, you sound like a Sicilian," which was exactly the wrong thing to say unless he took it in the spirit in which it was intended. Joe gaped at me for a moment and then snorted a couple of times and showed me that he appreciated we talked the same language by asking me to speak before a Knights of Columbus meeting for him. Before we were through, we had worked out a compromise where he would bounce only a couple of dissidents, just to let everybody know who was boss and, after a reasonable length of time had passed, take them back into the union too.

There were also the more or less personal obligations. Until the track opened, I was commuting to Chicago every Monday to tape five five-minute programs for my syndicated radio show and flying all over the country on a previously contracted lecture tour. By March I had also signed on to do a three-a-week commentary for WBZ-TV News, the local ABC affiliate. And always the speaking engagements around Boston. It wasn't unusual for me to hold seven or eight meetings and then go dashing off into the night.

The only way I could juggle it all was to hold my business meetings at the track, preferably over breakfast or lunch. Usually over breakfast *and* lunch. There were times, however, when things got so hectic that there was nothing to do but arrange to meet with somebody back at the motel at two o'clock in the morning.

Under the best of circumstances, as I had reason to know after my many years of operating ball clubs, any opening is going to be difficult. I don't care how detailed a checklist you make out, one or two things are going to be missed. That's why the opening ceremonies for a Shea Stadium can be held before anybody discovers that there are no water fountains, or how a multimillion-dollar housing development can be built without any doorknobs. A classic example is Fred Tucker's setting out to revolutionize the automotive industry with a rear-engine car and not discovering until after he had built his prototypes that he had neglected to put in a reverse shift.

I managed to spend a quarter of a million dollars renovating the ladies' rooms, and it had never entered my mind that we were going to need a couple of bucks' worth of doorstoppers. I had also forgotten that if you are going to encourage women to relax amidst luxurious surroundings, a certain number of them are going to sit back and light up cigarettes. That's right. No ashtrays.

Even more frustrating to those of us who still have the teeth to grind together is a phenomenon I shall call the Law of Immobility, which attaches itself, anonymously and impersonally, to any large organization. "All things tend to revert to their former shape and habitat," would be one way to put it. "Inanimate objects have a habit of returning to the scene of the crime," would be even better.

While I was making the morning rounds on opening day, I walked into the men's room on the second level of the grandstand and found myself face to face with a gross, ugly shoeshine stand, the same stand I had already yanked out of maybe half a dozen other men's rooms. The last time it had popped up, I had ordered the maintenance crew to drop it into the Atlantic Ocean, preferably upon the head of a giant cod. A month had passed, and here it was again. Back in the arms of that bourne from which it had sprung and to which some helpful soul knew it must be returned.

The same thing happened with the artificial flowers in the clubhouse dining room. I react to artificial flowers the way some particularly sensitive people react to real ones. I feel as if my chest is breaking all out in a rash. I can't stand them. I had personally lugged them out of there twice, the last time within the past twenty-four hours. Both times I had taken care to explain that fresh flowers would be arriving on opening day. On my first tour of the plant, they were still sitting out in the hall, waiting for the truckmen. On my second, they were right back where they had always been. Somebody had apparently looked in on the flowerless room and assumed that . . . Well, what can you do, he was only trying to be helpful.

We also had a dozen crabapple trees sitting out on the infield on the track, wrapped all around in their original burlap. For that, the blame or credit was mine own. I had made a decision, with malice afore-thought, to plant them in full view of all the customers. In part, it was to let everybody see—and, if they were the right sort, sympathize with —how rushed we had been. Sheer cop-outism. That was hardly the most compelling reason, though; my mind runs along far more devious paths than that. The real reason was to demonstrate to our customers that our program of renovation was alive and well and ongoing. That wasn't just twelve trees being put into twelve holes; that was a reforestation pro-gram.

Having gazed with moody introspection through the Paddock Club window, I headed back to my office in the administration building, a small white stucco edifice across the parking lot. One of the straw skimmers we had ordered to give our ushers a jaunty, debonair look was sitting on my desk. Now, gazing through windows isn't my only talent.

I have also gazed into enough mirrors in my time to know that Fred Astaire and his entire chorus line couldn't make me look debonair. Dress me in a top hat, white tie, and tails, put a cane in my hand and a white carnation in my lapel, and I'll look as if I just came in from watering the lawn. You do your best with what you've got. I put on my well-known irrepressible grin and settled for a rakish slant.

Enter Stan Isaacs of *Newsday*, with a dissenting opinion. "You look like the lascivious barker for a bust-out carny sideshow," he said. "The one who's trying to con you in to see the hootchy-kootchy girls." He also had some legal advice for me. "Don't ever wear that hat," he said, "if you're trying to beat a morals rap."

I could remember the exact moment in time and space when I first met Stan. He and I were seated in adjoining taxicabs on the way to Comiskey Field for the opening game of the 1959 World Series, waiting for a red light to change. I was sitting beside my driver in otherwise solitary splendor, and Stan was pressed in amongst an unsightly overload of fleshy, disreputable, but, on the whole, cheery sportswriters. The introductions had been shouted back and forth. He was a very young, very apple-cheeked fellow with a mischievous glint in his eye in those days, and with the passage of years he had become a not-so-young, not-so-apple-cheeked fellow with a mischievous glint in his eye. Young or not so young, he has been a kindred spirit. We share a common irreverence for sports, for bigness, and for Men of Great Moment, and a common reverence for H. L. Mencken. A reverence, if you want to get cynical about it, for the irreverent.

Across the room, Bea Furlong, my aptly named and amply talented secretary, looked out the window directly behind her. "Bill," she said, "shouldn't the gates be open by now?"

"They're not????" It was 11:50. "Those gates should have been opened at eleven-thirty!" I ran over to look out. Sure enough, there were a couple of hundred people huddled around the approach to the gates, dampening rapidly in the cold, misty rain.

A second later I was stumping out through the conference room and down the stairs and up toward the turnstiles. You have to picture the scene in your mind. Well, you don't have to, but it helps. The door of the administation building faces the track, and that meant it was the one area that had remained fenced off. Otherwise, anybody would have been able to walk right onto the track. As I was hurrying toward the gate, I could hear the people on the other side of the fence saying, "Hey, there's Bill Veeck." "What about it, Bill?" "What's the holdup here?" And such other remarks as brought into play the true racing fan's naturally inquisitive nature.

The holdup, the ticket-seller informed me, was that the Wells Fargo armored truck hadn't arrived with the change. Admission price was $1.50, see, and he wasn't taking any chance of getting caught short.

"Let 'em in," I shouted, waving my arms frantically. "Come on! Everybody in! Be our guests."

Wild cheers! "Attaboy, Bill." Warm handshakes. "The best of luck to you, Bill." Unbounded affection. "You're the tops, Bill." I tell you, it would have done your heart good.

As they were filing by, I suddenly became aware that Stan Isaacs was standing a little behind me, busily jotting down notes. I tell you, it did my heart good. I tell you, it took only that long for the concerned operator and beloved humanitarian in Attaboy-Bill to disappear and the hustler in me to take over. Hey, I thought. This was going to turn out pretty good. Bill Veeck, friend of the common man. Right in the old image. Too bad there weren't a few Boston writers around, though. Hmmmm. Obviously I would have to find a way of getting the word of my good deed around.

A little round old man with a heavy gray stubble touched me on the elbow and with a brogue that could have been coming right out of Barry Fitzgerald murmured, "God bless you, Bill. God bless you."

Stan gave me a half-wincing, half-mischievous grin as he closed in. "Oh, come on," he whispered. "You got that one straight out of central casting."

I beamed my own irrepressible, rakish grin right back at him. A grin which as much as said, *If I didn't, it was only because I didn't think of it.*

Fortune was smiling on me at last. In those few seconds I had a feeling that everything was going to be just fine. In the next few seconds I became aware of the pitter-patter on my face. And the sudden chill in the air. I held out the palm of my hand. Fortune may have been smiling on me, but not the weather. In the middle of April, it was hailing in Boston.

Not enough of my common men showed up. The attendance was only 18,940. The handle was $1,430,164. A slightly better-than-average opening day.

It was also, no fault of ours, a very bad day for privilege. The seats for our boxes, when they finally arrived, had been too large. Instead of putting four seats in a box, we had been able to put in only three. That in itself wouldn't have posed any problem if we hadn't already sent out the tickets. Rudie not only had to set up a whole new seating arrangement, he also had to set up a system so that the old tickets could be exchanged for the new ones. For some incalculable reason, that simple mechanical operation went so slowly that there was a massive pile-up at the exchange booth. Since the box-holders hadn't paid extra for the privilege of standing in line, they became understandably cranky. All through the day they stopped me on my rounds to let me know just how deeply they felt about it. "I'm sorry," was all I could tell them. "We'll try to do things better in the future."

The members of the Paddock Club weren't exactly sitting back in unrepentent ease and splendor, either. Given the damp weather outside and the air-conditioning inside, the same thing happened to the glass enclosure that happens to the windshield of your car. It kept steaming up.

The smartest thing I had done in getting started was to hire a private cleaning outfit, Allied Maintenance. The track hadn't been exactly run down, I discovered, it just hadn't been kept up. Allied had the know-how our people didn't have, and it also had the equipment. There was only one phase of the job that wasn't included in the contract. The Paddock Club windows required very specialized equipment, the only equipment Allied didn't have. We had, in fact, undergone a last-minute crisis in window-washing—and you can imagine what those windows looked like after three months of sand-blasting and repainting—before we finally managed to dig up an outfit that did.

For the crisis on hand, we threw the Industrial Revolution overboard and turned the job over to some guys with rags. And that was where we almost brought on a real disaster. One whole panel of glass collapsed upon a handsome young couple at one of the ringside tables. One minute, they were innocently eating their lunch; the next minute, they were covered with glass. Covered with it! How they escaped without a scratch, I'll never know.

Fortunately, it was only the upper transom-like section that had collapsed inside the room. The much larger section fell three floors and shattered all over the apron. By an even greater miracle, nobody was standing underneath it when it came crashing down.

Or maybe the fact that it was pouring rain had something to do with it.

The one bright spot in an afternoon of otherwise mixed notices had been the Lady Godiva Handicap. The race had attracted a lot of attention and, with the Red Sox game rained out, we could look forward to excellent coverage in the Sunday papers.

For lack of any better place, the conference room had been established as the unofficial press room. The post-mortems were well and noisily under way when the phone in front of me rang. A guy from the sports desk of one of the papers was on the other end, soliciting my opinion on the trade that had just sent Hawk Harrelson to Cleveland. "Who'd they get for him?" I kept asking. "Who?"

The difficulty was with my concentration, not my hearing. Harrelson had led the American League in runs batted in the previous season, and he was the mod hero of the town. A very bad trade for the Red Sox, as anybody with a modicum of intelligence could see. Or for the Indians, as any fool should have been able to see. What did I care? The real significance of the trade, as a man of my undoubted expertise could see, was that it was a very bad one for me. The trading of the hero, Harrelson, would take over the sports pages for the next day and week and month, and, more important still, it would take over the minds, hearts, and conversation of all sports fans.

And that, of course, was just what happened. We found out later that the *Herald Traveler* had a huge picture layout on the Lady Godiva set up for the front page of its sports section. Set up, locked in, and ready to go. The editor ripped it out, as any editor with a modicum of intelligence would have done, and went with the trade.

After all that work, our publicity had been most foully stolen away.

3

Waiting for Godiva

The girls had already begun their assault upon the jockey Establishment at the end of 1968, when I was unveiled to the Boston press. I would have been terribly disappointed in the editorial enterprise of the collected reporters if they had not asked me about it.

"Lady jockeys?" I replied in my carefully prepared ad lib. "Well, they do more for the silks than the boys do." If they also happened to be qualified to ride, I added with a shrug, why not?

I already knew that I was going to have the all-girl race on opening day, April 19. I also knew that it was a long, long time from November to April, and I didn't want to blow it.

From the beginning, I never thought of calling it anything but the Lady Godiva. When it comes to naming a promotion, I don't believe in being either cute or subtle or intellectual. The more obvious the name is, the more meaning it has for the most people. Nabokov is Nabokov, and Veeck is Veeck. We appeal to a different audience. (Notice the cute bit of subtle intellectualism there.)

To recapitulate for the historians, the siren song of equality had first been sung by a little girl from just outside Washington, D.C., named Kathy Kusner, after she had swept the equestrian events in the Women's Olympics. Miss Kusner, returning home full of ribands and honors, applied for a license to compete against the men, and when the Maryland Racing Commission gave her and her ribands the back of their hand, she took her case into the courts. By the time the verdict came down for her, though, she had taken a bad fall in a jumping race and broken her leg.

She had, however, won a landmark victory. If the gates still weren't completely open, they would never again be completely closed.

Onto the stage stepped Penny Ann Early, a pretty twenty-five-year-old divorcee who had been exercising horses for seven years. Flushed with Miss Kusner's success, Miss Early submitted her application to the Kentucky Racing Commission, and that citadel of the ever-improving breed trembled right down to its flimsiest blade of blue grass. Although the commission had no choice but to accept her application, the male jockeys didn't have to ride against her. They boycotted the first race she was scheduled to ride in, and it had to be canceled. Three more times Miss Early was listed as a rider in the overnight entries. All three times the trainers were pressured into taking her off.

Miss Early had discovered that the walls of tradition do not fall down at the first blast of the trumpet. Tradition is not just the way it has always been. Tradition is the truth by which those who have grown up within its protective walls have always lived. Challenge that central truth, and you are challenging all truth, every belief. You are challenging the truth, the purpose, the worth of their lives. The prospect of a woman jockey was so alarming to trainers, jockeys, sportswriters, and fans—in short, the entire male population—that their automatic response was to treat her application as either a bad joke or a tasteless publicity stunt. And that was to be expected, too. I have observed, in my wanderings, that whenever people are against something in principle, they level their attack upon the motives of the person who is asserting the principle. Not infrequently on the grounds that it is being asserted frivolously, for reasons of personal aggrandizement.

The attack that was leveled against Miss Early could have been made with far greater justification against me. I don't want to travel under false colors here. In retrospect, I can see where the Lady Godiva may well have been the first of the all-out Women's Lib events, even though it was run before there was such a thing as Women's Lib. But from my point of view it was a promotional stunt only. A gag. Something to get the people talking about us right away.

I didn't find anything outrageous about the idea of a woman jockey.

The fact that a woman had never ridden in a pari-mutuel race didn't mean that women hadn't been competing against men in the small, unlicensed circuits. Back in the late forties and early fifties, when I was moldering away on a ranch in Arizona, I had seen a girl by the name of Wantha Davis ride the tough, hell-for-leather quarter-horse races and more than hold her own against the best of them.

To enlarge the perspective even further, it would be well to point out that there have always been women around the racetrack. As exercise girls. As morning riders. It is customary—and not at all unpleasant—to think of the female sex as fickle and unreliable, but that is only because men are accustomed to dealing with women on a social basis, where they are operating on their glands as the enticers in nature's grand design. On the job, girls are dedicated and dependable. Since it's not that easy to find men who are willing to be dedicated and dependable at five o'clock in the morning for short money these days, the trainers are delighted to sign the girls on.

The girls have something else going for them. Any trainer will tell you that if a girl has good hands she can handle a fractious horse far better than any man. Especially in those early-morning hours. There is a relationship between a female and a horse that transcends anything that can possibly exist between a male and a horse. A man looks upon a horse as a form of transportation or a means of making money. With a woman it's closer to a love affair. You can take whatever Freudian implications you want out of that; I am simply recording a phenomenon which I myself had occasion to observe while I was running the ranch. Women and horses; men and mules. Women mother a horse. They fuss over him. They have a truly remarkable rapport.

While Penny Ann Early was by no stretch of the imagination as accomplished a horsewoman as Kathy Kusner, her contribution should not be minimized. Miss Kusner had the medals and the wherewithal to make the legal breakthrough. And she was operating in the backwaters of the sport world. The public at large looks upon steeplechase racing as a hobby indulged in by wealthy sportsmen. A girl jockey would serve them right. Miss Early hit the issue head on, and she had to have the toughness of mind to stand up to the constant attacks, disappointments, and humiliations.

Little Miss Early stood up just fine. She took the heat, and she kept the heat on.

That's where the situation stood as I came onto the scene. The court fights would be moving from the racing commissions to the Jockey Guild, and there was no possible way for the girls not to win. Yes, it was a long, long time from November to April, and if I played my cards right the timing would break just right for me.

In the meantime, I could only hope that the log jam didn't break so fast that somebody else would beat me to it.

By the time I had become president of Suffolk Downs, seven weeks later, a girl with the wonderfully English name of Diane Crump had filed for an injunction against the Florida chapter of the Jockey Guild to prevent them from interfering with her right to make a living. The Jockey Guild had dug its heels in and filed its own injunction to prevent her from interfering with the historical prerogative of the male to make a living on the racetrack without having to worry about a woman falling under his horse.

That didn't bother me a bit. As far as I was concerned, I had the formula to win the jockeys over. A week later I was flying down to Miami to meet with Nick Jemas, the head of the Jockey Guild.

"Look," I began, "the logical thing is to have an all-girl race. That way the male jockeys won't have to worry about their safety. And if the trainers are willing to take a chance with their horses, what do you care?"

But that was only the first half of the pitch. I wasn't proposing one race; I was proposing two. A doubleheader. The first four jockettes to finish in the Lady Godiva on Saturday would automatically become eligible to compete against four male jockeys in the Guys & Dolls Handicap on Monday. The Guys & Dolls was only going to be a $5000 handicap, which might not have sounded quite that tempting if it weren't that the winning jockey would also be winning a brand-new Cadillac (which turned it into the equivalent of an $80,000 race as far as his or her share of the purse was concerned). The first jockey of whichever sex was left would take home a Ford Maverick.

A bribe, pure and simple. I was making it worth their while to let me play with my all-girl race, and I was also enticing them—as part of my grand design—to race against the girls themselves. A package deal, gift-wrapped. Something for everybody.

Wrapped inside the package was the implicit question: *You don't think any of those girls have a chance of winning that Cadillac, do you?*

Nick Jemas was a very nice, very likable little guy. In very short order I was left with the distinct impression that while he may very well have been as outraged as anyone else at the first onslaught of the females, he had become mightily uncomfortable at finding himself cast as the conspicuous spokesman in what was being billed, undoubtedly to his astonishment, as a civil-rights issue. As far as my promotion was concerned, he took the position that although he was going to support any local chapter in any action it might chose to take, he had no intention of making life any more difficult for himself by encouraging it.

Good. That was as much as I could have expected.

The real problem, as the day of our opening was drawing nearer, was that the girls weren't coming out in anywhere near the numbers I had expected. We heard through the grapevine that Gulfstream in Florida was fiddling around with the idea of holding an all-girl race for its own opening day on March 4 (to be called, of all things, the Lady Godiva Handicap) but was probably going to have to give it up due to the flat unavailability of eight qualified girls.

As January was coming to an end, I had Tom Beedem, our general manager, check the situation out for me, and he reported back that there were only three licensed women riders (including the injured Miss Kusner), plus nine others who had submitted their applications. Beedem, who had made no particular effort to hide his distaste for the whole silly project, warned me that we'd have to run the race with a lot of exercise girls. Tom Beedem had been held over from the previous regime. Back in the fifties he had served as the chairman of the state Racing Commission. He was steeped in the tradition of racing. His advice to me was to forget about it.

Forget about it? I wasn't steeped in the tradition of racing. I wasn't even steeped in common decency. I'd have run it with exercise girls if it had come to that.

On February 7, Diane Crump, having won that suit in Florida, became the first woman to ride in a pari-mutuel race in America, which may not place her alongside Joan of Arc in the hearts of her countrymen but does make her the first woman to ride in a pari-mutuel race in America. The log jam had finally broken. Two weeks later Barbara Jo Rubin became the first woman to win a race. On March 1, Tuesdee Testa became the first woman to win a race in California and then came back East to bring New York into the fold. Penny Ann Early, having failed to beat the boycott in Kentucky, finally got to the starting gate in California.

Larry Howley, our racing secretary, and Nick Del Ninno began to contact the trainer or agent of every girl who had either ridden in a race or been recommended to us by a qualified horseman. Or a qualified newspaperman. Or a qualified busboy.

Long before we were ready to make the announcement, I had begun to talk it up as something I'd like to do. "Eight fillies on eight fillies," my line went. A broad smile followed by a sudden burst of infectious laughter. "I'd like to put eight maidens on eight maidens, but I don't think I'd be able to fill the race."

On March 28 we made the announcement, and the next day Diane Crump put herself right alongside Joan of Arc in the heart of this countryman by popping up on the winner of a $20,000 stake.

Getting the girls lined up was interesting because it illustrates so beautifully something that happens in any corner of a revolution. There are those who are willing to die for the cause, there are those who float along with the tide, and there are those who latch on to what they take to be a good thing. Whether a cause succeeds or fails just may have something to do with where the line falls between the true believers and the claim-jumpers.

We were offering to pay a bonus of $200 above expenses so that every girl who participated would come out with something. The guy handling Barbara Jo Rubin demanded that we cough up $2000 in "appearance money," *plus* a guarantee that she would get the best horse. Miss Rubin had been winning a few races here and there, and so it is possible that the poor deluded fellow thought he had us over a barrel. I didn't think so. My reading of the situation was that he looked upon her as too valuable a property to take that kind of a chance with. You see the irony there? Here was a young lady who was burning to compete as an equal, and her handler was taking the typical male chauvinistic attitude that while it was no disgrace to lose to a man her market value would drop to nothing if she should lose to mere girls.

With the week of the race upon us, we ran into two minor problems, neither of them having a great deal to do with the race itself and both rather funny if that happens to be the kind of humor you enjoy. You will now be informed that April 19 is Patriot's Day, a singularly Boston holiday which celebrates the midnight ride of Paul Revere. Now watch this carefully: Paul Revere was a noted horseman who had got himself involved in the whole nasty business because of a mild dispute that had arisen out of oppressive British taxes. Lady Godiva, in her unexpurgated form, was a noble horselady who had taken her equally celebrated ride as her own contribution toward lowering the local tax rate. Now that the passage of time and a couple of wars had eased the tension somewhat, it seemed to me we could do a world of good for Anglo-American relations by inviting a descendant of Lady Godiva to add a touch of tone and elegance to the festivities by presenting the trophy to the winning owner and, if she burned with the zeal of her daredevil ancestor, drum up a little goodwill for her beleaguered little country (and a lot of publicity for us) by making the radio and television rounds.

Evie Johnson of Nick Del Ninno's office called the British consulate, where they scratched their blooming heads and referred her to the British Travel Association, who told her to hold the phone.

Fortunately for us, the transatlantic operator took a somewhat more enthusiastic view of our excursion into English history. A dedicated lady she was and, if the quality of her laughter was any indication, a delightfully ribald one. At length, after many an unanswered call, she succeeded in rousing someone in one of the eighty-three historic museums that seem to dot the little town of Coventry and was told that for the love of heaven it was two o'clock in the morning, and he was only the janitor and what did he know about things like that?

Who would know about things like that? The director would know about things like that.

"Well, wake him up," said our operator in imperious tones. "This is a transatlantic call."

So the janitor woke up the director—it was a transatlantic call, what else could he do?—and the Director woke up his Lady Godiva expert, and that's how we came to learn that Lord and Lady Godiva had died without heir or issue.

"The Lord of Godiva was a very old man before he took a wife," he explained with impeccable British tact. "And his lady was most devout. According to legend, her favorite activity was visiting the surrounding monasteries, most notable among them being the Benedictine monastery, a superb example of eleventh-century architecture."

Which would seem to cast a whole new light upon the event. But then, I always had my doubts about Paul Revere too.

The other problem came to belated light when Rudie chewed down on his pipe and asked where we were going to have the girl jockeys dress. Holy smoke! As if we didn't have enough troubles! Well, there was the old jockeys' quarters. It had been used as a storage room for twenty years, and we had five days to yank everything out and then clean it up, paint it, bring in couches, chairs, and mirrors, patch up the plumbing, and provide new shower facilities and washbasins. Also an electric hairdrier and a spinning wheel.

A spinning wheel??? Well, yeah. The regular jockey room had a pool table, a feature I was sure would be of little interest, either functionally or ornamentally, to the girls. We were preaching equality, weren't we? If it turned out that our girls didn't have quite the hang of spinning saddlecloths out of hay, we could always utilize it to spin out some publicity releases.

We just about made it. The washbasins were still being installed on Saturday morning when the jockettes came in to look the facilities over.

We had met the girls at a press party the night before, and a most attractive group they were. Attractive and competent and very, very earnest. They ranged in age from Brenda Wilson, a nineteen-year-old girl who had just ridden her first race at a little Delaware track, to Lawrece Grube, a forty-nine-year-old Californian who was married to a jet pilot turned horse-trainer and had a twenty-four-year-old son in Vietnam. Most of them had been riding since they were little girls. Tuesdee Testa had ridden quarter horses when she was five years old, and worked the horse shows in her teens. As an exercise girl, her great asset was a perfect sense of timing. If her trainer told her to take his horse through a forty-six-second half mile, she could be counted upon to hit forty-six seconds right on the button.

Connie Hendricks and her husband were former rodeo stars who had carved out a very successful new career for themselves by opening up a spa for neurotic racehorses. Yes, you *did* hear me right. Neurotic horses. Their system was to take problem horses and reschool them, from the bottom up, through tender loving care. No, I am *not* kidding you. A patient named Fleeting Thought, who had become so terrified at the sight of a racetrack that he would throw himself over backward and roll around in the dirt, had returned to the races earlier in the month and romped home, a $117 winner. Obviously a useful, functioning, well-adjusted member of society.

Lawrece Grube had been brought up on cavalry horses. Her father, an Army colonel, had tied her to a saddle when she was two years old, and she had been riding ever since. For years she had been the only woman licensed to exercise Thoroughbreds in California. In the previous few weeks she had been receiving a great deal of publicity as the "exercise boy," the term she preferred, for Majestic Prince, the undefeated three-year-old who was to go on to win the Kentucky Derby and Preakness within the month.

It was with Mrs. Grube that the generation gap showed through most clearly. She had competed in the traditional exhibition events for women from time to time, winning the Powder Puff Derby twice and finishing second to Wantha Davis countless times. Unless every horseman and jockey in California was wrong, she was by far the best woman rider in the country. And yet, she was more than content with being a wife and a mother and an "exercise boy." She wouldn't have entered our race, or anybody else's, if we hadn't gone all out after her.

Unhappily, Mrs. Grube traveled the three thousand miles for nothing. The morning of the race, we were told that her horse wasn't coming in. The trainer who handled the filly at Suffolk had presumably been acting in good faith when he had promised her to us, but another trainer was handling the horse in Maryland, and he had entered her in another race. All I could do was promise Mrs. Grube that I would get her another horse in a couple of days and, of course, pick up the added expenses and pay her guarantee. Mrs. Grube was just great about it. She watched the races from up in the press box and captivated everybody who talked to her. No fires were burning in her, that's all.

Robyn Smith was a horsewoman of another generation. The activist generation. Robyn Smith was a tall twenty-four-year-old beauty who had chucked a movie contract with MGM to become an exercise girl for zilch. She knew what she wanted and she was obviously willing to pay the price. It is not really surprising, then, that Robyn Smith has been the girl who has stuck to it most steadfastly. From time to time she would return to Suffolk, always listing herself under the name of R. C. Smith in order to put herself on an equal footing with the bettors. When last I looked, she was riding in New York's Big Apple against the best in the business, and picking up more than an occasional win.

And yet, when it comes right down to the essence of femininity, the generations show no gap. The Lady Godiva was run in the rain over a track that had become a quagmire, and as soon as it was over the jockeys reverted to being girls. They refused to stop to have their pictures taken out on the track, all muddied up like that, and the photographers who hadn't got them while they were waiting to weigh in were out of luck. They insisted, one and all, upon showering and primping and attending to their make-up before they would meet with the press. A whole roomful of reporters was kept waiting for an hour. Diane Crump, who had finished second, didn't show up at all. Her horse had stumbled in the mud, across the finish line, and thrown her. She wasn't hurt. She had jumped right up and ridden the horse back to the unsaddling area. But she had suffered a little cut on the lip, and she wasn't completely satisfied that her make-up covered the mark.

The winning jockette, rather fittingly, was Penny Ann Early. The girl who had been the first to be actually entered in a race had finally ridden her first winner. She did it easily by holding her horse in the middle of the track, away from the mud being kicked up in front of her, and then taking her horse wide at the far turn and running down the leaders. She should have won. She had the best horse.

And that takes us back to one racetrack tradition that I hadn't been allowed to tamper with. In extending our original invitations, we had told our contacts that we would, of course, provide the horses. It had been my intention, frankly, to have the girls draw their horses out of a hat. The agents didn't want any part of that. An agent exists for the sole purpose of hustling around among the trainers to get his "boy" the best possible mounts, and they had no intention of surrendering their function. Penny Ann Early, who was hardly the most highly regarded of the jockettes, had ended up with the best horse through circumstances that were not wholly unconnected with diplomacy.

In the Guys & Dolls, the diplomacy was even more flagrant. There was a stickout horse in the race, Just A Baker, and Tony DeSpirito, who had been the national jockey champion in 1952, got the mount by making a deal with the trainer to sell the Cadillac and split the proceeds.

By the time of the race, however, another interested party had apparently been heard from. After Just A Baker had breezed home by seven lengths, DeSpirito bought the trainer's half from him at list price and gave the car to his wife.

The first jockette to finish was going to win the Maverick regardless, but Tuesdee Testa came roaring down the stretch to finish second, so it worked out perfectly.

You will notice that the best horse won in both races, regardless of the sex or ability of the jockey. You will also notice that the girls ended up with both cars. Which would seem to indicate that one woman's Liberation is another woman's 1969 Cadillac.

4

But Is It Promotable?

The finances of a racetrack are well worth talking about, if only because they are so widely misunderstood. You pick up the paper and see that the track handled $1 million yesterday, and you assume that the lucky stiff running the place is whistling all the way to the bank. If you know something about racing, you are aware that the take-out has been 15 per cent—split evenly between the track and the state—with the remaining 85 per cent going back to the bettors, although this varies in some states. Knowing that much about racing, you think, *Well, 7.5 per cent of a million ain't bad for a day's work. The lucky stiff running the joint is whistling all the way to the bank.*

And if he was really keeping $7.50 out of every $100, he would be. Let us see, though, how much of the $7.50 actually gets to the bank. The contract with the horsemen calls for 46.5 per cent to go toward the purses. There goes $3.49. The payroll takes $2.68. We are now left with $1.33 to pay the American Tote Company for letting us use their machines; to apply toward the general maintenance and operation costs; and—something nobody ever takes into consideration—to pay our property taxes. In outlying areas, where the taxes are reasonable, you would still be able to get by on the handle and the concessions. Our property taxes alone came to just a shade under $1 million. Not the pari-mutuel tax; that's something else. The property taxes.

A million-dollar handle is just about what we needed before we could begin to work up a pucker.

That leaves you to make your profit out of the money that accrues to you from the presence of the people in the park: the box-office receipts, the sale of your programs, the parking, and the concessions. The great problem there, as I had discovered in my surveys of the national scene, was that racing was operating on a steadily dwindling attendance base. The handle had been going up, sure. But that was due entirely to the increase in the number of tracks, the number of races per track, and, of course, inflation. And even there, the increase in the handle, track by track, had not begun to keep pace with the skyrocketing expenses.

In every other business you simply pass increased costs on to the consumer. Tracks are caught in the squeeze because nobody has been able to figure out a way to raise the figures on a $2 bill. You could, of course, raise the minimum bet to $3. They tried that somewhere and it was a disaster.

You could also raise the price on admission, parking, and programs. You could, but I wouldn't advise it. Where gambling is involved, you find a tremendous resentment to the charges you already have. Take parking. You go to the theater in downtown Boston, and it's going to cost you $4.50 to park. But you expect that. The whole night might be going to cost you $50—tickets, baby-sitter, parking, dinner—but you know that's what it's going to cost you ahead of time, and, more significantly, you know it isn't going to cost you any more.

Where gambling is involved, an entirely different set of attitudes comes into play. We were charging $0.25 for general parking and $1 for preferred parking, and you should have heard everybody scream. Well, the customers reason they're giving you a shot at their money too, and to take any more from them seems to make it an unequal battle. They don't understand that they're not betting against the track. They do not understand, no matter how often you try to explain it, that the track's cut of the handle is only enough to meet expenses.

The other way to increase the box-office receipts is by increasing the attendance. Which was just fine. My thinking has always been directed toward people, not dollars, anyway. My operating principle has always been that if you put on a good enough show the people will come, and that if the people come, the dollars will take care of themselves.

The first time I was able to get my hands on a Suffolk Downs balance sheet, I suffered a rude awakening. Theoretically, the prices were pegged at $1.50 for the grandstand and $2.50 for the clubhouse. Theoretically. Out of a total attendance of 804,000 people the previous year, almost 500,000 had come in on passes. Out of a total clubhouse attendance of 200,000, fewer than 30,000 had paid the full price. The others had come in through the grandstand entrance on passes and paid $1 each to pass through the transfer gate. As nearly as I could discover, 50,000 free grandstand passes had been sent out every day. Judge Pappas, one of the earlier owners of Suffolk Downs, had been a liquor distributor, and every liquor store had passes by the stack. Every little paper in New England was sent what were laughably called press passes, although they were, in reality, the same as any other free passes. The sports editors of any papers of appreciable size were sent a minimum of 20 passes a day. The legislators were getting 500 passes, and every peanut politician was on the list for 100 or more.

Economics aside, you are cheapening your product by giving it away and you are insulting every poor shnook who has to pay. Economics to the fore, it was perfectly clear to me that I wasn't going to be able to make the thing work unless the guy sitting on either side of him could be brought to pay too. Every new regime tried to cut off the free passes, I was told rather indulgently. Between the drop-off in attendance and the flak it caught from the politicians, none had been able to gut it through the first week. The pols had come to count upon those passes as largesse for the faithful and the prospective faithful. The bettors had simply refused to pay for something they had been conditioned to look upon as their due.

Fine. In making the announcement I took care to sweeten the pill for the old customers by framing the no-pass policy within a one-price structure. A buck and a half for either the grandstand or clubhouse; there was no distinction between them.

Just as I had been warned, the politicians screamed to high heavens. The Communist Manifesto may have been more provocative in its time and place, but not much. In theory those passes represented a minimum of five hundred votes to each of those dedicated public servants, and a lioness who is fighting for her cub could learn a few things about biting and clawing from a politician who is fighting for his constituents' inalienable right to continue to vote for him.

For each and every caller I had the same answer: "If my dear old mother asked me for a pass, I couldn't oblige her. There *are* no passes.

We didn't print any up." As far as he personally was concerned, I would add, we would be honored to have him as our guest any time he wanted to come. "All you have to do is call."

Look. Maybe I was a little frisky, but I wasn't crazy. To make a politician pay for anything would shake the very foundations of our civilization.

It was, of course, a calculated risk. My bet was that while there would be an initial drop-off in attendance, the soreheads would come drifting back once the word got around that nobody else was getting any passes either, and the over-all loss would be negligible. It's hard to say. So many other things were going on at the same time that comparative attendance figures would be misleading. And, I think, are. For what it's worth, the figures show that our attendance was, contrariwise, higher over the first half of the season than over the last. My seat-of-the-pants feeling as we were going along, however, was that the no-pass policy worked out pretty much as we had expected.

I am, as I have hinted from time to time, essentially a promoter. My method has always been geared to charm, intrigue, or—where resistance is encountered—inveigle people to the box office. The question at all times, as far as horseracing is concerned, was, "Yeah, but is it promotable?" That wasn't the question I was asking, I want you to understand. It was the question everybody else seemed to be asking me. It wasn't even a question, really. It was the most diplomatic way of making known the other person's opinion that it was not. The basic argument goes that the last thing the dedicated bettor wants is to have a guy blowing a horn in his ear when he's a few bucks out on the day and trying to handicap the next race.

I could have pointed out, and it's points for me in heaven that I didn't, that everybody had been sure that baseball wasn't promotable either. The argument then was that the dedicated baseball fan came out to watch the finer aspects of the athletic contest unfold, and that throwing some extra entertainment in would be as boorish as intruding upon the meditations of a Trappist monk. So we broke attendance records—if we can be big enough to rise above the disaster in St. Louis—everywhere. So the owners who were most outraged when I put in an exploding scoreboard now have exploding scoreboards of their own. So all the general managers who groaned when we first held Bat Day now find that Bat Day brings them their biggest gate of the year.

It's not even a matter of philosophy, really; it goes to the genes. I operate the way I operate. A far more realistic question, to my way of thinking, was, "If it isn't promotable, why would they want me?" The woods might not exactly be teeming with racetrack operators, but they most certainly could have got an experienced one a lot cheaper than they were getting me.

During my long winter of procrastination, I had weighed the pros and cons very carefully. If I would be moving into an area I knew little about, there is a stimulation in going into something new. It is healthy, I think, for any man to turn it all over at a certain age. The similarities were fairly evident. I would be dealing with the public, just as I had always done. The work was seasonal. The fate of the Empire would not be hanging in the balance.

There was one vast difference. When you are operating a baseball team, your customers have a strong rooting interest in your success. There is a personal identification with the team that is representing their city—meaning themselves—against the rest of the country. There is a strong identification with individual players. When you go out to speak, the questions are: "Why aren't we winning?" Or, "What do we need to win?" They want to know about the physical condition—and sometimes even the mental condition—of specific players. They want to hear about the behind-the-scenes maneuvering that did or did not bring something about.

You don't have that personal identification in racing. You don't have an overpowering personality like a Willie Mays or a Vida Blue. People don't really identify with a jockey, and with the best will in the world it isn't very easy to identify with a horse. As the final limiting factor, there is nothing like the continuity of interest that comes with a pennant race in baseball. In horseracing there are ten winners every day, and if you didn't have a bet on one of them, who cares?

Against all that, it did seem to me that I was in a unique position where I would be able to use my reputation, my visibility, and my availibility to personalize the operation around myself. And since I couldn't identify myself with horses or jockeys or with a winning team, I would have to identify myself with an establishment that was well run.

On January 9, three days after I had moved into Boston, I went to the Arlington Touchdown Club to make my first speech. In two years I spoke before four hundred different groups all over New England. It may be said of me that I have frequently been at a loss for a word or a phrase but never for something to say. Before I was finished, I found places in Massachusetts which no Kennedy had ever reached.

Once you decide to go that route, you can't pick and choose. You can't leave some guy feeling that while you are delighted to speak before almost anybody else, you don't think he and his group are important enough.

It isn't an imposition, it's an opportunity. In order to get new people into the track, you have to find some way to make contact with them. The vast majority of these people are tuned out to your advertising because the subject is so completely outside their interest and experience. To all practical purposes, they don't know the racing page exists. It's nothing to them except some blocks of print in the back of the paper which their eyes flick over as they are turning the page.

There's another thing that happens. If you have an unusually good night, you're quoted. And this is like a stone in the pond. You're not just reaching those people who are in the hall now, you're reaching a lot of other people. And you are reaching people who are asking, basically: Why in the world would he come all the way out there to speak for you? What are you paying him?

Nothing. He paid his own expenses and he cost us nothing.

And the ripples widen. To prove that they widen, the requests came in, in increasing numbers, as I became more and more of a local personality and less and less of a baseball figure. (This is the guy who gets involved in charities, who is on TV, who seems to show up wherever there's action. And he plays tennis, even though he's got a peg leg. And he will speak for us. For free.)

The only thing about it is that if you don't enjoy it, you'd better stay home. The audience will know it before you have ten sentences out of your mouth.

Rudie didn't think that racing was basically promotable. Nor, I suspect, did Nick. To put it another way, they felt that there couldn't possibly be a return that was at all commensurate with the way I was knocking myself out.

I couldn't see anything but good coming from it. Provided, again, that you enjoy it. And provided you survive.

Obviously, I look upon salesmanship as being synonymous with promotion. I'll take it even farther than that. The line I draw between promotion and operations falls somewhere between thin and nonexistent. Promotion is too intrinsic a part of my operation to be thought of as a separate category.

Item: Suffolk Downs had developed such a notorious reputation for holding the start of its races long enough to catch every last possible dollar that if the final race wasn't much more than an hour late everybody thought he was getting home early. We instituted the policy of punctual post time, while at the same time cutting the interval between races from thirty minutes to twenty-seven minutes. Would you call that operations or promotion? Well, we got good publicity on it, but I don't see how anyone could argue that it wasn't a vital part of the operations. On the other hand, anything that improves the operation of the track also improves the image of the track and that, you will remember, was precisely what I was setting out to do.

Item: We presented potted petunias to the first five thousand women to enter the track on Mother's Day. A promotion? No. It would be a promotion, under the customary usage, only if we had advertised it ahead of time in the hope of drawing people to the track. We didn't advertise it. It was part of an ongoing operating policy of providing fun, excitement, and surprises to our customers. But since the operating policy was aimed toward having people thinking, "Hey, let's go out to the track and see what that nut Veeck is up to now," it could be looked upon as long-term promotion. See what I mean?

Promotion is nothing but salesmanship with a funny hat on its head, that's all in the world it is. It doesn't matter whether it's a day promotion or a week promotion or a season promotion, it is a means of selling your product. Whether you chose to do it by delivering a direct pitch or by making the surroundings as attractive and relaxing as possible or by going for laughs becomes a matter of personality, individual predilection, and, in the end, semantics.

Item: We bought several hundred folding chairs and stacked them in the concourse so that people could carry them out onto the apron and watch the race in comfort. That was certainly operations. It was also promotion. Not because there is anything so remarkable about giving your customers a place to sit, but only because it was being done in a way that showed we were thinking about them. In the beginning, everybody warned me that half the seats would be stolen before the week was over. Over the entire year, we lost no more than a couple of dozen. Not to spoil us too much, the customers paid absolutely no attention to the signs requesting them to return the chairs to the runway on their way out. Okay. We could put them back for them. Give a little, take a little.

There is one clear distinction I do make in my own mind. It isn't between promotions and operations, it's between Special Events and promotions. A Special Event is a promotion which is advertised ahead of time. It is a Special Event, in short, precisely because it does fall outside the normal operating procedure. In our second year, we planned two particularly spectacular Special Events: a reproduction of the chariot race from Ben Hur, and a re-enactment of the massacre of Custer. Only one of them came off.

All promoters have one thing in common. They are able to convince people that they are engaged in a common enterprise. In reshuffling the stakes line-up at the beginning of the year I had, with malice aforethought, dropped a $20,000 Beef Stake Handicap into the final month. Throughout the week we inserted a page into the program, with my smiling kisser on top and the question "What's your beef?" underneath. Suggestion boxes were set up at all the exits. "Make your beef now," we proclaimed, "or forever hold your peace." Why hire a consultant firm to tell you how to make your operation more efficient for your customers when you can ask the customers themselves?

We held out the promise of a "big prize" for the best suggestion. We also made it clear that anonymous raps would be equally appreciated.

We anticipated perhaps a thousand entries and ended up with more than four thousand. We also expected that about a third of them would qualify for instant disqualification by either asking for "more winners" or making blunt and perhaps even pungent commentary about the historical connection between horseracing and highwaymen. Only about half a dozen of them had to be thrown out, a reminder—and a very useful one—that it never pays to underestimate the customer. What really pleased me was that almost all of the beefs were addressed directly to me as "Dear Bill."

The largest number of complaints, no contest, was about the food. The descriptive word most often used was "lousy." We already knew that, and we couldn't do a thing about it. We were, however, able to follow one suggestion and put a concession stand across from the escalator for the people coming down from the second level. We should have thought of that ourselves. We also should have realized, as a couple of ladies were good enough to inform us, that if we were going to have kids at the track (see next chapter), we should have had the foresight to install a few ice-cream and milk bars.

Third on the list was something I could not possibly have known about. There was a concerted, and possibly organized, campaign for us to sell Moxie, a local soft drink which is so steeped in tradition that it had long ago given rise to the expression, "Hey, that kid's got a lot of moxie," meaning that the little rascal had a lot of guts.

Number Two on the Beef Parade was the public-address system. We had known that there were dead spots in the acoustics, caused by the shape of the stands, we hadn't been aware they were quite that bad. So we brought in some sound engineers and spent more than $25,000 on repairs and new equipment. While we were about it, we installed a couple of open mikes above the grandstand apron and piped the crowd noises into the Paddock Club. It is amazing how the level of vocal enthusiasm is in inverse proportion to what in most tracks would have been the price of the tickets. The decibel sound could be charted in a direct line from the people standing along the rail—who really root their horses home—up through the apron, back into the grandstand, over to the clubhouse, and, finally, up to the Paddock Club, where the clientele sat through the races in glass-enclosed dignity. Cheering is contagious. As soon as we began to pipe in the uninhibited cheering of the groundlings, the whole atmosphere of the Paddock Club came alive.

Another excellent suggestion was to mark the posts in the parking lots so people wouldn't go crazy looking for their cars. Immediately, we posted numbers on the light stanchions. By the second year, Rudie's mercenary instincts were clicking along so well that we were able to turn the thing into an ongoing commercial by posting the names of our stakes on them. What better way to impress our future attractions upon the minds of our prospective customers, after all, than to encourage them to memorize them?

There were so many excellent suggestions that we decided the only fair way to do it would be to pick the winner out of a hat. The one we plucked out read: "How about giving more fans a chance to look at the horses in the Paddock?"

Lucky but also very worthy. It was, once we came to think about it, a suggestion that fitted right into the mood we had tried to establish through the entire refurbishing operation; i.e., to take the curse off the place as a betting factory.

The winner, a gentleman named John Savage, was going to get a Brahma bull and a couple of calves. We didn't tell him that, though. I simply extended an invitation for him and his wife to be my guests at the Paddock Club for the day of the race, and did nothing to disabuse him when he assumed that was going to be his prize. The bull and the calves were grazing in the infield all through the afternoon, and nobody paid the slightest attention to them. After the race, Mr. and Mrs. Savage were called to the winner's circle to take part in the presentation of the cup. And then the track announcer said, "Mr. Savage, there is your beef on the infield. Please pick it up and take it home with you."

We handed him the lead-string and waited to see what his reaction was going to be. He was great. "Look," he said. "I'll ride the big one, and my wife can ride a little one, and drag the other home behind her."

To everyone else who had submitted a suggestion, I wrote a letter of thanks for their constructive criticism and sent it along with a coupon for a hamburger and french fries at McDonald's, which was McDonald's part in the promotion.

As a continuing diversion in the fun-and-games department, we would place certificates under seats in widely scattered areas, with prizes going to the people who were lucky enough to be sitting there. What a joy it was to watch. After the third or fourth race, Jim Hannon, the track announcer, would announce that we were playing L-1-1-lucky Chairs, and you could see everybody jump up, turn around, and throw up his seat in such perfect military precision that it came to you in one great *callumping* sound. To maintain the integrity of the thing we'd have to space our Lucky Days far enough apart so that the fans wouldn't be looking for them. We succeeded so impressively that the surprise and excitement not only maintained themselves but seemed to become greater every time we did it. That's the bonus you get out of a running promotion. To the normal excitement of the treasure hunt, there is added that special joyful buzz of ten thousand people congratulating themselves on having hit the lucky day.

When we wanted to exercise a certain amount of geographic control, purely for a gag, we changed the game to Lucky License Plates, making it clear in our announcement that we had picked the license numbers from the parking lots—and not necessarily by lot. There was one time we picked out licenses from three different states, just so that we could give one guy a thousand hot dogs, another guy a thousand buns, and the third guy a thousand Cokes and then help them resolve the question of what to do with a thousand hot dogs, buns, and Cokes by suggesting that they get together in neutral territory for a block party.

The guy never did pick up his Cokes, which left us to resolve the problem of what to do with a thousand Cokes. If there's anything I hate, it's a sore winner.

The best of the Lucky Chair Days by far—the best promotion of any kind in our first year—was held in honor of Joe Fan. We had tipped our mitt on it somewhat by changing the name of the Suffolk Downs Handicap (sheer inspiration, that) to the Joe Fan Handicap, and if anybody wanted to anticipate we had something on our minds we did nothing to either encourage or discourage them. Not until we were ready to go to work on it, anyway. The Saturday before the race was coming up, we started counting down the days on the program. Seven days to the Joe Fan Handicap. Six days . . . Five days . . .

Let me tell you, a lot of planning went into it. The Joe Fan Handicap was not only the first of our big promotional stunts, it was the first race of the year on turf and therefore the opening shot of the publicity campaign for the $200,000 Yankee Gold Cup. We had it planned in such detail that we had a script written out for Jim Hannon, right down to the good-natured chuckles.

After Hannon had announced that the previous race was official, he intoned: "Ladies and gentlemen. Today in honor of each and every one of you we are holding the Joe Fan Handicap. The first race of the year on turf. To make our Joe Fan a real special occasion we have selected today to play L-l-l-lucky Chairs. Certificates have been placed under some seats throughout Suffolk Downs for prizes."

To make it seem as if we were still gagging it up in the grand old what's-he-going-to-do-with-it tradition, the first three prizes were one thousand cans of beer, two thousand (good-natured chuckle) coloring books with a box of coloring crayons, and a lifetime supply of balloons accompanied by a hand tire-pump with which to blow them up.

The fourth prize was the big one. What would any Joe Fan want more than anything else? You betcha. We were giving him a racehorse to race under his own colors. And this time, it wasn't to answer the tantalizing question of what an average guy is going to say to his wife when he comes home with a horse under his arm. There were seven weeks left to the meeting, and we were going to pick up all training costs and entry fees.

You should have heard the roar that went up from the crowd at that announcement. A roar which very quickly tailed off into a kind of mass groan as everybody in the racetrack gave himself a mental kick for not having had the foresight to be sitting in the right chair. Yes, everybody does want to own a racehorse, and what better way to realize that ambition than to have it handed to you without any of the attendant risks.

The risks were even less than the fans thought. We didn't want to take the edge off the presentation by announcing it then and there, but since the last thing we wanted was to leave our Joe Fan with a horse on his hands we were going to buy it back from him for $3500 when the meet was over. The plan was to relieve any misgivings our guy might have on that score by telling him about it as soon as we had him alone, but to hold the announcement until the day after we closed, in order to give needy sportswriters a chance to rerun the never-to-be-forgotten story of how Joe Fan had, all unexpectedly, found himself in possession of the valuable piece of horseflesh he was now so regretfully surrendering.

The holder of the lucky certificate was told to come to the winner's circle. Nick went up to the grandstand gate to escort him through, and . . . Holy Toledo, if we had sent out scouts to beat the underbrush we couldn't have done better. He's coming down the aisle wearing a soft hat with the brim turned up; a pair of binoculars are draped around his neck, a copy of the *Morning Telegraph* is rolled up in his hand—and he's black. And I'm not going to try to tell you that his being black wasn't the first thing we noticed. It was like the Barry Fitzgerald scene on opening day. The world is full of cynics who will never be convinced that we hadn't planted the guy there. To begin with, there aren't that many black guys who come to the races in New England, for the very good reason that there aren't that many blacks who have both the time and the money. Our guy was Robert Morgan, forty-five, who owned a restaurant on Columbus Avenue in Dorchester, and a rather well-known one: Bob the Chef's the Home of the Soul Food. On top of that, he came to the track three or four times a week and, like all regulars, always tried to sit in the same seat. No matter which way you looked at him, he was perfect.

We had set it up so that as soon as Hannon made his announcement that the race was official the groom would begin to walk the horse down from the stable area. The horse arrived in the winner's circle just in time for Rudie to take the reins and place them into the new owner's hands.

Some little work had gone into the selection of the horse. For openers, we had to find a horse that was available at the price we had in mind. The price we had in mind was: not too expensive. The cheapest claiming price at Suffolk was $2500. (The claiming price, I should explain, has nothing to do with the purse; it is the price at which any other owner running horses at the track is entitled to buy the horse from the owner who has entered it in the race.) We didn't want to palm a cheapie off on our winner—we were willing to go all the way up to $3000—and we most certainly didn't want to hand him a stiff. If the horse didn't have a chance to win, we'd have done better to call the whole thing off. The best we could get, at our price, was a three-year-old chestnut filly named Buck's Delight. She'd had a win, a second, two thirds, and two fourths down in Florida, but she had done nothing in two starts at our track and after running for as high as $4000 had been dropped down into $3000 claiming races.

It was, then, a horse which figured to get into the money a couple of times, and if Mr. Morgan got real lucky, maybe even win a race for him. Which meant that he had a very good chance of making somewhere between $500 and $2500 on top of his guaranteed $3500.

The money wasn't the main thing, though. What we were really offering him was the thrill of becoming a part of the horse scene. Because this wasn't play-acting; it was the real McCoy. The first thing they were going to do, Nick told him when the ceremonies were over, was to go to the Racing Commission's office at the track and apply for a license. They would then hustle over to Security to pick up an ID card, with his picture on it, so that he could get into the stable area. And then a pass for the owners' parking area, and a box seat in the section reserved for horsemen. The whole shmeer.

But Morgan was so excited that the first thing he had to do was phone his wife. Now, that isn't as easy as it may sound. For security reasons, there are no public telephones in a racetrack. Only one line is kept open in the administrative office while the races are being run, and that one is monitored. (Not only is the phone in the jockeys' room monitored at all times; all calls are taken or placed by a security agent, and even with all that, it's cut off an hour before the first race.)

Nick took Morgan to the administration building. "Hello, Mama," he shouted into the phone. "You got the air-conditioner thing on?" And right away you could visualize his wife sweating over a stove in the kitchen of a ghetto restaurant and being less than thrilled when he gurgled, "Sit down, I've got something to tell you. Guess what . . . I've won a racehorse!"

She must have said, "You're drunk," or some similar expression of wifely devotion, because his next words were, "No, I'm not. Listen to me, I've won an honest-to-goodness racehorse. I need a name for our stable. How does the R & W Morgan Stables hit you? The both of us."

R & W Morgan Stables it was. With red and gold colors. The only person rooting harder for the R & W Morgan Stable's sole asset was me. Or dreaming wilder dreams. To turn the Joe Fan award into a real triumph, all the $3000 plater had to do was to turn into an overnight champion.

Morgan ran her right back four days later, which was the smart thing to do, and Buck's Delight finished fourth. Not quite a championship performance, to be sure, but worth $150. On her fourth start, four days before the closing, Buck's Delight went off at 47–1 and pulled it out for all of us by finishing a good second. Morgan had won himself another $650, and we had a highly satisfactory if not smashing ending to an excellent human-interest story.

But, there was something we hadn't figured on. We had wanted a typical fan and we had got him. Bob Morgan had been coming out mornings to walk and saddle his horse. He had been feeding her. Rubbing her down. Talking things over with the other horsemen and trainers. In short, he was hooked.

Nick saw it coming. "Hey, don't go overboard on this," he kept telling him. "You've got a free ride. Enjoy it."

No good. When the meet ended, he decided not to sell the horse back to us. Even before Buck's Delight had finished second, he had been negotiating to buy a second horse. He shipped them both to Finger Lakes in upper New York State, won a race, turned his power of attorney over to his trainer, and in no time at all found himself with a nine-horse stable on his hands.

But now he was operating on his own bankroll, and since he had to stay with his restaurant most of the time he had the expenses without the pleasure, an exact reversal of the situation we had set up for him. By the time his wife finally told him he was going to have to make a choice between her and his horses, he was more than ready to disband the legendary R & W Morgan Stables.

The R & W Morgan Stables had won $25,000 in purse money, and even though he was able to sell all his horses, he still ended up a loser.

He made a very interesting comment. "It's like any other business," he said. "You have to know what you're doing, plus you have to be there yourself. Or at least have someone who also has a financial commitment running the business for you."

There was one other Lucky Chair whimsy which stands out, most vividly, in my mind. Our harness season started a week before Halloween. Harness races are run at night. Is there anyone in the audience who can doubt for one minute that I was going to call my plucky crew together to find out what we were going to do about it? Half a dozen ideas suggested themselves immediately. All of them obvious. Twenty gallons of cider. A truckload of pumpkins. A dozen ghosting sheets. A gross of witches' brooms. And then I said, "Come on, let's not fight it. We have to have some black cats."

To tell you the truth, we tried to figure out a better way to do it, if only because we suspected that our fans would be closely enough attuned to my thinking by then to anticipate that we would be pulling a Lucky Chair night on them. To throw them off the scent, we flashed the following cryptic message on our tote board on opening night:

WANTED: 100 BLACK CATS

No, we weren't going to load anybody down with a hundred cats. I'm mean and rotten but never sadistic. We weren't going to be giving away *live* cats, if only because I was afraid nobody would take them. My devious plan was to implant the idea that we had a hundred cats tucked away somewhere, so that when we did begin to hand out all those other prizes our fans would be able to chuckle in amusement or cringe in horror in the sheer anticipation that we were going to perpetrate so foul a deed on some devout taxpaying and perhaps even law-abiding citizen. And then, in a crescendo of anticlimax, we'd present the terrified winner with a hundred stuffed black cats.

I didn't know what I was letting the office in for. The AP picked up the story of our "advertisement," and we were deluged with calls. Not to offer us any cats, which was what we were afraid was going to happen, but to ask us, in tones that varied from polite inquiry to flat accusation, whether we had found, bought, or stolen their particularly beloved or talented black cat. We received letters from all along the East Coast, plus Phoenix, Arizona. I can tell you, from the data of an impromptu but otherwise scientific survey, that there are more lost cats in Virginia, or at any rate more ladies who are worrying about them, than in any other state in the Union.

We didn't want to blow the thing by telling the callers that we wouldn't have taken their cats on a bet, and that led to even more trouble. One woman, who was apparently unsatisfied with what she had apparently taken to be a less candid answer than she deserved, came storming into the publicity office. "I want my cat," she shouted at Nick and Evelyn. "Don't lie to me! I know you've got it!"

Her son had been threatening to get rid of her black cat for years, it seemed, and now that we had suddenly provided such a ready market for him, she knew—absolutely—that he had spirited it away and sold it to us. She didn't look like a nut. She was a young woman, well dressed and not at all bad-looking. She was also, for reasons that may well be superfluous, accompanied by her mother. With one thing and another, Nick and Evie weren't sure that she hadn't been put up to it by one of their playful coworkers—Rudie was the logical suspect—or even that she wasn't a practical jokester with a rather fey sense of humor of her own. Until she started screaming. That's when they knew that humor wasn't quite the word for it. Or fey, either. She was going to have the police after us. And her friend the Governor. And her parish priest.

Sure enough. Twenty minutes after she slammed out of the office, leaving her best wishes of something behind her, a call came from the desk sergeant at Revere Police Headquarters wanting to know what the ————was going on down there. Fortunately, it was Sergeant Pasquale, an old friend of Nick's, and after Nick had had his fun, he assured the good sergeant, with a scrupulous regard for the truth, that while we were indeed trying to find black cats, we had not, on his honor, been able to find one.

I had my moment too. A couple of days before Halloween I happened to be sitting in the publicity office with Evelyn when in marches a guy all decked out in his SPCA uniform, with a holster yet, and just all full of authority and self-importance.

"Mr. Veeck, I'm here to investigate the hundred black cats you have here."

"Yes . . . ?"

"Well . . . ?"

"Well what?"

"Well, what do you intend to do with them?"

"Why?"

Already, he'd kind of deflated. "Well, we're concerned about their welfare down at the SPCA. Are you taking good care of them?"

"Why should I tell you?"

And now he's badly deflated. This isn't at all the attitude he expected. Evelyn is keeping her head down, smothering her laughter and half turned away from us so that she can scribble it all down.

"Because a lot of people have been calling," the guy says. He wanders through a long explanation about all the calls that have been coming in to the SPCA, and, having girded himself back up again, he snaps, "I'm asking you officially. What do you intend to do with them?"

"I might eat them."

"What?"

"All up."

The guy deflates again. "All right now. How do you intend to take care of them?"

"Why? Do I ask you how you take care of your children?"

"That doesn't have anything to do with it. That's something else."

"Then why are you asking me how I'm going to take care of my cats?"

Now he's sure we have the hundred cats. "Well, how will you take care of them? Why don't you answer me that?"

"We have hundreds of horses here. We have a vet. We can take care of cats. What do you want to bet that we have more horses than you have cats."

That gave him pause. Yeah, now that he thought about it, we could take care of cats. But where were we keeping them?

"We have them in clean, warm surroundings. The vet looks in on them four times a day. After every meal."

His chest sagged. His holster hung uselessly from his waist. "Yes, but . . . well, what do you intend to do with them? That's what I want to know."

"We haven't made up our minds." I gave it deep thought, knowing that I had to make up my mind on the spot or suffer the terrible wrath of the SPCA. "I might give them away. Maybe all to one person."

"*One person?*"

"Sure."

He was horrified. "Do you realize that some people drink and are not . . . well, not capable of competent cat care."

"Well, personally I don't have much respect for anybody who doesn't take a drink now and then."

"*Don't look at me, Mr. Veeck. I like a drink as well as the next fellow.*"

Well, that was different. Now that we recognized each other as fellow tipplers, a new warmth and conviviality entered into our relationship. He had marched in like Napoleon, and he departed with my invitation to drop in at the track any old time as my personal guest.

As soon as the door closed, Evelyn looked at me, I looked at Evelyn, and we both doubled over with laughter.

We never did have to come to grips with the problem of what we were going to do if hordes of children came marching in to dump their cats and kittens on us. Amazingly, we were never offered one cat. Not one. As a matter of fact, we had a terrible time finding any stuffed ones. Evelyn called all the novelty stores in town. Some had red ones. Some had green ones. Some had white ones. But nobody had one single black one. We were down to the day before Halloween and wondering what kind of miserable excuse we could offer to our fans. And cursing, for once, the circumstances that had got us so much unexpected publicity on it. And then, there occurred one of those incredible coincidences that keep happening in life and are always laughed out of a court of law. In the midst of all our moaning and groaning, Rudie got a call from some guy he had known back in Milwaukee and hadn't heard from in years. Rudie's friend was now workng for Fannie Farmer's in Boston, and he had only just discovered that Rudie was working in Boston too. In the course of bringing each other up to date, Rudie casually mentioned that he was currently involved in a hopeless search for stuffed black cats. And the guy said, "We have a whole warehouse full of yarn kittens. With ribbons tied around their necks. Would that do you any good?" I became aware of the turn the conversation had taken when Rudie bolted upright in his chair. "Are any of them black?"

"All of them."

Rudie asked him only one other question. "How fast can you get here with them?"

We arranged them tastefully in two big baskets. When the time came to make the long-awaited announcement, Jim Hannon's script read: "And, finally, the big prize of the night. You've heard about the hundred black cats all week. Well, we've got news for the person in the lucky seat in the grandstand. You've just won those hundred black cats. Please, for heaven's sake, clear your prize with the SPCA before you take the cats home. Would the lucky winner please report to the finish line at the track to collect his hundred black cats."

It turned out to be not a man but a woman. A marvelous woman, who was delighted to be a winner of anything. She hadn't heard a thing about the cats, so she didn't know what she was supposed to be relieved about.

After the next race, a message appeared on the tote board saying, "Anybody who finds a black cat will please contact Nick Del Ninno."

Nick knew that it had to be Rudie because the two of them had been playing jokes on each other about the cats for days. So Nick rushed up the announcer's booth on top of the roof, grabbed the mike from Jim Hannon, and began to howl: "Meeeeeeeeeoooooooowwwww. Meeeeeoooooooowwwww. Meeeeeeeoooooooooowwwwww." Oh, we had a lot of fun, us kids.

Is racing promotable, though? I can't prove it by the record, but having spent two years laboring in those vineyards I know absolutely that it is. I don't think it is; I know it is. Call it a basic feel of the mood that had been developing, or call it the gift of prophecy, but I know that we were just on the brink of cashing in on all that work when the rug was pulled out from under us.

5

It Was an Artistic Success;
We Ain't Running It Any More

On Friday morning, the day before the first annual running of the $200,000 added Yankee Gold Cup, I sprang out of bed (a litttle hyperbole never hurt anybody), strapped on my artificial leg, took a couple of steps toward the john, and—*boinnngg!* The hinge at the knee didn't do what a hinge is supposed to do, and the whole leg split down the middle like a ripe tomato. And that, racing fans, was the best thing that happened to me all weekend. The weekend before the closing of my first season at Suffolk Downs.

I could remember that I had one old leg kicking around in a closet back in Maryland, and while Allegheny Airlines refused to take it as freight, they did agree to let us buy a passenger ticket for it. First class. Since they did not think any of the other passengers would be overjoyed at having a leg as a traveling companion, it became necessary to buy two first-class tickets. Which has to make me the only guy with a wooden leg that travels better than he does.

It was, as I have suggested, a very old leg, which had been ordered before the last slice had been taken off my stump and therefore it was a little shorter than my right—or tourist-class—leg. I was, it seemed, going to face my big day listing somewhat to starboard.

Now, no promotion is ever going to go smoothly, and the bigger the promotion, the more difficulties are going to crop up. Usually when you least expect them. That's all right. Aggravation is good for you; it keeps you on your toes. But, you know, it really shouldn't be that difficult to give a quarter of a million dollars away.

The first question I was asked after I had been unveiled to the Boston press as the new president of Suffolk Downs was what I intended to do about bringing a better caliber of horse to New England. Viewing myself with my usual cold objectivity, I reminded them that while I am perhaps better known for having mounted a bizarre promotion or two during my days as a card-carrying Lord of Baseball, I would hope that the more discerning among them had not overlooked the fact that it had all been toward the greater purpose of improving the product; i.e., building a winning ball club.

In racing, the quality of your horses depends entirely upon the quality of your purse structure, and your purse structure depends entirely upon your average daily handle. Suffolk Downs, with its $1-million daily handle, draws a grade of horse which is better than the horses that run at the Rhode Island tracks, which have a $750,000 handle, and not nearly as good as the horses that run at Belmont and Santa Anita, which have $2-million handles.

All I would be able to do coming in, therefore, would be to demonstrate that there was a new day a-dawning. During my days as Low Lord on the Totem Pole, I had always operated on the principle that while you can't buy a winner, you sure as heck can buy respectability. The only way I was going to buy respectability at Suffolk Downs was to buy it in superlatives. What better way to buy instant respectability, I decided, than to present the hard-working, downtrodden citizens of New England with The Richest Race in the World?

Tell me, Doc, where did I go wrong?

For reasons that seemed good and sufficient to me, I decided to run the Yankee Gold Cup over the turf; that is, over a grass course instead of the conventional dirt course:

(1) In the galloping inflation of the late sixties, the difference between a $100,000 race and a $200,000 one wasn't necessarily going to impress the kind of stable which had the kind of big-name stake horses that

could run for a minimum of $100,000 any time they pleased. That kind of stable opted for tradition and the old graceful racetracks and the old and valued connections.

(2) Turf horses, on the other hand, ran for big purses often enough so that their names were familiar to the average racegoer, but infrequently enough so that they would be eminently available.

(3) I had always felt—now that I thought of it—that turf racing was the purest form of horseracing, reeking of respectability, hedgerows, and class.

(4) Throughout the rest of the world the richest races and the great distance races are run over turf, which would give us a good shot at an International Extravaganza and—as I realized on the spot—my heart had always leaped with joy at the thought of putting on an International Extravaganza.

The first minor disillusionment came when we learned, only a couple of weeks before our race, that there had been a turf race in France the previous year, the Arc de Triomphe, for a purse which, translated into American money, had come to a gauche and unseemly $354,000. Well, we still had the richest race ever run in America, which wasn't so bad either.

For the benefit of the uninitiated, $200,000 added means that the track puts up the $200,000 and the horsemen put up the added: $150 to nominate each horse, $1000 to "pass the box" (which means to draw for a post position), and another $2000 on the day of the race to send the horse to the starting gate. We had been very anxious to put together not only a class field but a full field; first, to establish the attractiveness of the event, and second, to build the purse up to $250,000. We had every horse we had gone after except one, Fort Marcy. We had four former national riding champions, Johnny Sellers, Walter Blum, Angel Cordero, Jr., and Tony DeSpirito. We had four French horses, including the three we really wanted—Pardello, Petrone, and Samos 3rd—who had finished 1, 2, 3 in the Ascot Gold Cup. We had an Argentine-bred from Venezuela. We had the American champion, Czar Alexander, an Irish-bred with a Russian name.

Larry Howley, our racing secretary, had assigned Czar Alexander the top weight of 128 pounds, which wasn't unreasonable when you consider that the Czar had been breaking track records almost every time out, but was a bleeping outrage if you happened to be his owner, Gustav Ring. Ring had been on the phone from Washington, D. C. every day, threatening to pull his horse out of the race unless we knocked a pound off. Well, badly as we wanted Czar Alexander, we weren't going to cheapen the race or humble ourselves by taking an ounce off anybody. Howley's job was to assign weights in a way that would even up the field as much as possible. My job was to listen to Ring's moaning with as much sympathy as I could muster and then congratulate him on the fine piece of horseflesh he had there.

We had not only filled the field, we had flooded it. Sixteen horses had been entered on Thursday, and we had a starting gate which could accommodate only fourteen of them. And the starting gate fitted so snugly into the head of the stretch where the race was going to start that there was no room to start them outside.

That left us with two alternatives. The first alternative, highly favored by the horsemen, was to split the race into two $150,000 sections. I couldn't see how it was going to help us at all to put up an extra $100,000 *not* to run the Richest Race in America. The other alternative was to forget the starting gate and go back to the old walk-up starting tape. (The tape extends across the track between two poles. The horses walk up to the tape, and when the starter yanks the loose end the tape slides up to the top.)

Billy Mills, our starter, had informed me the previous night that he was reasonably certain they had a starting tape tucked away somewhere in Belmont Park in New York. As soon as I had settled the complicated business about having the leg flown in from Maryland, I called Billy's contact at Belmont and was assured that the starting tape would be delivered to us as early as possible on Saturday morning.

By this time, of course, I wasn't so sure we were going to need it. It had begun to look as if we were going to get down to fourteen horses in the worst possible way: by losing two of the French horses.

One of the French horses, Petrone, had been on the grounds for a week. A big black, stunningly beautiful horse. If you had come to the track knowing nothing about horses, you would take one look at Petrone and go running to the betting window. Pardello and Samos 3rd had been caught in a wildcat airport strike the previous Friday, just as they were about to be flown to New York. Happened all the time in France, I was told, They'd be out the next day. For four straight days they were going to be out the next day.

Pardello, who had been bought by an American syndicate, had arrived in New Jersey on Tuesday and had been kept in quarantine until

Wednesday night. His new owners had been waiting for him at Belmont. The last time we had heard from them, their plan was to give him a couple of stiff workouts on Thursday and Friday mornings and van him into Suffolk on Friday afternoon. For two days it had been pouring in New York. While I was still waiting for my leg to arrive, the head of the syndicate called, heartbroken, to tell me that since they hadn't been able to work Pardello at all, they were going to have to scratch him. He also confided to me that their intention had been to run Pardello this one last time before retiring him to stud. We had not only lost the winner of the Ascot Gold Cup, to say nothing of his colorful Australian-born rider, Bill Pyers, we had lost that greatest of all sports-page stories, the old champion's farewell appearance.

Samos, who had a reputation as a tough-luck horse, had left on Tuesday too. And—true to his reputation—his plane had developed motor trouble over the Atlantic, and he spent another day in London. The last we had heard about him, he was still being held in quarantine in New York. Larry Howley had been on the phone all morning, getting minute-by-minute reports, and almost immediately after the loss of Pardello the word came through that Samos had cleared quarantine and was being vanned to Boston. His trainer, Albert Klimscha, a Hungarian-born Swedish citizen who was living in France, had a transatlantic call in to the horse's owner, a French *comtesse*, for instructions on whether to run him. Klimscha had been at the track for a week, and he had charmed us all. A fascinating man. Before a bad fall ended his career, he had been the riding champion in every country he had ever ridden in. He had won eleven Derbies in almost as many countries and he spoke about eleven languages fluently, including English. In faultless English he told me that Samos was a big, ungainly, long-legged horse who would have had trouble handling the sharp turns on our grass course even if he had been in top condition. Fortunately for us, it turned out that the *comtesse* had been looking forward to her trip to the United States and she was perfectly willing to blow another $2000 to watch her horse run. So Klimscha shrugged as philosophically as only a Hungarian-born Swedish citizen from France can, breezed his horse in the heat of the early evening, and pronounced Samos 3rd to be spectacularly unfit for the great test ahead.

The heat of the evening, I said. In the great promotional test that lay ahead for me, the weather had suddenly become a factor. In my dreams, I had been looking forward to an overflow crowd and a handle of $2.5 million, which would break the previous record by a cool $75,000.

The race had created such interest around the country that ABC-TV had approached me indirectly about telecasting it live on *Wide World of Sports*, which would have meant a windfall income of something like $50,000. The catch was that they wanted me to delay the race for an hour so that it would fit into their programing. And that I wasn't going to do. I had instituted a policy of Precision Post, which meant that the races went off scrupulously on schedule, not when the last dollar was shoved through the betting windows—a radical departure at Suffolk Downs. I certainly wasn't going to throw it away on the big race of the year. Besides, television may run the world but it doesn't run me. There is, I think, a not-so-subtle difference between having the TV people point their cameras at your race—which is a form of reporting—and subjugating your race to their programing. When you accommodate yourself so docilely to their direction, your race becomes a TV show, your track is reduced to a backdrop, and your customers become props.

"You want to telecast the race?" I told them. "Fine. But it's our race you'll have to telecast, not yours."

With the big weekend coming up, the weather had turned hot and humid, with predictions of more to come. The kind of weekend weather that traditionally sends Bostonians flocking to the Cape. Saturday came up even hotter, and, to make it the worst of all possible worlds, it rained off and on during the morning to discourage any casual racegoer who might have been planning, or trying to decide this late in the game, to come on out. To discourage him even further, the Weather Bureau was predicting "possible thunderstorms." I had made arrangements to rent extra parking facilities along the routes of entrance, if need be, and to rent some shuttle buses to go with the jitneys we already had for transporting the customers back and forth to their cars. I waited to see. I still wasn't ready to back off my prediction of a record crowd, mind you. I wasn't sticking to it, either. Just between you and me, I didn't have the slightest idea what to expect.

And then there was the starting tape. You have already guessed by now that the starting tape didn't arrive, haven't you? Wrong. The starting tape was delivered late in the morning, as promised, in plenty of time for us to discover that it didn't even begin to extend across the track. I ordered the ground crew to knock out the railing alongside the starting gate so that we could start the number 15 horse outside the gate.

A chinchy way to do it, to be sure, but I didn't have any other choice.

Shortly before noon, I bumped into Larry Howley coming up the stairs of the administration building. "You can call off the crew, Bill," he said, beaming. "Harem Lady has been scratched." Harem Lady was a little mare who had been one of the surprise entries. As we found out later, Allen Jerkens, the bright young trainer, had gambled $1000 on the chance that he'd force us to break the field into two sections. Quite obviously, he wasn't willing to spend another $2000 to run the little mare in such a huge field—and off an unaccustomed walk-up start, at that.

With the final entry fees from the fourteen remaining horses, the Yankee Gold Cup was worth $252,750.

For one tantalizing moment after the scratching of Harem Lady, I was seized by the sweet illusion that our fortunes had finally taken a turn for the better. But not for long. Within minutes my wife, Mary Frances, arrived at the track with the bad news. She had left the motel somewhere around noon, later than she had intended to. "The cab-driver never really had to slow down," she said, and that told me all I had to know. By that time, if we were going to come anywhere near the crowd I had been anticipating, she should have hit the beginnings of a massive traffic jam. All I could do now was hope for one of those late crowds. It never came. It continued to be a day of terrible heat, with the thermometer flirting with 100 degrees. Between noon and 1:45, the post time for our first race, thunderclouds gathered off to the east and lightning flashed through the skies. The humidity was unbearable. One of those days where your pants stick to your legs if you take three steps.

The crowd was 18,680, routine for a Saturday.

We had reserved a box for the *comtesse,* and even she didn't show. I have a feeling that she got off the plane, staggered a couple of steps backward, and said, "Take me to the Cape."

As the horses entered the gate for the Yankee Gold Cup, only a little more than $198,000 had been bet. For the only time in my entire stay at Suffolk Downs, I was not rooting for them to get right off. I was rooting for a long, long delay, because it's in those late flashes that you'll usually find some big money thrown in. And there was indeed a long delay while Billy Mills was getting the big field settled. Long enough for six or seven new totals to be flashed. The total crept up by no more than a hundred or two hundred dollars with each new flash. Not thousands, hundreds. It is still the most remarkable thing I have ever seen on a racetrack. The final flash showed that $198,750 had been bet, and I am absolutely convinced that if we had waited another hour it wouldn't have gone up to $200,000. For whatever it was worth, I could congratulate myself that our customers had come to believe that we had meant what we said about Precision Post. Every dollar that was in the track to be bet had been bet.

The race itself was a classic. Czar Alexander went right to the front but began to fade after three-quarters of a mile. Gustav Ring had been right. The weight was just too much for his horse. In that weather, anyway.

The French horses were both far back in the early running. Samos's lack of conditioning was painfully evident. He was still running gingerly the second time the field passed the grandstand, as if he couldn't quite get his footing. After a mile, he had fallen back to eleventh place, just behind Petrone. But then, as they went into the turn for the last time, Samos dug in and began to sweep around the field in great, ground-eating strides. As they hit the sixteenth pole, he caught Czar Alexander, who was still holding gamely onto third place about five lengths behind the two leaders, closed to within a couple of lengths in the next few strides, and seemed to have dead aim on them. And then the lack of conditioning told, and he hung. A hard-luck horse. His reputation held.

The real hard-luck horse in the Yankee Gold Cup, though, was his countryman, Petrone. In a classically run race, one horse gets a bad break which he either overcomes or doesn't. When Samos had begun his big move from way back, Johnny Sellers on Petrone had taken right out behind him. But just as Petrone began to move, the two horses directly in front of him quit cold—both of them together. To keep Petrone from running up their heels, Sellers had to pull Petrone back sharply, swing him around them, and, to all practical purposes, get his horse back in stride again. By the time they hit the final stretch, Petrone was under a full head of steam again and flying. When Samos hung in the final yards, Petrone went roaring on by him. If the two front horses hadn't been running so strongly, he would have caught them. In another twenty or thirty yards he probably would have won, regardless.

The winner was Jean Pierre, a Kentucky-bred with a French name. The irony was that Jean Pierre had been losing so consistently to Czar Alexander all year that his stable hadn't intended to enter him. They had, instead, run him in a handicap at Monmouth Park in New Jersey the previous Saturday. Jean Pierre had run such a big race at Monmouth under a new jockey, Walter Blum, that his people called Larry Howley on Wednesday, the day before the drawing, to let us know they were thinking very seriously of running him back in the Gold Cup with only a week's rest.

A second irony was that the horse he had to beat off was the fourth, and virtually ignored, French horse that had been entered in the race, Taneb, a front-runner who had shown very little ability to hold his speed over a distance. Having astonished everybody by knocking off Czar Alexander early, Taneb continued to race stride for stride with Jean Pierre for another full turn around the track. It wasn't until they were straightening out for the stretch run that Jean Pierre was able to get his nose out in front, and it was only in the final few strides that he was able to open up daylight.

I still run into people who want to talk about that race. It's too bad there weren't enough of them.

I had to go down to the winner's circle to make the presentation. Not because I had planned it that way, but only because I had neglected to plan it any other way. I had been so occupied with more serious matters during the week that I had completely forgotten to call anybody from the distinguished list of prospects I had in my desk drawer.

Leading the long list of notables who were conspicuously absent from the winner's circle was Jean Pierre's owner, Thomas Nichols. I made the presentation—a gold cup and a check for $164, 287.50—to the trainer. Nichols was billed as a New York financier and Kentucky horsebreeder —which sounds like a pleasant way to make a living. He also turned out to be a man of mystery. None of the out-of-town writers who tried to get in touch with him had any success. Even his trainer wasn't able to tell them very much about him. That's the way it goes when it's going bad. I give the guy a check for $164,287.50, and I can't get a line's worth of publicity out of him.

There is a Thomas Nichols, though. His name was written, plain as day, on the back of the check when it came back.

We were throwing a champagne party in the Paddock Club, our fanciest restaurant, after the race, and I did my very best to let everybody see how much fun it can be to preside over a disaster. "So I just blew $200,000," I said, laughing through my tears. "I've blown that much on a ballplayer."

I didn't bother to mention that I had also managed to prove how it was possible to take a moderately successful sixty-five-day meet and turn it overnight into a moderately unsuccessful-sixty-six-day meet. Or that the Yankee Gold Cup, hallowed be its name, was about to be retired with honors.

6

An Issue of No Significance

Thirteen days after our opening, I sued the Racing Commission. There were not many subsequent days during my two-year stewardship that we didn't have a suit in the courts against either the commission or the Attorney General.

We are just beginning to skate along the edges of Massachusetts politics here, and some small input of basic background would be useful. Just the lay of the land, so to speak. The shape, as it were, of the terrain.

(1) The tax on racing is the easiest kind of tax for politicians to levy because (a) no property value is affected, and (b) none of their constituents is going to be paying the tax except those who enter the track voluntarily and, indeed, pay for the privilege.

(2) You would think that politicians would be eager to realize as much as possible from this pool of painless revenue. And they are. Except where the Commonwealth's interest comes into conflict with their own personal financial interest.

(3) The pols believe that horseracing was created by a bountiful heaven as their own private grazing grounds. And not without reason. The control of racing is in the hands of the state legislature. Your license to operate comes from the Racing Commission, which is the creature

of the legislature. Your racing dates, which are what you live by, also come from the Racing Commission. The commissioners are appointed by the Governor. Their legal adviser, whenever a problem arises, is the Attorney General.

(4) In Massachusetts, with its puritancial background, horseracing has always been looked upon as being somewhat disreputable. People *gamble*. Right out in the open. And worse of all, in the daytime when honest people should be working or cooking dinner or picketing. The operator of a racetrack is in no position to assume a righteous stance. He is supposed to be quiet, accommodating, and invisible.

The first thing I discovered was that the Racing Statute of Massachusetts had put me in a straitjacket. To begin with, Thoroughbred racing was limited to 90 days a year. Suffolk Downs had 66 of those days. Berkshire Downs, a ramshackle little track in the western part of the state, had the other 24. The statutory straitjacket squeezes tighter because of the limitations that are placed upon those 90 days. For openers, we had to apply for our dates by January 5, and the commission had to award them by January 30, an arrangement which allowed the Rhode Island and New Hampshire tracks, which operate more than 70 per cent on Massachusetts clientele, to decide where and how they wanted to run against us. What it comes down to is that for reasons I couldn't possibly imagine, the Rhode Island and New Hampshire tracks had more muscle with the Massachusetts legislators than we did. We are going to take that up, in nauseating detail, in the next chapter—that's where we step up in class and sue the Attorney General, folks. In filing your application, it is well to keep in mind that (1) you cannot start before April 1, (2) there is a six-week hiatus between August 10 and the second Saturday after Labor Day and (3) you cannot run after November 30.

The six-week blackout in the middle of summer is a "protected sanctuary" for pari-mutuel racing in what are humourously called "agricultural and horticultural fairs." The blackout applies only to Thoroughbred racing. Not to the dogs or the harness horses, which are running at night.

Although these six-day "fair racing meetings" enter only peripherally into the suit against the commission, they are perfect illustrations of the hypocrisy and corruption of the political scene. The farm vote doesn't mean that much. Massachusetts is an industrial state, not an agricultural one. The fairs are fronts for other interests. Fair racing exists for no other reasons than that influential citizens and powerful politicians profit mightily from it.

Item: Berkshire Downs was getting the extra six days by running the Hancock Fair, the only profitable part of its operation. It bought the racing license from the fair for $30,000. All that is required from the sponsoring agricultural society is that it be certified by the Agricultural Department, hold exhibits, and present awards.

Back in 1963 a special legislative investigating committee came to the conclusion that "it is difficult, perhaps impossible, to name a single fair which is truly agricultural and which conducts racing purely for the fair's gain." Governor Endicott Peabody asked for a complete overhaul of the enabling statute, which was really a Christmas tree of special privileges. And that was the last that was ever heard of that. The bill never got out of committee.

Who kills Santa Claus?

And yet, because the fairs themselves are technically "nonprofit organizations," they didn't have to pay 7.5 per cent of their handle to the state like the commercial tracks; they were paying only about 4.5 per cent. The difference was costing the Commonwealth more than $700,000 a year.

Nor were there any federal taxes. As a matter of fact, the Brockton Fair owned sixty-five acres of prime land in the middle of the city and for years didn't even have to pay property taxes.

Here's how favored these "fairs" were. As originally drawn, the law had not only knocked out daytime competition from the Thoroughbreds, it had given the fairs an absolute right to bring about the cancelation of any dog or harness meet anywhere in the state on the mere assertion that it constituted unfair competition.

In addition to whatever money just might have crossed their sweaty palms, insiders could profit from good advice. As you might expect, these six-day meets are hit-and-run affairs. There is little supervision of the races. Security is almost nonexistent.

Back to the suit: There were signs all over Suffolk Downs saying: NO MINORS PERMITTED. As the week of our opening approached, those signs began to vex me. In our original plans, my wife, Mary Frances, and our six kids were going to remain down in Maryland until school ended, with a couple of the kids coming up to pay their old man a visit during the first week of racing. I looked at all those signs and thought to myself: *Where am I going to put them?*

And then I thought: This is ridiculous. I don't want them to bet, but why shouldn't they be permitted on the grounds?

And then: Where does it say in the rules and regulations that they aren't?

A quick reading of the Racing Statute turned up only one relevant clause: "Any licensee permitting any minor to participate in the pari-mutuel system of wagering at a racing meeting . . . shall be punished by a fine of not more than a hundred dollars."

I called our lawyer, Joel Kozol, and asked whether there was any reason we couldn't have minors at the track.

A very good one, he answered. It was prohibited.

"Where is it prohibited?"

"Lookit," he said, "the Racing Statute has been on the books since 1934, and I've never been in a track in the Commonwealth or in New England that didn't have those signs posted all over the place. It must be there in the statute."

Not the way I read it. As far as the signs were concerned, we had inherited them from the previous management. "You'd be surprised," I told him, "how fast I can pull signs off the wall."

In due time, he called me back. The Racing Commission's own rules and regulations were worded very similarly to the statute's. "There is a provision against their gambling," he said. "But that wasn't your question."

And then Joel asked a question of his own. Why did I want minors at the track?

"Because I am not going to have my own kids thinking their old man is involved in something so nefarious that they can't watch him at work."

True enough. But not the whole truth. There were long-range economic prospects that were involved, too. For years, I had been known among my more classical-minded admirers as baseball's Cassandra, forever leaning against a Doric column and warning that doom was close at hand unless we lifted the game out of the horse-and-buggy age and brought it into line with the quickening rhythm of American life.

Now, the Thoroughbred is the fastest thing on four feet. Once we swung into action, my line went: "Unlike baseball, we can guarantee action nine times a day."

Well, yeah. But how could I ignore the ominous intonations that are set up by the very term "horse-and-buggy"? The horse itself is an anachronism. There's no other way to put it. If the horse is an anachronism, what does that make horseracing except an exercise in ancestor-worship, an outdoor museum with betting windows.

Almost from the beginning of recorded history, the horse was the center of the economic, social, and military might of every powerful nation. It was so interwoven into the texture of knighthood and the Age of Chivalry that the word itself is an anglicization of *cheval*, the French word for horse.

In our country, the horse was a partner to the winning of the West. The wagon train, the stage coach, the pony express. To the cowboy, the horse was so vital to survival that horse-stealing was a hanging offense, with or without judicial sanction. To the settler, the horse was the power that pulled the plow. To the military, the cavalry was the elite striking force.

From the beginning of recorded history, right down to us. If you're not very much under fifty, you can still remember, however dimly, the horse-drawn ice wagons and milk wagons and junk wagons as a routine part of daily life.

If you're under forty, you don't know what an ice wagon is and you never saw a milk truck that didn't come equipped with an internal-combustion engine. The last faint signature of that longtime partner to man's destiny is in the word "horsepower." A kid growing up in the city today could spend his whole life without seeing a real live horse except for a trip to the zoo or racetrack. So, for that matter, could a kid growing up on a farm.

The horses they do see are mostly show horses and Thoroughbreds, bred to be not man's associate in conquest but only man's toy. The Thoroughbred has become so domesticated that a mare is unable to foal without help. It is such a fragile animal that—well, you've noticed what happens to the leading contenders for the Kentucky Derby every year, haven't you?

An anachronism. An old champion hanging on. The mystique that once surrounded horseracing has passed on to automobile racing and turned it into the fastest-growing sport in the United States. Especially among young people. And while it's true enough that the stock cars that

are raced on the big-time circuit have been "modified" out of all relation to anything you'll see on the road, it's also true that stock-car races
are being conducted on fairgrounds all around the country that are
exactly that: races of stock cars. The guys who race against each other
on Sunday morning will be driving the same cars to work on Monday.
Listen to me now: I have absolutely no doubt that we are going to have
pari-mutuel betting on automobile racing one of these days. And sooner
than you think. If it weren't for the historical accident that set the
hotbed of auto racing in the Piedmont area, the heart of the Bible Belt,
we'd have had it already.

I don't know for sure what the average age of the spectators on the
stock-car grounds would be, but I'd be pretty safe in placing it, at the
outside, at no more than twenty-five.

I do know what the average age at the racetrack is. Over thirty? Yup.
Over forty? Yup. Over fifty? Yup. It's fifty years, six months. Nationally.

When you think a little about it, it's not as surprising as it may have
seemed at first glance. The average man gets married at the age of
twenty-two. Before he knows it, he has a mortgage and a couple of kids.
He is not only immersed in family life but he has the feeling—which
isn't really true—that he can't afford to go to the track because that's
the place where you lose your money. For the most part, then, you've
lost him completely until he hits his mid-thirties. With the vast and
varied opportunities that are available these days to develop an interest
in other forms of recreation, you may very well have lost him forever.

No matter how you sliced it, it added up to only one thing. Our
clientele was aging fast, and we weren't doing a thing to develop anybody to replace it.

No. I could see nothing wrong with permitting minors onto the premises, and a great deal to be said in its favor as far as our remaining in
business was concerned.

We didn't move precipitously. Although there was nothing in the
statute that specifically barred children from the track, the commission
had been given broad powers "to prescribe rules, regulations and conditions under which all horse or dog meets shall be conducted in the
Commonwealth." I began to taking an unofficial and very casual sounding among the commissioners. The two associate commissioners, Peter
Consiglio and Mike Holovak, couldn't have cared less. Mike Holovak,
the ex-Boston Patriot football coach, who had been appointed only a
month earlier when his predecessor's term ran out, was moved only to

reflect with obvious pleasure upon how he and his wife used to bring their daughter to the track with them in California when she was a little girl.

The chairman of the commission was Dr. Paul F. Walsh, a New Bedford dentist. Dr. Walsh turned out to be a different set of molars entirely. Clenched. Firm. Resolute. In other words, Dr. Walsh was vehemently against it.

Dr. Walsh is a thin, reserved man with white-blond hair, who bears a startling resemblance, in both looks and speech, to that good solid actor Arthur O'Connell. Despite his slightness of build, he had been the star running back for the crunching, single-wing Georgetown U. football teams of the early 1940s. Unless I am very much mistaken he and Mike Holovak had played against each other when Georgetown came to Boston and defeated an equally powerful Boston College team coached by Frank Leahy. I had met him socially at a luncheon that had been thrown for me in New Bedford during my first weeks in Boston, a wild and wooly affair that had carried on through dinner and hadn't broken up until the morning light was on the windows. A perfectly delightful affair; the best and most enjoyable affair I attended during my entire stay in Boston. Since New Bedford is Dr. Walsh's home town, we had ended up as sort of co-guests of honor and he had unbent as much as such a quiet and reserved man ever unbends.

Four days before our opening, we sent out a press release to announce that minors "accompanied by their parents or guardians, and under their direct control at all times, will be admitted to view the horse races" at Suffolk Downs. Children under twelve were to be admitted at half-price.

The wording, as you can see, was very carefully phrased to defuse any possible objections. "The state Racing Commission rule of prohibiting minors in the betting area is an excellent one, obviously, and will be strictly adhered to," I said, pulling a forelock in the direction of Chairman Walsh. "In fact, we're going to make sure the rule is enforced."

"At the same time," I added, getting in a blow for my own side, "we feel children are tremendously interested in horses. I think it's wrong to deprive them of the chance to view the colorful pageantry which surrounds the sport."

The announcement went out on Tuesday. The Racing Commission meets every Wednesday. Rain or shine. Agenda or no agenda. We didn't have to wait even that long. From his unofficial headquarters in

New Bedford, Dr. Walsh issued a bristling manifesto of his determination to fight to see that our wicked design never came to pass. It was okay for the kids to come out to the morning workouts, the way he saw it, but he was unalterably opposed to having them at the track when the pari-mutuel machines were in operation.

Most disheartening. And also most revealing. We had a chairman who believed in his bones that betting was evil. So evil that he took it as his duty to protect innocent children from the indifference and neglect of their parents. We weren't requiring children to come to the track, after all. We were simply allowing their parents to bring them in, if they wanted to.

Sure enough, Dr. Walsh opened the commission meeting the next day by introducing a motion to bar anybody under twenty-one. The motion died when neither of his fellow commissioners would second it.

It didn't stay dead for long. After the real business of the meeting had been disposed of, Dr. Walsh did a little evangelizing among his colleagues and succeeded in getting them to go along to the extent of issuing a statement that we were being allowed to go ahead on a "probationary" basis only, and with the clear understanding that policing the kids would be the sole responsibility of the track. If the commission wasn't satisfied with our performance in that regard, we were warned, it would put an end to the new policy forthwith.

I just love being put on probation. I just love these political agencies who know what's good for you better than you do. Gritting my teeth, I explained to the press that we had gone ahead only after an exhaustive study of the practices in all parts of the country. "Obviously, policing is our responsibility," I said snappishly. "And if I thought we couldn't do the job properly, we wouldn't admit the children."

Did I really think I was going to be able to keep every minor in there from betting? Of course I didn't. All we could do was to instruct our people to try. Thirteen-year-old kids we could take care of. How are you supposed to tell the difference between a twenty-year-old young man and a twenty-one-year-old one? What were we going to do, ask everybody to show us a birth certificate? I'm not going to be a hypocrite about this. If an eighteen-year-old kid can be sent into battle—to use that frayed but telling argument—who am I or the Racing Commission or King Farouk to tell him he isn't old enough to bet on a horse?

It was just as well that I was able to forbear from mounting my soapbox to make that speech publicly. I had said quite enough as it was.

The word came winging back to us that the state police had been instructed to be extremely vigilant in their surveillance of the betting lines. There was an implicit warning that if they turned up any kids in there they'd go after our license.

Well, good luck to them. The one thing I was sure of was that they weren't going to be doing anything forthwith at that stage of the game. In order to adopt a new regulation, the law requires the commission to hold a full public hearing. And then only after it has published a notice of intent in an accredited newspaper, sent us a copy of the proposed regulation, and given us twenty-one days to prepare our rebuttal.

On April 29, ten days after we opened, Dr. Walsh called the commission into emergency session and threw the kids out. The vote was 2–0. Mike Holovak had just signed on as backfield coach for the San Francisco Forty-Niners, and it was such an *Emergency!* they couldn't wait for him to get back. To this day, I don't think Peter Consiglio cared one way or the other. Consiglio is a very bright, very successful businessman. His company, Parker Manufacturing, turns out a wide variety of products made of wire. Disposable items mostly, the best kind. Any time you steal one of those shopping carts from your supermarket, you are probably making him a little richer. With the chairman making such a personal issue out of it Consiglio had, in my opinion, simply shrugged his shoulders and paid him the courtesy of going along.

In order to pass an *Emergency!* rule, an administrative body such as the Racing Commission has be be convinced that:

(1) immediate adoption or amendment of a regulation is necessary for the preservation of the public health, safety, or general welfare, *and*

(2) observance of the requirements of notice and public hearing would be contrary to the public interest.

By admitting kids to the track, we were—by a unanimous 2–0 vote —attacking everything near and dear to the decent people of the community *and* placing the Commonwealth in such imminent peril that a delay of twenty-one days would have proved fatal.

Incredible! At a time when the mass disaffection of our children was a real and present phenomenon on the national scene, when drugs had saturated their environment and the credibility of the government itself was under attack, Dr. Walsh's world was coming all apart at the prospect of a kid sneaking in a two-dollar bet.

Did the man really think that any kid in Boston couldn't get down a bet with the corner bookie any time he wanted to?

I don't think so. Aware though I am that dentists lead a sheltered and sometimes even monkish existence, I just can't bring myself to believe that. The marvelous thing about the Watch-and-Ward morality of Massachusetts is that the reality is never as strong as the pretense. The Great Commonwealth has always been able to balance a pervasive political corruption against an official piety that somehow blended its Puritan heritage with the rigorous theology of a latter-day Irish Catholicism. Against the evidence of their eyes, the communicants are easily able to persuade themselves that an absolute morality does exist. Inviolable. Irreducible. Unchanging. Cotton Mather never really went away. The idea—religious orthodoxy become political salvation—that governmental agencies are the appointed keepers of everybody's morals still runs pretty rampant in the Great Commonwealth.

Viewed in that light, a reading of the *Emergency!* rule becomes most instructive. It consists, in its entirety, of two short sentences. The first sentence reads: "No person under the age of twenty-one years shall be admitted as a patron to any racing meeting licensed by the Commission." The second sentence reads: "This rule shall not apply to racing meetings conducted at State or County Fairs where racing is not the sole attraction."

So here we are, back at the fairs.

I have never questioned the depth of Dr. Walsh's sincerity. Nobody, after all, makes himself look ridiculous on purpose. He is an honest man, incapable of subterfuge, and, within the limitations placed upon him by the practicalities of politics and the bonds of friendship, an honorable one.

And yet, to get his ruling, Dr. Walsh had been willing to palter with his conscience where the fairs were concerned. If it would corrupt a child to enter our lavish plant, where the racing was closely regulated and the facilities quite attractive, why should he emerge, pure and shining, from the fair? The children were going to be exposed to the pernicious influence of pari-mutuel machines there too, weren't they? The same tickets punched by the same company's machines? If we had happened to have a fair at Suffolk Downs, the kids would have been able to come in, *with or without* their parents, and wander around at will. No, I am not indulging in idle speculation there. Berkshire Downs, you will remember, does have a fair. Children would be going in. They had been going in for years. The same grounds, the same facilities, the same machines.

Two of the three dog tracks and the other harness track had fairs too. The same grounds, the same facilities, the same machines.

The question, as I don't have to tell you, is a rhetorical one. We know the answer. Fairs are predominantly family affairs. If you barred the kids, the fairs would have to shut down, and there'd be a lot of politicians and faithful contributors to the commonweal with longer faces and thinner wallets.

The practicalities of politics, I said. Commissioners are political appointees. Where politics rears its many heads, Dr. Walsh does as he is told.

It was no dentist's hand that had so carefully appended that clause to protect the fairs. That was the hand of a lawyer. Nor was it a dentist's mind that had clamped upon the *Emergency!* gimmick. An assistant attorney general is assigned permanently to the commission. After Dr. Walsh had convinced Consiglio that he should go along with him, he would have automatically gone to the Attorney General's man to write the new regulation for him. A logical reconstruction of what happened from there would go something like this: The assistant attorney general would probably have cleared the *Emergency!* meeting with the Attorney General himself, both as to the legal approach and, because the fairs might be involved, the political considerations. Attorney General Robert H. Quinn, was, as we shall see, in the habit of improvising quite freely on the law. Dr. Walsh would have been assured that the *Emergency!* approach was beyond reproach. Absolutely legal. No problem at all. He also would have been told that, like it or not, he had to take the exclusion on the fairs. Considering what that did to his lofty moral position, I am willing to assume that he voiced some reservations.

What did he have to worry about, anyway? Nobody had ever sued the Racing Commission before.

We had to decide whether we wanted to take them on. And we had to decide fast. By going the *Emergency!* route, the commission didn't have to give us a hearing for ninety days, by which time the meet would be over and we would be arguing about 1970. Assuming there was anything still there to argue about. Our information, which was generally very good, was that the *Emergency!* rule was only a holding operation. The over-all plan was to follow it up by whipping a bill through the state legislature, a rather strong indication—we felt—that somebody was very well aware he was playing fast and loose with the legalities. Because we had been hit with the ban so suddenly, the commission had given us a week of grace to get the word around. If we were going to sue, it seemed like a mighty good idea—a strategic imperative, really —to cut them off at the pass by filing before the ban went into effect. Our thinking went something like this: Once the bill was in the hopper, the Attorney General could argue that the courts should leave legislative matters to the legislature. If we beat the commission to the punch, and it was *still* foolish enough to file the bill, it would be inviting us to assume a posture of indignation and accuse it of making a cheap and obvious attempt to usurp the power of the courts.

If it had been only a question of the kids, there would have been nothing to think about. What we were thinking about was my future relationship with the entire political structure. In my three months in town, I had already upset a few of the established patterns. The elimination of the politicians' passes, as we have already seen, had not been looked upon as a particularly winning bid for friendship. There had also been the matter of placing our insurance, which is generally accepted in the upper echelons as a legal way of playing the political game. Or hasn't it ever occurred to you to wonder why so many politicians with a passsion for helping their fellow man run insurance agencies on the side? An account like Suffolk Downs is a nice way to start the day. The premiums had amounted to $268,000, and the man who had been waking up to them was Sonny McDonough, a longtime member of the Governor's Council. Considering the symbiotic relationship between insurance and politics, I had to figure that my predecessors hadn't been giving them to him for the love of the game. Let me put it this way: When you're sending out checks with big numbers on them, you don't feel at all bashful about placing a call and saying, "Hey, Sonny, I've got a little trouble here. I wonder if you can help me out . . ." Don't misunderstand me. There was nothing I would have liked better than to have been able to tell Sonny my troubles. What happened was that Realty Equities came up with their own guy in New York. They were playing their own games. In my first brush with life on the underside of a conglomerate, I was discovering that when the name of the game is Moneyball, the parent company owns the ball. I made it very, very clear to them that taking the insurance away from a man who had a seat in the Governor's Council was a hurtful thing to do to us. I did manage to salvage some of it for McDonough by insisting that, at the very minimum, their guy should lay part of it off with him. It couldn't have been very much. I know it wasn't enough to make McDonough happy.

Or me. I could just imagine what they'd be saying in the State House corridors when the word got around, in the distorted way these things always get around, that I had taken the insurance away from Sonny McDonough and farmed it out to a friend in New York.

And, finally, I had been rocking the boat as far as the commission and the interlocking racing interests of three states were concerned by asking for more dates and going to the legislature for a whole new set of laws.

To sue now over an issue as insignificant as a few kids coming into the track would be taken as the final proof that I had come to town so eager for battle that I wasn't going to play along in even the most minor of things. On a more personal basis, none of the commissioners had enjoyed being attacked in the press and they were not going to jump with joy about being sued. What, after all, was the use of being a commissioner if they couldn't tell you what you had to do? But that would pass. It wasn't an emotional issue with Consiglio and Holovak. Before it was over, they would be as impatient with Dr. Walsh for pushing me to a showdown as they'd be with me.

And right there you had the most worrisome thing of all. There were only two people in the entire Commonwealth to whom the issue of admitting kids to a racetrack was not such an insignificant thing. One was Dr. Walsh. The other was me. I had already informed Joel that my children were coming into the track, regardless. "I'll go to jail if I have to. Under no circumstances am I going to obey a rule that's based on nothing more than the narrow personal morality of one man, elected by nobody." Greed vs. greed makes for the kind of lawsuits that are settled between the lawyers as soon as both sides decide to take what they can get. Principle vs. principle is a holy war, and no holy war has ever been settled out of court.

I was incensed that they had rammed this through without giving me so much as the courtesy of a hearing. I was furious at the implication that the chairman of any regulatory board was a better keeper of my children's morals than I was. Let Dr. Walsh worry about his incisors and root canals, and I would tend to my children's upbringing. For my part, I wouldn't take a fifteen-year-old child of mine to the dog races, because the dogs run at night. But neither would I presume to impose my own code of child-rearing upon any parent who thought it would be the greatest experience in the world for his fifteen-year-old.

The first question I had asked Joel was, "What about the judges in this state?" Joel had assured me that one thing Massachusetts did have was a strong and independent bench. From that moment on, I suppose, I knew what my decision was going to be.

I said, "Joel, I think they're wrong. I think they're wrong morally. I think they're wrong legally. I think they're wrong about what's good for racing. And I think they're tragically wrong, over the long run, about what's good for the state."

I said, "Let's take the commission to court."

You think I wasn't ready to make a federal case out of it? Oh, I had constitutional issues that would have kept the Supreme Court in session through the summer. The rights of parents. The rights of children. The discrimination against the Thoroughbreds *vis-à-vis* the harness horses and dogs. The discrimination against us *vis-à-vis* Berkshire Downs, which *did* have a fair. "Insupportable," I growled, doing my well-known imitation of Clarence Darrow. "Absolutely discriminatory. Clearly unconstitutional." I always did want to be a lawyer, you know. I always did see myself roaming a small Arizona courthouse (which looked suspiciously like a Warner Brothers set), fighting the good fight for the underdog. What better underdog to fight for than myself?

Underdog? Why not underhorse? Insupportable! Absolutely discriminatory!

Joel's somewhat more professional attitude was that while the constitutional issues made good window-dressing, courtroom battles, like football games, were won on the fundamentals. The average spectator might come away thinking you had won with your passing game, but the pros in the audience knew you had won it in the line. Our best strategy, he felt, would be to attack them on the narrowest possible grounds.

Question: Did the commission have the legal authority to bar children from racetracks? For any reason.

Commission Answer (projected): Yes. Our authority comes out of our broad power to prescribe "rules, regulations and conditions." Especially conditions.

But Joel thought he saw something. Did not the provision in the statute that said minors were not to be permitted to wager carry the strong implication that the legislature had, in fact, contemplated their presence on the premises? If the legislature hadn't wanted them there, why hadn't it simply said so? Just as the Racing Commission was now so unmistakably saying so? This being true (and it became true to us the moment Joel gave voice to it), the commission had clearly exceeded its powers by going beyond the statutory scheme.

Commission Answer (projected): We can play that game, too. If the legislature had wanted them there, why hadn't it said so? Just as we are now so unmistakably excluding them.

Easy. Either the legislature had deliberately refrained from spelling it out, in order perhaps not to rile up the anti-racing elements any further, or it had simply overlooked it. If the omission had been inadvertent, no administrative agency had the right to rectify it. If it had been deliberate, the commission had no right to add a meaning that had not been intended.

We filed our suit on Friday, May 2. We also petitioned for a temporary injunction to stop the rule from going into effect until after we had had our day in court. The judge wouldn't go that far for us, and the kids were out. What he did do for us was almost as good. He put us on a standby list that would guarantee us an almost immediate trial. The date was tentatively set as May 13.

Right away, it got rough. On Tuesday, the secretary of the Racing Commission, Larry Lane, notified Frank Kozol, Joel's father, that the commission was going to append additional reasons to those already on file to explain why it had felt it necessary to institute *Emergency!* proceedings. Oh no, it wasn't! In issuing its ruling, the commission had listed four reasons, ranging from philosophically vague to vaguely philosophical. To our astonishment, there hadn't been a word in there about minors having been found betting. The only two charges which by any stretch of the imagination could be called specific were:

"Numerous complaints have been received by the Commission that these minors have been disturbing the patrons at the track."

"Once they are inside the track there is little or no supervision exercised over them by said parents or guardians."

It seemed quite clear to us that the Attorney General's office had advised Dr. Walsh that he was going to have to do better than that to justify an *Emergency!* And that told us something, too. Since the AG's office would have drawn up the Reasons for Emergency itself, it told us that our resistance had come as a complete surprise.

Joel found his father's memo about the commission meeting on his desk when he came in Wednesday morning. The meeting was scheduled for 11:00 A.M. There was no time for cuteness. Tom Beedem, as a former commissioner and former chairman and longtime racing official, was our natural contact with the commission. We sent Tom hustling over to the hearing room to warn them that if they tried to play games with us we were going to instruct our lawyers to tear them apart. The message was that the reasons for adopting an *Emergency!* measure were insufficient to the moment thereof, and that we were more than willing to fight that issue out with them on its merits. If they tried to beef up their case, after the fact, we were going to take it as an outright admission of bad faith and go after them personally and individually.

It was down to the bare knuckles, and they backed away.

The trial was pushed back for two consecutive days. Whichever judge was free when our case came up was the one we'd get.

One little sidelight—and it's worth bringing up here as a reminder that none of this was taking place in a vacuum—was that the case was coming up during the same week we were going to run the Joe Fan Handicap. Day by day, Joel had become more and more nervous about the possibility that the Attorney General might retaliate by ruling that the way we were giving away the horse constituted a lottery. After the trial had been put off for the second day, he paid a personal call on Attorney General Quinn, told him what we were up to, and asked him for a ruling. Although Quinn refused to give us anything in writing, he did assure him, unofficially, that we had nothing to worry about as far as any action by his office was concerned.

That's all we were after. To get him committed before the trial. We were confident that we were going to blow them right out of the courtroom, and we didn't want the Honorable Robert Quinn to pick up the paper on Sunday morning, still smarting from defeat, and get any bright ideas.

On Friday we drew Judge James L. Roy, a relatively new judge. A very fastidious old-Yankee type, who lived in Louisburg Square on the Hill and dressed in an aristocratic Victorian manner, morning suit and all. Joel had very little book on him, but he turned out to be a very human judge, with a minimum of pomp and an occasional twinkle in his eye. From time to time I had the feeling that he thought we were both pretty ridiculous—they with their nervous breakdown over kids at a track, and we with our high-flown constitutional grounds.

I took the stand and testified as to why I believed the spectacle of racing would be enjoyable and, by heavens, educational for the kids. A marvelous opportunity for families to spend a day together. I reminded him that in colonial days racing had been exactly that, a family affair. I also made it clear that my interests did not run parallel with a social worker's. Unless we did something to develop new fans, I said, I did not think racing could survive.

We were able to show that seventeen states did allow children on the track, including New York, California, Maryland, Kentucky, New Jersey, and Ohio. Against that, only one state, Florida, specifically banned them. Far from weakening our case, the Florida situation was dead in line with our main attack. The children were barred there not by edict of an arrogant racing commission but, in the highest tradition of democracy, peace, and freedom, by legislative action.

The state's only real witness was a lieutenant detective of the state police, who testified that he had seen about fifty minors in the line between opening day and the implementation of the *Emergency!* rule. His testimony was considerably weakened, though—nullified, really— when Joel brought out the reason why nothing had been said about this in the commission's original ruling. Nobody had asked him, that's why. Oh . . . ? Was the commission now claiming that it had been forced to take *Emergency!* action because of something it didn't know about? From there, his testimony was a shambles. Had the lieutenant pulled any of the fifty minors out of line? No. Had he taken any of their names? No. Had he asked any of them how old they were? No. He had permitted them to go right ahead and place their bets, was that it? That was it. Which meant that, if he had judged their ages correctly, he had, in clear dereliction of his sworn duty, stood idly by and permitted them to break the law. Tsk, tsk, tsk.

The trial didn't take one full day. Two weeks later, Judge Roy handed down his decision. He did it in 350 words, all stinging.

He began by stripping the case of all the nonessentials, and the way he did it was fascinating. After the commission had backed away from its rewrite job on the Reasons for Emergency, it had filed notice that it was going to hold a public hearing on June 18. Instead of waiting the full ninety days, it was going out of its way to give us our hearing before our meeting closed, see? But not, you will notice, before we came to trial.

It was a ploy, and a very obvious one, and Judge Roy picked it up and rejected it. Since the hearing would be coming up so shortly, said the judge, "no useful purpose would be served by exploring the dubious emergency action of the commission." Having rebuked the commission's tactics by the use of that one word "dubious," he then proceeded to perform a neat vasectomy on the upcoming hearing by holding for us in every regard. For all practical purposes, he could have copied his findings straight out of Joel's brief.

He adopted completely—"inescapable" was the word he used—the notion that, in limiting its restrictions to betting, the legislature had provided what it regarded as a reasonable protection for minors. *"The rule in question does not seem to implement but, in effect, prohibits that which the legislature saw fit to permit."*

Joel had been right about fighting it out on the narrowest possible grounds. And just as he had predicted, the window-dressing had played its part. For without departing from the narrow line he had chosen to base his decision upon, Judge Roy wove *my case* into his findings and, still ostensibly hewing to the question of the commission's authority, found in my favor. The operative words this time are "in this day and age." Listen.

"If the presence of a minor at the track in company with his parent is to be deemed dangerous to the well-being of youth, inimical to the public interest, or offensive to the public morality in this day and age, this should be the decision of the legislature (theoretically, at least, more responsive to the public will than an appointed board) rather than that of the commission."

His ruling was that the *Emergency!* rule was "in excess of the jurisdiction and authority of the commission and is invalid."

Would you believe that the commission voted unanimously to appeal? Or that the Assistant Attorney General came into court himself to ask that the kids be kept out of the track until the appeal could be heard. What he was saying was that even though the judge had ruled that the commission had no right to overrule the legislature, the judge should now overrule it himself.

Predictably, Judge Roy refused. Kids came back on the track, and the Commonwealth still stands undiminished in all its majesty.

Dr. Walsh went ahead with the June 18 hearing anyway, and the commission repassed its rule so that it would be ready to sweep the kids out the moment it got a favorable ruling on its appeal. Dr. Walsh's attitude toward me could best be described as cold and correct, much as if he were informing me that he would do his best to be fair to me at all times, whatever he might think of me personally. In the course of the hearing, he kept letting us know, both officially and unofficially, what a terrible thing he thought we had done. After everything that had happened, the man still could not understand that although we had beaten him on the purely legal issue, we had been challenging his moral right to impose a kind of censorship based upon his personal beliefs. At one point, when he was stating for the record that he certainly wouldn't want *his* children exposed to a racetrack environment, Joel popped up and said, "Bill Veeck is not unfamiliar with the problems of a family man. He's got nine kids of his own."

The sad part of it was that although Dr. Walsh couldn't understand me, I was beginning to understand him almost too well. Our kids had quite obviously become the occasion for fighting a much larger issue. He had found something symbolic in it, something central in his life. I should have been able to see that from the beginning just in the way he had pursued it, gnawing at it, bringing everybody on his side into line, using up all his credit, refusing to let go of it. Just as he was, even now, refusing to let go of it.

The greater issue was everything that was happening. It was riots, it was immortality, it was bombing. It was drugs. It was Revolution. It was all our problems and heartaches. It was you-couldn't-tell-the-girls-from-the-boys. The commission offices at 1010 Commonwealth Avenue were only a few blocks up from Boston University and its huge sidewalk campus aswarm with kids. Hairy kids, dirty kids, grimy kids. Flaunting their disrespect for their elders. So sure they had the answers that they jumped the questions. Distorted history. Rejecting the hard lessons of centuries of civilization. Sneering at authority. Spitting on the flag. Dr. Walsh could look out the window and witness the Decline and Fall of Western Civilization. In that context, I set off resonances too. I was Bill Veeck, who had come to town with a billing, taken off a book blurb, as an "incorrigible maverick." Always trying to change things. Announcing right off the bat that I was coming into his bailiwick to change things.

Yes, I should have been able to see it. He had taken his stand in the one place where he had the power to hold the barbarians off. And he had lost. To make his stand—and *lose*—would hold the greater meaning to him that there was nothing he could do about things. Nothing. Anywhere.

You could see the wound that was on him as grimly and meticulously he got his rule cleaned up for the great day when he would be vindicated by a higher court. You wanted to cry out: It's over, Walsh. There's nothing you can do about it. For the love of heaven, man, do yourself a favor and let it go.

You wanted to take him aside and say: The snows of yesteryear have melted. The ship has sailed. The moving finger has writ. It's not that bad. It's really not that bad. And, anyway, there . . . is . . . nothing . . . you—or I, or any of us . . . can . . . do . . . about . . . it.

Too bad. In many ways he was the best and most decent of the political men I came across in Boston. For two years, the face he presented to me was cold and correct. A sad face, a well-meaning face trying so hard to be fair and closing up when, every now and then, he failed. Well, I hadn't forced the issue; he had. I hadn't put the wound there; the world had. A man with so bruisable a conscience should never have taken a political appointment to begin with.

The appeal hung until early in the fall, when Attorney General Quinn called Joel to tell him he was dropping it.

Dr. Walsh still wasn't ready to let it go. When the legislature reconvened, he marched up to the State House and introduced a bill on behalf of his commission to bar minors from the racetrack.

7

The Great and Glorious Commonwealth

The first question I was always asked—invariably, anywhere—was how I found horseracing as compared to baseball. My answer—invariably, anywhere—was that, fans excluded, you met a nicer brand of human being in racing. That gave me a chance to do a fast ten minutes on the fools, scoundrels, and mountebanks who operate the Grand Old Game, tip my skimmer, show some teeth, and, eyes agleam, dance off. The truth, however, was that the politicians of the Great Commonwealth had become to me, in my middle years, what the baseball owners were to my youth. The second question was usually about Eddie Gaedel. I carry a midget on my back, you know.

The questioners were quite correct in their basic assumption that everybody sees the world through his own frame of reference, and that baseball was mine. The first great difference I had come upon in my fascinating new career was in my relationship with the politicians. It is the difference, looking out through my own somewhat clouded frame of reference, between pitching and catching. Baseball is regarded as a civic enterprise; racing is a barely tolerated activity. When you're operating a baseball club you find the politicians coming around, tails awagging, to get their pictures taken with a ball in one of their hands and a cap on top of one of their heads. (One of my more depressing memories is of Adlai Stevenson in a baseball cap, smiling stoutly. I mean, there are some of us who are supposed to help the world along on that careening journey that is taken in a handbasket, and there are the chosen few who are supposed to be out there trying to save it.)

When you're operating a racetrack you find the politicians coming around, eyes agleam. They don't want their pictures taken and they expect you to sign every tab. It's a different ball game. You're looked upon as a little bank to shake something out of.

It is impossible to get involved in something as closely tied to politics as horseracing without coming out with the distinct impression that politics is the principal industry of Boston and, quite probably, the whole of the Great Commonwealth. The politicians come at you like a swarm of locusts.

The odd part of it is that everybody else I came into contact with (the 80 per cent of the populace which is not connected with politics, officially or unofficially or hopefully) applauded any victory over what used to be called the entrenched political interests and is now, I suppose, called the power structure. But always, you know, with the kind of dread amusement that says, "Of course, you're going to get yours in the end." It was always difficult to tell whether they had become totally resigned to the futility—or fatuity—of any attempt to buck the system or whether they weren't secretly proud of it in the perverse way that people are so frequently prouder of their vices than of their virtues. It's like hearing over the six-o'clock news that today has been the hottest July 2 of all time. It makes it seem, you know, that you haven't been sweltering all day to no purpose. As long as you're going to have a corrupt political system, you might as well swelter under the most corrupt one around.

When a man makes that categorical a statement about such a highly competitive area of human endeavor, I suppose he has obligated himself to put up or shut up. Okay, let's talk about tax abatements, otherwise known as the friendly little tax-abatement dodge. The way it works is: (1) You open your mail one morning and find that the City of Boston, through its duly appointed agency has increased the assessment on your property by some ungodly sum amounting to, oh, half a million dollars, thereby bringing on a corresponding ungodly leap in your tax bill; (2) you file for an abatement based upon the old evaluation; and (3) they say, "Yeah, you're right; we were wrong," and reduce your taxes back to where they were supposed to be in the first place. Then the next year you go through the same charade again. In order to cut down on the paperwork at the Board of Assessors, you never at any time have to actually send in the money you have been overcharged. It's not a rebate; it's an abatement.

Question: Now, why do big boys play games like that?

Answer: Big boys play games like that to make big money.

Would it help at all if I confessed that I skipped a step between (1) and (2), or had you already suspected that? First clue: You don't have your own law firm—that's the firm of highly skilled attorneys you are paying an annual retainer to—handle such a highly specialized chore. It doesn't quite have the "in" and the expertise. No, there is a very exclusive, very prestigious group of lawyers who "specialize" in this line of work, possibly to the exclusion of all others. They tend to be former chief assessors and close personal friends of the mayor or the lieutenant governor or someone, and, as proof of their professional competence, they never, but never, fail. Everybody knows who they are, and everybody knows what the standard fee is. The standard fee is 20 per cent of what they are saving for you in the form of the abatement, and, since they are men of impeccable professional ethics, none of them would dream of undercutting his brothers. That would be almost as bad as advertising for clients.

Normally, as I understand it, all businesses are overassessed as a matter of sound fiscal policy at the time of their first appearance on the tax lists, and, as a matter of sound actuarial practice, the assessment is never changed. Not that the system is foolproof. New enterprises, moving in from out of town, have been known to raise havoc with the system by actually paying the original levy in full for a year or two before somebody—possibly even a guilt-racked underling down at the Board of Assessors—slips them the word. And, of course, there are always those fortunate few who are somehow overlooked. My predecessors at Suffolk Downs seem to have been particularly fortunate in that regard. Some of them, anyway. From what I can gather, Suffolk Downs hadn't qualified for an overassessment until Dave Haber came in from New York to take over from the local regime of Judge John C. Pappas. Just our little way of saying *Hello, Dave, and sorry there's no Welcome Wagon.* I was greeted with open arms, too. In our first year, our tax bill from the city of Boston was roughly $613,000, and we got an abatement of $58,500, which, taking the rising tax rate into consideration, was pretty much in line with what it had always been.

The next year, with the tax rate still rising and perhaps a generalized distemper setting in, they hit us with a bill for $859,339.47—these things, as you can see, are computed to the infinitesimal decimal. No, the tax rate hadn't gone through the roof. Only our assessment. Take heart. Do not despair. Our highly specialized legal expert whirred off some lightning mental calisthenics and advised us to make out a check for $623,823.63, which he thereupon submitted along with his request for an abatement of $166,499.73.

His legal fee for all that mental exertion was, at the going rate for all-that-mental-exertion, only $33,296—a steal. A year earlier it had been a giveaway $10,800. When all the check stubs had been filed away, our real-estate tax had gone up only $10,800, and our legal fee had gone up $21,600.

A racket? A political pay-off? I wouldn't know about things like that. All I know is that it's a legal fee for services rendered. Which shows, kids, why it is better to go to law school and get a license than to become a drop-out and maybe fall into a life of crime.

Just as a mental exercise—I want you to submit a theme, class, of no more than five hundred words—how would it be possible for the Board of Assessors or the mayor or any of their assorted hirelings to justify this kind of legal extortion should anybody like, say, a crusading editor put them to the test? If the abatements aren't legitimate, they can only mean that millions of dollars are stolen from the treasury every year. This means that the tax base has necessarily been rising to cover the loss. It means that every other taxpayer has been forced to make up the difference and, as the tax base rises, the 20-per-cent legal fee is being taken—the final indignity—from a larger and larger pool. If, on the other hand, the abatements are legitimate, why should it cost you thousands of dollars to rectify the Board of Assessors' error? An error which it frequently concedes and regularly repeats?

No matter how you look at it—up, down, or around—there is a goodly amount of money being skimmed off the top of the *potential* tax revenue that might just as well be going to the public purse, in these times of urban crisis, as into the political sausage-grinder.

Where are the newspapers, you ask? Where did all those crusading editors and enterprising reporters go? To Providence, I guess (see Chapter 15, "The Third Wheel"). Second clue: The newspapers are playing their own games. There are more webs running through the Great Commonwealth than my friend quoted at the beginning of Chapter 8 dreams of, and the strands can mingle and intertwine. If I were a gambling man, I would be willing to place a small wager that in the face of everything I have written here the Boston press will continue to avert its eyes. I would then hedge my bet just a little by predicting that if, by chance, the editorial boards of the Boston newspapers should feel called upon to shake their heads in collective horror to hear of such goings-on, it will amount to no more than an obligatory, formalized show of indignation with absolute sincerity and no follow-up. How, after all, can any self-respecting Boston editor waste his time worrying about what's going on down at the Board of Assessors when there are so many problems in Cambodia that are clamoring for his attention?

The one thing the politicians have succeeded in doing has been to create an atmosphere in which it is felt that nothing can be done without paying somebody off. And that is the kind of atmosphere which gives rise to a second infestation. An infestation of opportunists. The guys who have an uncle who is a friend of a friend of the governor. It can be said about Boston that nobody has ever left his house looking for somebody to pay off without finding just the man he's looking for standing on the corner.

We didn't have just Boston to deal with, either. Our stable area was in Revere, and everything we were doing had to be approved by its City Council as well. The sad part of it there was that Revere had a remarkably good mayor, a man named George Colella, who was really trying to turn his decaying city around. Most of the City Councilmen were workingmen who had become involved in politics to try to do something for the city, if only to keep it from falling down. Unhappily for Mayor Colella, if we may return for a moment to our seminar on urban blight, that was the full extent of their vision: to keep things from getting any worse. How about trying to make things better? Good intentions are not to be dismissed lightly. Good intentions are better, more often than not, than bad intentions. Not more profitable, just better for you. Good intentions have succeeded in keeping the road to hell well paved, according to many an unnamed traveler who presumably took a wrong turn at the fork. In practical politics, I'm not so sure that good intentions will pave your driveway. Whenever we at Suffolk Downs were in the dock, the well-meaning amateurs were outmaneuvered and outtalked and, in the end, effectively shouted down by a couple of professional politicos of the worst kind. Loud, stupid ranters.

The kind of men who made you realize that those old Anglo-Saxons knew exactly what they were doing when the coined the word "blowhard."

The stable area we had inherited was an affront to the eye and an assault upon the nostrils. Admittedly. Since nobody had as yet come up with a practical way to tear down all the stables and still keep 1350 horses out of the rain, we had instituted a five-year improvement plan, at $50,000 a year, to rebuild it in sections. The "blowhards" were hardly going to let us get away with anything like that. Having done not a thing to prevent the place from becoming the mess that it was, they were now going to settle for nothing short of palatial splendor, instantly materialized. Obviously I was supposed to come up with the brilliant idea that I could save myself a lot of aggravation by working out some kind of a deal. In case I didn't, they insisted upon being taken on an inspection tour before they would vote on whether to grant us our operating license. It was pitiful. Some of them were such second-rate opportunists that they apparently hadn't been able to figure out what their cooperation was worth. The best they could come up with, at length, was a few jobs for their friends, relatives, and—oh yes—their wives. They didn't get even those. No matter. They continued to live on heavy breathing and great expectations.

A week or so after I had taken up my new duties as Lord of the Suffolk Manor I paid a call on Governor Sargent, partly as a gesture of courtesy and partly out of curiosity. He was, like me, a new man on the job, a lieutenant governor who had succeeded to the governor's mansion when John A. Volpe became Nixon's Secretary of Transportation. It was strange. I mean, strange. The Governor wasn't unfriendly, and yet there was something hanging in the air. Something perched there: watchful, wary. Listen, either you trust your instincts in these matters or you don't, and it is my business to size up a situation in a hurry. Clearly, I was suspect. All through our rather inconsequential conversation I had the distinct impression that Governor Sargent was measuring me. What made it so weird was that I could never quite shake the feeling that it wasn't just one man who was looking me over so carefully; it was the whole political body he represented. "They" thought anyone who wandered around making speeches for free had to have something more nefarious in mind than drumming up customers for his operation. Given the political atmosphere which so completely blankets the city, everything I subsequently did confirmed their worst suspicions. I had my own TV show; I continued to pop up all over the radio dial; I joined gladly in the work of any civic committees and charity drives who would have me. All that activity, all that public exposure, could add up to only one thing. I was out to make a political career for myself. Never mind that I had operated the same way everywhere else I had been. Never mind that I was completely nonpolitical and, in fact, overtly and obstinately apolitical. It isn't what you say, it's what you're doing. As time went on, I rarely could appear on one of those telephone shows without some caller purring, "You ought to run for mayor, Bill." I would chuckle modestly and twirl my hair and mutter playful interdictions about having all the troubles I needed without placing myself athwart a stampede of buffaloes. In any other city, that kind of unspectacular public exchange would have been taken for exactly what it was, the caller's way of saying that I had made a favorable impression on that part of the populace represented by himself and his friends and my way of trying to endear myself further to him and any other susceptible listeners or viewers. In Boston, where everybody is running for mayor, in and out of season, it can actually get people to worrying.

Whether or not I was successful in my game attempt to remain so cordially apolitical, it had been impressed upon me from the opening gun that it was going to be impossible to ignore the political realities. Politics is such an intrinsic part of the racing scene that in order to protect our interests in the halls of the legislature we had a full-time lobbyist on the payroll, a fellow named Peter Fallon. Along with the rather stupefying discovery that I had my very own marker in the influence game, I was advised that if I was really interested in playing to win I had better "dump" Peter Fallon and replace him with somebody who had more clout. Well, I can't fire people. And anyway, all the heavyweight representatives were already in the service of the other racing interests. Being stubborn by nature and optimistic by design, I felt that with the best legal counsel I just might be able to get the job done on merit alone. As far as Fallon's relationship with his friends in the legislature was concerned, I was well aware that by rocking the boat I wasn't going to be making his job any easier. Except for recommending more caution and a more sympathetic approach to the status quo, Fallon never complained. At least not to me. If Peter Fallon didn't exactly help us, I'm certain he never intentionally hurt us. He is an honest person. And that, I might add, I looked upon as somewhat of a victory.

The dogs were king in Massachusetts because they were first on the scene. Wonderland and its lobbyist, Clarence King, had written the legislation, and it is not so very surprising that they wrote it to favor themselves. And isn't it wholly typical of the Great Commonwealth that the original settlers had hit upon the scheme of legalizing pari-mutuel racing not through the Thoroughbreds which are always somewhat suspect (have you ever read a story about horseracing which didn't involve chicanery at the heart of the plot?) but through dogs, which are well known to be the friends of mankind, the companions of children, and the protectors of the home. Thirty-five years later, the astute and canny Mr. King was still at the old stand doing his good works, by far the most influential lobbyist in the Massachusetts legislature.

In dictating the statutory framework at a time when racing was considered so disreputable that it had been deemed politic to provide that all the tax revenue be applied for old-age assistance and agricultural development, Wonderland track had restricted pari-mutuel racing to 200 days for the dogs, 90 days for flat racing and—later—90 days for harness horses (now increased to 150 days for flat racing, 120 days for harness racing, 250 days for dog racing). Those figures have never changed until recently. Other populous states had seized upon pari-mutuel racing as a welcome source of additional revenue. Florida, the only other state where greyhound racing is so popular, was leading the list with a total of 1954 days. New York was running 1273 days; Illinois, 744 days; California, 929 days; Ohio, 804 days; Pennsylvania, 615 days. All of it without any dog racing at all. In every case, the number of racing days had been steadily increasing.

Massachusetts hadn't lifted a restriction in thirty-five years.

Everybody was wallowing happily inside the status quo because everybody had come to regard the status quo as the best insurance for continued fun and profit. The dog interests, and Wonderland in particular, had prospered mightily from the beginning, and they assumed, with a logic that was matched only by their shortsightedness, that they must be doing something right. The leaders of the legislature were happy because it allowed them to play intermural games with the out-of-state racing interests as well as intramural kneesies with the all-powerful dog-track operators of the Great and Glorious Commonwealth. The run-of-the-aisle legislators were happy because it protected the poor fellows from being placed in a position where it might look as if they were helping the gambling interests. And so a policy which had been born of timidity in the narrow, corseted thirties had been perpetuated into the final days of the rocking, riotous sixties out of a combination of greed, drift, and good old-fashioned arteriosclerosis.

Everybody profited, according to his own lights, except the taxpayers of Massachusetts, who were being systematically fleeced by their elected representatives and the licensed operators of their tracks. Well, not quite everybody. Suffolk Downs, which should have been the dominant track in New England, had been locked into the status quo. Nor had anybody gone to any heroic lengths to hide who was calling the tune. During my predecessor Dave Haber's first year at Suffolk Downs, when he was still sounding as if he intended to maybe institute a few changes, Dick Johnston, the publicity director of Wonderland, collared Nick Del Ninno at a meeting of the New England Breeders Association at the Rolling Greens Hotel to offer the following heartfelt words of advice: "Tell that Haber not to go getting any funny ideas. Because we control the legislature and we control the sportswriters."

8

The Interlocking Machine

It's like a web, Bill. Nobody can see it, but everyone knows it's there. Brush up against it and the whole web quivers. Snap one strand and you can feel something gathering itself together, and it has a hundred legs and a thousand eyes. It's like a web to hurt any individual, whether you're trying to or not. Because you couldn't. It's almost like they're intangible. Like they're ghosts. You see what I'm saying? You know they're there, and you know that it's a power structure, and all I said was that any time somebody is doing something for the over-all good, some of that power has to leave. These people in this power structure, they might donate the money to the politicians, which is what keeps them that way. And donate where it counts. I don't want to go into that. You work just the opposite. I've thought this over in my mind, what we're discussing now. If you get enough of the smaller people, then you begin to make a little impact. You've got some people scared pink, Bill. They're really scared pink. It's like anything else; when people have something wrapped like this for so long, somebody comes in and these people don't necessarily have to see how selfish they are, or what they're doing to the over-all picture. They don't realize it. Maybe later on if they sat down and thought about it, they might

see what harm they're doing to the over-all stake, which affects
each and every one. You know? Like different interests in different
parts of the state. I don't want to get into that. But wouldn't you
say some of the people in this power structure might have interests
in other states, possibly? I have thought about these things. Maybe
you're big enough to overcome it. I hope you are. You're not sup-
posed to create waves in this state.

—A veteran New England horseman, whom I would not
dream of identifying

What my friend thought of as a web, I always saw as a network of
interlocking ownerships, friendships, and private arrangements. There
were nine tracks, encompassing three states and involving eleven racing meets. Five Thoroughbred meets, three harness meets and three
greyhound meets.

The three dog tracks are all in Massachusetts:

Wonderland
Taunton
Raynham

Flat racing:

Suffolk Downs (Massachusetts)
Berkshire Downs (Massachusetts)
Rockingham Park (New Hampshire)
Narragansett Park (Rhode Island)
Lincoln Downs (Rhode Island)

Harness racing

Suffolk Downs (Massachusetts)
Foxboro (Massachusetts)
Rockingham Park (New Hampshire)

Except for Berkshire Downs, which was a small two-bit operation in
the western corner of the state, all the tracks fall within a fifty-mile
radius of Boston. Wonderland is in Revere, almost across the street from
our stable area. The other Massachusetts tracks—Foxboro, Taunton,
and Raynham—lie from fifteen to twenty-five miles south of Boston,
either directly on or close to main highways.

The original out-of-state tracks are just over the borders of their respective states. Rockingham Park is in the little town of Salem Depot, the first sovereign patch of New Hampshire you hit on a straight line, twenty-five miles up from Boston. Narragansett is in Pawtucket, the first city you come upon as you cross into that little salient of Rhode Island that pushes into Massachusetts along Route 1.

Lincoln Downs came along later, after the war. It is on the other side of Providence, perhaps fifty miles away.

It is not by accident that they are where they are. They were built to catch Massachusetts money. Rhode Island and New Hampshire have fewer than a million inhabitants. The Greater Boston metropolitan area has 1,750,000; Massachusetts has 5 million. Surveys have consistently shown that 70 to 72 per cent of the clientele of the out-of-state tracks comes from Massachusetts. My own unofficial survey, which was accomplished by checking all the license plates in our parking lots and computing in a subway count, showed that 26.8 per cent of Suffolk's customers came from outside Massachusetts. With their tracks living off the citizenry of Massachusetts, the legislators of Rhode Island and New Hampshire had been more than content to sit back and leave it to the machine to protect everybody's interests. And why shouldn't they? The Massachusetts legislature had shown itself to be so solicitous of Rockingham's welfare that it had built a superhighway practically to its door. For years you knew you were in New Hampshire when the paved highway turned to a couple of hundred yards of narrow macadam.

Politics isn't imposed upon racing from time to time; it's in the weave. It's in the statutory straitjacket; it's in the geography, history, and calendar of New England racing. And, when everything is said and done, it's in the interpersonal relationships and internal maneuverings of the resourceful, politically potent men who own and operate the various tracks. Two of them were in their eighties, and three of the others were in their seventies. Remarkable old men they are: impossible, amiable, stubborn, and, on occasion, slightly silly. All of them have a bit of the swagger of the entrepreneur, and each of them has a character and a fascination all his own. The one young man in the group was more fascinating still, because, unlike the old men, who like old men everywhere had become set in their ways, he was bright, noisy, and unpredictable.

The oldest of all the old were Lou Smith (now dead) of Rockingham Park and George Reynolds of Wonderland, the two men who had got racing under way in New England. Which reminds me—I left out one very significant descriptive adjective up there: mysterious.

If you asked anybody in Boston who owned Wonderland Racetrack, and I'm talking about the regular customers, not the last living dowagers, the odds are overwhelming they couldn't tell you. George Reynolds is the Howard Hughes of Boston. I never laid eyes on him myself. I know of only a few people, all intimately connected with the dogs at the highest level, who have. But if Reynolds is willing to see a few more people than Howard Hughes is in the pursuit of his business, he has been far more successful in hiding his identity. Even the last living dowager knows who Howard Hughes is.

With Reynolds so invisible, you were far more likely to think of superlobbyist Clarence King when you thought about Wonderland and, speaking of remarkable old men, King must be up there in the seventies himself. In describing Clarence King as the most influential lobbyist in the state I was probably doing him an injustice. He is, in all probability, the most powerful single figure in the legislature. In addition to sustaining the happy alliance between the legislature and the dog tracks, he is the lobbyist for the power companies, some banks, and I don't know who-all else—except that they're lucky to have him. He is astute. He is much respected. He knows what it takes. He holds the whole chamber in his hands. I'd have hired him in a minute if I'd had the chance.

You still don't believe that a lobbyist can wield as much power as I'm giving King credit for, though, do you? All right. At the time I came to Boston, the Attorney General was still Elliot Richardson, who was about to go winging off to Washington to serve the Nixon Administration as Under Secretary of State and, eventually, as Secretary of Health, Education, and Welfare. Under the peculiar laws of the Commonwealth, his successor was appointed not by the Governor but by the collective wisdom of the state legislature. The theory seems to be that if the Governor and the legislature are of the same party the Governor will exert a strong and probably decisive influence on the selection, and that if they aren't, the will of the people as indicated by the make-up of the legislature will be better served. The Governor was a Republican; the legislature was Democratic. Robert H. Quinn, who happened to be King's friend, was the Speaker of the House. Offhand, you might think that having a Speaker of the House as a friend ain't bad if you happen to be a lobbyist. Off the other hand, having Clarence King as a mentor is better than staying up all night to wait for the votes to come in from the outlying precincts if you happen to be a politician. Representative

Quinn's meteoric rise, which had seen him rise to the Speaker's chair in record time, continued unabated. Clarence King's friend became the Attorney General. Yes indeed, we'd have had much smoother sailing through those choppy waters if I had been able to hire Mr. King.

My first chance to see Mr. King jump the legislature through the hoops came while I was attending a joint committee hearing on a bill to increase the number of harness days from 90 to 150. About the bill itself I knew nothing; it had been drawn up by Foxboro and my predecessors at Suffolk. About harness racing I knew even less. The panic was on to get Suffolk in shape to open in another month. The harness meet was still six months away. Between one thing and a hundred others, I hadn't even thought about thinking about it. What I'm saying is that in one of the great upsets of modern parliamentary history I was able to overcome my natural instincts and refrain from making a public display of my ignorance. I was there strictly as an interested spectator. And a very interesting spectacle it turned out to be.

Potentially (I was to discover) harness racing offered the greatest possibilities for increased profits if only because it had come on late in Massachusetts and hadn't really caught on. Potentialities aside, the harness interests, hereinafter to be known as the good guys, were pleading that they had been operating marginally through the years and were in desperate need of the added dates to meet increased expenses.

That wasn't quite the way King saw it. "Harness wants an absolute monopoly on harness racing in this state!" thundered King, forgetting in his rage and indignation that his own clients had more dates than the harness and flat horses put together.

According to the spokesmen for our side, the Commonwealth would realize a minimum of $1.5 million in additional revenue, which seemed to be a modest enough projection until King moved in to place the matter in its proper perspective. Far from increasing tax revenues, the additional 60 days of harness racing were actually going to cost the Commonwealth $2 million—if you can follow this—through the loss of revenues on the dogs. Now, when you realize that the Commonwealth's cut was on 7.5 per cent of the handle, he was telling the members of the committee that the hitherto faithful and even dutiful bettors would become so impoverished, sated, or perhaps bewildered at being confronted with all those extra opportunities to indulge their hobby that they would balk, turn sullen, and strike back by withholding $30 million that they had been accustomed to shoving through the betting windows.

"Just because some harness people can't feed their horses is no reason why we should tax the people of Massachusetts," he growled. "Why, it's the most ridiculous argument I've heard in my thirty-nine years here."

The committee members must have found that argument most compelling, because it reported the bill out adversely. The House of Representatives must have found some overwhelming merit in it too. Why else would it have voted the bill down, 60–6? Considering the sparkle and clarity of King's logic, to say nothing of its triumphant gall, one can only marvel that he didn't get a standing ovation.

For reasons undoubtedly arising from my own deficiencies, I didn't have quite as galvanic an effect on the Ways and Means Committee when I appeared before it a short time afterward with a bill that would have revised the racing statute to allow for more racing dates and take us out of the straitjacket. An enormous amount of work had gone into drawing up the bill and then finding a representative who would be willing to sponsor it. I offered the committee a plethora of statistics to show that our operating expenses, purses, and real-estate taxes were all climbing out of sight. The bill never got out of committee. The response to my plea for help came on the last day of the legislative session when the lawmakers slipped through a bill to increase the take-out from 15 per cent to 16 per cent, with the extra 1 per cent going entirely to the state. They jammed it through both the committee and the House so fast that our lobbyist, Mr. Fallon, didn't know what they were doing until the deed had been done.

The extra 1 per cent came out of the take at Wonderland too, of course, but what did the Wonderland people care? Their expenses weren't skyrocketing. A dog track bears absolutely no resemblance to an Oriental palace. It looks more like something you race Kiddie-Kars on. The back area required to kennel the dogs is relatively meager, and Wonderland was paying the almost negligible Revere taxes. Unlike the horsemen, the dog-owners are very reasonable people, possibly because nobody ever told them they were the heirs to the Sport of Kings. The upkeep on a greyhound is no more than you would expect it to be; there are no jockeys to split the purse with; the owners are sometimes their own trainers; and there are only a few states in which they can race. Taken altogether, they are more than willing to take what they can get. The total purses on any given night are a percentage of the handle on that day; that's right, a winning owner doesn't know what he's won until the night is over. And if that makes it exciting for him, it kind of takes the suspense out of it for the operators. Also the risk.

Wonderland has far more than that going for it. To return to the committee hearing for a moment, King's motives for pulling out all the stops on the harness dates went beyond the purely philosophical question of maintaining the status quo. By the nature of the interweaving Thoroughbred and harness circuits that had grown up through the years, Suffolk Downs would have been running its entire 30 days head-to-head against Rockingham's harness meet and—we're into the interlocking ownerships again now—Wonderland owns 50 per cent of Rockingham's harness meet and runs 100 per cent of it. Louis Lobel (now dead) who started harness racing in New Hampshire, was the legal counsel for Wonderland and he remained its legal counsel while he was conducting the meet at Rockingham. If there's any tighter relationship than that, it requires a license and a minister and a ring. When Lobel died, Dick Johnston, the public-relations director of Wonderland, moved up as director of operations, and when he bowed out of the picture, Donald Young, Wonderland's auditor, took over. Under those circumstances, it is perhaps not so surprising that Mr. King's anti-monopolistic fervor diminished rapidly as it approached the border. From the 32 days it had run in its inaugural meeting in 1958, the Rockingham harness meet had increased so steadily that it was now running two meets totaling 106 days. As many, you might say, as the traffic from Massachusetts would bear.

On the surface, Lou Smith and Reynolds were complete opposites. Lou Smith was the most visible of the owners—the only visible owner, really. He had broken the ice in New England in 1933 and paved the way for Wonderland to open in Massachusetts a year later. In point of fact, Reynolds and Smith complemented each other very nicely. Reynolds is a natural manipulator, the man behind the scenes. Uncle Lou was a promoter, the pitchman out front. My impression is that he had batted around the racing world most of his life, starting tracks on short bankrolls, making it big and losing it big before he hit the jackpot in New Hampshire. The general consensus seems to be that it was Reynolds who set him up in Rockingham to pave the way for racing in Massachusetts.

By the time I came along, Uncle Lou was eighty-three years old, and he saw himself as the patriarch of New England racing. He was. He had made his pile, he had no children to leave it to, and, unlike the other old men of the combine, he was no longer interested in fighting the battle for the sake of the battle. Where the New Hampshire Racing Commission would have been only too happy to give him all the flat dates he wanted, he had been settling for fewer and fewer and leaving it to the harness meet at Rockingham, under the more energetic leadership of the Wonderland folk, to pick up the slack. In a conscious attempt to upgrade the image of racing, Uncle Lou had been presented to the public as a kindly old philanthropist spreading his largesse around, interacially and interdenominationally, to the meek, the needy, and the worthy. Glowing publicity, while harmless to the young, can turn virulent and deceptive when contracted late in life. Something like the measles. In one of those triumphs of public relations that have become so prevalent in American life, Uncle Lou had come to cherish the picture of himself that had been built up in his press clippings. He had become the benevolent dictator of the castle he had built, casting the glow of his goodwill toward all mankind upon all comers. Having finally won acceptance, he wanted to be beloved. He believed his press notices.

Uncle Lou had been the only operator of any track to pick up the phone when I arrived in town, and he alone welcomed me to the fraternity. He had dropped in on us, unexpectedly, to lend his presence to our opening day. And still, when I had the temerity to brush against the web by applying for ten extra days (which everybody knew I had not the slightest chance of getting), it was Lou Smith, serving in the same role as front man for the machine, who led the press to believe that I had turned down an invitation to meet with the other tracks "as has been done for thirty years" to work out a schedule that would be agreeable to everybody. "Had there been a meeting," Lou said, "I'm sure the no-conflict schedule which has been in effect for sometime now would have continued."

Absolutely false in both regards. Nobody had invited me in for as much as a cup of coffee. There had been plenty of conflicts in the past, never by Suffolk's choice. Suffolk Downs had customarily run 66 days (or less) starting on April 19. Just as, as Uncle Lou well knew, we would be doing again that year. I was the new boy in town, though, and it was never too soon to show me what a mistake it would be to "go getting any ideas." Or have a big mouth. B. A. Dario of Lincoln Downs had been screaming that I was out to start "a race war" (the man sure did have a gift for the shuddersome phrase) where, in fact, it was he who had already jumped the gun by applying for dates that were going to take him past our opening and well into May. In responding to Dario, I had committed the ultimate indiscretion of suggesting that maybe everybody had better take his best hold because I saw no reason why Massachusetts money shouldn't stay in Massachusetts. Clearly, loose talk like that wasn't going to be tolerated.

I was quite fond of Uncle Lou, though. When he died a year later, I asked his widow for permission to inaugurate a $15,000 Lou Smith Memorial Stakes in his honor. And so B. A. Dario, who has a racing stable of his own, shipped his best horse in from Lincoln Downs and romped off with it. Maybe Lou had something there, after all. I always did have a big mouth.

While Wonderland, with its long and many-tentacled reach into the halls of power, is clearly the kingpin of racing in New England—the lynchpin, more accurately, which holds the various elements of the machine together—George Reynolds, wherever he is, is not quite an absolute monarch. The owners of the other two dog tracks, Joe Linsey of Taunton and George Carney of Raynham, are powerful, independent forces in their own right. Linsey and Reynolds had a falling-out some years ago for reasons no man seems to know, but they made up and that is long past. What held them together was a common conviction that there should be no more racing in the Commonwealth—recently modified by a legislative grant of more racing dates to each of them. George Carney, the baby of the lot at thirty-five, was chafing under the restrictions that the old men of racing had imposed on him. He was young and restless and bursting with ambition. Still and all, Carney had been content to push for the breakthrough within their private councils and join with them in presenting a united front whenever the pre-eminence of the dog tracks was involved. In the hearing to increase the number of harness dates, Carney had been even louder in his opposition than King. No matter. George Carney, a brash young man on the move, was so atypical that we are going to save him for a while.

Joe Linsey, the whilom overlord of Suffolk Downs, owns a dog track in Denver, Colorado, in addition to the dog track at Taunton. Among the companies in his personal conglomerate was a Ford agency, in which his partner was B. A. Dario, owner of Lincoln Downs, and a company which operates carnivals and midways at fairs.

Linsey has moved onward and upward through the years until he has achieved a position of awesome power and respectability. The power was exercised quietly behind the scenes as a powerhouse political broker between his old world and his new one. Out front, he has been one of the city's leading businessmen-citizens, and an open-handed philanthropist on a level far surpassing the fondest dreams of Lou Smith. Linsey was one of the founding fathers of Brandeis University, and he was a leading fund-raiser and faithful personal contributor. A couple of years earlier, he had contributed to Brandeis the construction costs toward a new gym, called, appropriately enough, the Joseph M. Linsey Sport Center. Governor Volpe spoke at the dedication ceremonies. A classic example, it would seem, of the conjugation of man's journey through life which goes: to get on, to get honored, to get honest. After all, the cause of higher education was being served. It was so important that Suffolk's annual $5000 contribution had already been drawn against us for 1969 when we assumed control in the very first week of the year. The next year, Linsey called me, hard upon a grueling battle over a switch in our harness dates in which Linsey had been our last and most irreconcilable opponent, to remind me that I had been a bit tardy about sending our contribution to him. No thanks, I told him. If we wanted to be philanthropists, we were entirely capable of doing it without an intermediary.

(One sidelight: Although Linsey was no longer interlocked with Suffolk Downs, we had remained interlocked, after a fashion, by being represented by the same law firm, Friedman and Atherton, one of those typical Boston law firms which still carry the names of two men who died a while ago. Taunton was represented by Frank Kozol, the senior senior partner, and we were represented by his son, Joel A. Kozol. Linsey and Frank Kozol were close personal friends; Joel and I had become close personal friends. Take a complicated office tie, compound it with a tie of blood, drop some trouble into the caldron, and you can understand just how interlocking things could have got.)

E. M. Loew of Foxboro is as diverse a businessman as Linsey, and as atypical in his own way as Carney. Loew had been the only operator standing outside the machine, not aloof but in opposition. In case you have been wondering, E. M. Loew is indeed the same E. M. Loew whose name has decorated the marquees of so many theaters. He is an easy man to underestimate at first glance because he speaks with a very heavy accent and in the labored syntax of a man who is transposing literally from his basic language. Never underestimate him. He is a very shrewd, very crafty manipulator. So shrewd that by the time the old theater chains had faded into memory, he had set himself up very nicely with an even larger chain of E. M. Loew drive-in theaters. He is also a very tough old man. Among his holdings was the Latin Quarter in New York. I said, *was.* When the chorus girls struck for higher wages, one of the more misguided strikes in the history of the labor movement in view of the shaggy state of New York night life, the old man simply wished them good luck in their precarious pursuit of the ever-rising cost of living and shut the place down.

He viewed me, now that I think of it, in much the same light he viewed those ungrateful chorus girls. As far as E. M. Loew was concerned, Foxboro was the copyright owner of harness racing in Massachusetts, and Suffolk Downs had plagiarized 30 days from him. It was crazy. In the first place, he had never had those 30 days. Foxboro, operating by itself, had never been granted more than 66. And while it was true enough that Foxboro had pioneered the sport in New England, E. M. Loew hadn't. E. M. Loew had come in through the side door, a maneuver he is very proficient at. The pioneering spirit had been Paul Bowser, a longtime wrestling promoter who had apparently wanted to move up in class, but not very. E. M. Loew had come into Foxboro as concessionaire for Bowser and had advanced him some money in the form of a mortgage against the land and the plant. It was only after five years, with harness racing showing nothing more than a marked inability to buck the dogs, that he had exercised his rights and taken over.

Nevertheless, he took the attitude at every commission hearing that we were interlopers. And here again, the dogs probably had more than a little to do with it. The way the harness circuit was drawn up, there was a six-week gap between the close of Rockingham's early harness meet in early May and the opening of the Foxboro meet in mid-June. For years E. M. Loew had been going to Racing Commission hearings, in that stubborn, relentless way of his, to ask for the extra 30 days that would enable him to fill that gap, and for years he had been turned away. The soft nights of early summer were the exclusive property of the dogs, who were chasing Swifty at Wonderland and the Chief at Raynham. George Carney was willing to compete against Wonderland, mostly because he had no choice. Wonderland's 100 days blanketed the entire warm-weather spectrum from the middle of May (the day after its partners at Rockingham shut down) to Labor Day (a few days before the fall harness meet at Rockingham opened). You can be sure that George wasn't going to stand still for yet another competitor—and practically in the same neighborhood, at that.

That left E. M. Loew with nothing very much to do except to try for our 30 harness dates in the late fall so that he could run them over our 30 dates. Sure, it sounds crazy. Except that E. M. Loew is crazy like a fox. For all the political power of the dogs, E. M. Loew had been around the city forever and he had strong connections in the legislature himself. Not strong enough to buck the dogs, to be sure, but plenty strong enough to take care of us. Looking back, I can only assume that with my appearance he spotted a double vulnerability. With Linsey out of the picture, he would no longer be bucking the power of the dogs. When the word got around that Veeck wouldn't play games, I can only assume further, he saw a lot of interesting channels of exploration opening up. And not only in the legislature. My appearance coincided very closely with the appearance of a brand-new Governor; a Governor, as luck would have it, who had never really run for elective office. Sargent had come to office in the first election in Massachusetts in which the candidates for governor and lieutenant governor had run as an entry rather than as individual candidates, voted upon separately. Francis Sargent had been plucked from his job as the head of the Bureau of Conservation to fill out the underside of the ticket. Two years later, Volpe shuffles off to Washington. The former head of the Bureau of Conservation is now sitting in the Governor's chair, and the Governor is the man who exercises the ultimate control over the Racing Commission. Consider the opportunities. As a man who had never run for high public office on his own, Sargent may very well have been the only elected official of rank in the country who could truly say that he was under no obligation to anybody. Which is a nice way of saying that there had never been any occasion for him to seek financial backing, or for financial backers to seek him. E. M. Loew, who moves around the political game very well, moved in to woo the new Governor. And while he was about it, he put himself in the best possible position for an all-out assault on us by launching a rebuilding program at his track.

I can appreciate that if you're going to be a promoter you have to set your eyes on an objective and convince yourself, by something akin to autohypnosis, that you are going to succeed. I have always operated on pretty much the same principle of Optimum Optimism myself. But there does have to be some seed of logic in the initial concept, and some hope of success in the pursuit. It was beyond me how E. M. Loew could have convinced himself, in the first instance, that our dates belonged to him.

But then, I have never been able to understand the inner compulsions of those people to whom acquisition is the very blood of life. My total effort has always been concentrated on one operation, to the exclusion of everything else, including family life, sleep, and a balanced diet. E. M. Loew is a natural empire-builder. It takes no more than the barest working knowledge of the early gold-rush days of the theater industry to picture a young E. M. Loew piling acquisition upon acquisition; one baroque, balustraded, chandelier-dangling monstrosity upon another. A quick cut to his middle years, and we find him operating at the same old stand, acquiring lot after lot for his drive-ins. The concession business itself is the best possible vehicle—if history is any guide —for acquiring the property you have hired yourself out to serve.

Suffolk Downs' 30 days had become the Moby Dick of his old age. He pursued his objective with a single-mindedness that cared nothing for the odds, would employ any tactics, and was indifferent to repeated rebuffs and failures. We were the bigger track; we were the better track. We were in the population center he was drawing from. We were paying the heavy real-estate taxes and he was getting off cheap. And even with our far less desirable dates in late fall we had outdrawn him, on an average nightly basis, for nine of the twelve years we had been in competition. Nevertheless, he was always plotting and scheming, threatening and cajoling. Why he thought he had a divine right to our days, I will simply never know.

George Carney, a slim dark-haired Irishman, has a little of the empire-builder in him too. Carney is by far the most interesting of this predatory crew to me and by all odds the most appealing. The first time I saw him, which was during the commission hearing on the dates, he assaulted the commissioners in blunt, exuberant language out of nothing more than high spirits and the sheer joy of harassing the Establishment. At the legislative hearing on the harness dates a few weeks later, he had me in stitches, even though the new target for his affections had turned out to be me. "Veeck doesn't know which end is up!" he roared. "All he knows is what those idiots around him tell him. He's been up here for about three months and he's got everybody fighting with each other."

Obviously, the boy had style. The endearing thing about George, beyond the sheer relief of finding someone on the other side who wasn't eligible for Social Security, was that all the while he was advancing the game plan by depicting me as an arrogant outsider, and an ignorant one at that, you could see that he didn't believe a word of what he was saying and wanted everybody to see that he didn't believe a word of it. A bravura performance. "Hey," I told him afterward, "there I was, minding my own business, and all of a sudden the shiv. I'd better warn you right now, jealousy will get you nowhere."

Most encouraging of all, once I got to know him, was the discovery that he wasn't hung up on the mentality of the 1930s. He wanted more dog dates for himself at Raynham, and on an even longer-term basis he saw a chance of inserting himself into the Thoroughbred picture. Bright and energetic as he was, he had been maneuvering himself into position to exert some influence on Wonderland's stultifying policy without confronting the dominance of Wonderland head on, by buying up a huge chunk of its stock. He had dealt himself a hand in the Thoroughbred circuit by buying Rockingham and Narragansett stock, and he was the major factor in the Brockton Fair. Being young and bright, he could see that the state was so strapped for money that time was on his side. Being young and very bright, he could see that when the log jam finally broke, it was going to break wide open. The plan that had been simmering in the back of his mind was to jump right in and grab a license for a flat meet at Raynham, with the understanding that he would immediately begin construction on a multimillion-dollar luxury track.

Obviously, a natural ally. And he was fun. One story, apocryphal or not, gives you the flavor of the man. As a young man in his twenties, with a father who was a saloon-keeper (shades of the Kennedys) with a strong voice in Massachusetts politics, George discovered that the Liquor Board of his home town hadn't given out a license in years, and whether it was because a reform movement had stacked the board or because a combination of reform and natural attrition had reduced the board to one last, disapproving member, I can't really remember. Anyway, George went to the Mayor with a proposition. The Mayor listened and found himself so intrigued that he immediately appointed him chairman of the board. George thereupon hied himself to the Town Hall and placed a call to a retired motorman who had been pestering his father for a political appointment that would require no more work than he was qualified by experience and temperament to perform. In short, none. "If you can get down here to the Town Hall within fifteen minutes," George began, "I've got just what you've been looking for, a commissionership." To the background of delirious gurglings at the other end, George imparted job specifications that were so bountiful— an appointment that was prestigious beyond his wildest dreams and yet requiring only one day's work out of the year—that the motorman was out the door and heading for his destination before George realized that he was completing his pitch to a dangling earphone.

Ten minutes later, when the guy came flying through the door, George swore him in, called the Liquor Board into session, and, having taken a roll call and declared a quorum to be present, introduced two motions. The first was to award a new liquor license to the Mayor. The second was to award a new liquor license to George Carney. Both motions passed unanimously. Down crashed the gavel. Meeting adjourned.

Round one was over. The next half-hour or so was spent completing his administrative chores, i.e., performing all the paperwork necessary to insure that everything was in apple-pie order. Having given the motorman ample time for a more leisurely journey home, George placed another call to inform him that he had displayed such a deplorable inability to withstand pressure that he was clearly unsuited for a career in public life. "I'm going to give it to you straight," George told him. "Your appointment has been withdrawn."

"Yeah," the guy said. "Do I get paid for the whole year, though?"

"You get paid for one day. That's the whole year's work. Just like I told you."

The only thing left now was to whip off a telegram to the Mayor: DUE TO AN UNEXPECTED OPPORTUNITY WHICH HAS JUST COME MY WAY AND IS SIMPLY TOO GOOD TO TURN DOWN I MUST REGRETFULLY TENDER MY RESIGNATION. PLEASE DO NOT THINK ME UNGRATEFUL.

Whatever the truth of that story, the mere fact that people take such delight in telling it about him is a testimonial to his style. However the story may have been embroidered in the retelling, it has to be a story he originally told on himself, and that tells you there's a bit of the rogue in him. It tells you that he took the game the way he found it and takes his pleasure from playing it to the hilt. And yet, I wonder whether it doesn't also tell you something else. I wonder whether there isn't a reservation about the game built into the fabric of that story, a stutter at the center. *Look at the ridiculous system we have,* he seems to be saying, *if I could have got away with anything as outrageous as that.* The better I got to know him, and I got to know him quite well, the more of that abiding, deep-seated reservation I came to see in him. He played the game as well as it could be played, and yet he played it with the overbalancing bravado of a man who was laughing to maintain some core of personal honor—pure and intact—inside himself.

"The rising young executive must be prepared for emergency and opportunity alike," he would say. "Should I happen to be fallen upon by a marauding gang of a desperate highwayman or a covey of dedicated public servants, it would be the height of folly to let them go away mad." After I had left Suffolk Downs, I was back in Boston to complete some business with Joel Kozol. Joel had bumped into George coming down the hill from the State House, which wasn't so remarkable in that the State House is only a few blocks from Joel's office, and George had walked back with him to say hello. As it happened, I had been away from home for a couple of days and I had run out of money. The cashier at Joel's office had left, and so it was the most natural thing in the world that I would turn to George and ask him to cash a personal check for $100. He didn't have it. "George!" I gasped. "But you're always so loaded."

"Bill," he said, in much the same tone of quiet exasperation that might be used on a backward child, "you know where I just came from." To this day I don't know whether he was kidding or not.

The really admirable thing about him is that once he has determined in his own mind that he's in the right, he can't be moved. As I have already said, George was the principal factor of the Brockton Fair, that wholly tax-free, fully subsidized gold mine. While I was getting to know him—it was toward the end of our first flat meet—the police department of Brockton, which was providing his security at the fair, came in and demanded higher salaries. George didn't like the way the case was being put to him, which he took to be closer to extortion than to a request for collective bargaining—although I will readily concede that the distinction can sometimes be a rather fine one. The Brockton Police Department couldn't believe it was being turned down. It was so insistent in its disbelief that he threw the police out of the place and hired his own security force.

Now, that kind of treatment can be annoying to people who have become accustomed to being the throwers not the throwees. The

Brockton police were so annoyed that they came up with the perfect combination of antidote and retaliation. And so it was, boys and girls, that precisely at this stage of history the chairman of the Senate Ways and Means Committee, who happened to be from Brockton, revealed in rounded tones of outrage that his beleaguered city was not realizing one cent in real-estate taxes from all that prime land, something he had presumably stumbled across while browsing through the tax rolls down at the City Hall that morning. Well, boys and girls, you can be very, very certain that the Senator wasn't going to tolerate anything like that. No siree. Not on your life he wasn't. On behalf of the downtrodden taxpayers of his and similarly situated communities—and of straight shooters everywhere—he introduced a bill to do away with the tax exemption on all fair property that wasn't actually being put to use for agricultural purposes.

The strength of the fairs being what it was, everybody assumed that this was just another political foray—or foraging expedition—that would very quickly fade away. The extremely knowledgeable legislative reporter for the Berkshire *Eagle*—which always, incidentally, covered any legislation pertaining to racing revenue far more fully and far more accurately than any of the Boston papers—wrote that while the Chairman of the Ways and Means Committee was "one of the most powerful men in state government . . . even he may not have the muscle to bring the comparatively tax-free agricultural fairs to book. He's dealing with an 'institution' that is as untouchable as the billboard."

The reporter had not the slightest way of knowing what was going on behind the scenes, and yet he was right enough in the end. Almost. The Chairman of the Ways and Means Committee does wield enormous power. George wouldn't move. He doesn't back away. The bill proceeded to a hearing. The fair interests and the racing interests mobilized all their power. The Chairman of the Ways and Means Committee presumably mobilized all his. The Chairman of the Ways and Means Committee doesn't lose many battles. His opposition had never lost any battles. Once again, the power of the fair and racing interests prevailed.

And then one of those things happened that renews your faith in the whole political system, provided that you don't happen to be running fair racing in Massachusetts. A door had been opened. The light had been let in. A pair of twenty-seven-year-old freshmen legislators—the youngest legislators in the House, as a matter of fact—had become so outraged upon reading about the "untouchability" of the fairs that they had determined to do something about it. What they did first was to stay up late into the night boning up on parliamentary procedure. What they did next was to tack a rider onto the general tax bill just before it was to be voted on, putting fair racing on an equal footing with the commercial tracks on the split of the handle. Two hours later, the bill was passed. A day later, it was up before the Senate. With no hearings, and no chance for pressure to be exerted, the Senate approved the entire tax package.

Truth, virtue, and equality under the law had come to the Great and Glorious Commonwealth because George Carney had refused to knuckle under to a handful of cops. Instead of paying them a couple of thousand dollars, George was going to lose the difference between 12.5 per cent and 7.5 percent of his handle, a matter of something in excess of $90,000 a year.

The whole fair scene changed that day. The ironic twist was that George, who had never felt he was required to run his fair within the "privileged sanctuary" just because he had a right to, had already completed his six-day meet earlier that same week. In the first year of the new order, his fair was about the only one that wasn't affected. The next year, he tried it under the new rules and found the profits weren't worth the trouble. Since the Brockton Fair is a legitimate fair, the biggest and best of them, he just shrugged his shoulders and put it on that year without any pari-mutuel racing. His stubbornness, his refusal to be sandbagged, had cost him—projecting it out through the years— a tidy little fortune. It had earned him powerful enemies and friends, in and out of the legislature. There were other things, quite clearly, that were far more important to him.

It's too bad that story hasn't been told up to now. Otherwise, the mutuel clerks at Raynham might have thought twice before they struck Raynham two years later. George's reaction was to bring in a crew of women, and they turned out to be superior workers in every way. Joe Arena had beaten the Teamsters at Suffolk Downs, which is not a bad credential for any labor leader. But the clerks couldn't beat George Carney when George got his back up. The national headquarters sent up its biggest guns and most expensive lawyers in one final, all-out attempt to straighten him out. George is more than willing to take on the big ones. He moved not an inch. The cops were out at Brockton. The union is out at Raynham.

That's what I liked about George. He has a code of honor—you have to know how to break the code, that's all—and you don't find many like that around these days. Somehow or other, I have the feeling that you didn't find many of them around in the good old days either.

B. A. Dario I have saved for the last because we are going to meet him again in the next chapter. Dario is the owner of Lincoln Downs, more commonly referred to as "Dario's little gold mine." He was eligible to attend the hearing of the Massachusetts Racing Commission only because he also happened to own a third of Berkshire Downs. Dario comes out of an entirely different box from Reynolds, Linsey, or Loew. Back at the dawn of the forties, he was Dario Bacchiocchi, the owner of a couple of beat-up taxicabs in Providence, Rhode Island. When the war came along he began to make some money by filling the cabs up with servicemen and shuttling them back and forth to the Army camps and naval bases that ringed the area. With that bankroll, he leased a fairground on the outskirts of Providence and, this being a time when anything that purported to be entertainment and had a box-office window in front of it was an automatic success, he did well enough so that he was able to buy a weed-filled lot closer to town and swing some dates from the Racing Commission—which in Rhode Island means directly from the Governor. To finance the construction of the track he floated an attractive stock-debenture, in $10,000 packets, for anyone interested in investing in the proprietor of a taxicab stand, a racing license, and an empty lot. For those visionaries who did, it turned out to be the investment of a lifetime. Lincoln Downs was so successful so quickly that Dario was able to buy back the debentures during his first season. His investors had all their money back and they still had an absolutely free ride on an equal amount of stock.

In strict noncompliance with the public image of the other old men, Dario is a gay old dog. B. A. Dario in his seventies is a dancing fool, and while the young lady on his arm never seems to be the same young lady, his taste is always impeccable. The same, alas, cannot be said for his taste in toupees.

My affection for Dario was admittedly stunted by his screaming when I applied for the ten extra days. The nerve of the guy. Not only was it the other way around—I wasn't competing with him, he was competing with me—but Dario had himself done exactly what he was accusing me of doing. There had been a circuit in New England at one time, and it was B. A. Dario who had come in, full of vim and vinegar, and broken it by running against Rockingham and Suffolk Downs. Still, he made so much noise and received such sympathetic coverage from the Boston press that if you ask anybody in Boston today, I suspect they will tell you that yeah, Bill Veeck came to town and right away he started a race war.

9

Nine Deals + Two Lawsuits = Twenty-Four Dates

Before the kids suit had become final, I had started negotiations on a deal that would win me two lawsuits at a single bound, a new New England record.

Berkshire Downs, I had discovered, was an insolvent track with a very checkered history and a very spotty reputation. It was put to me that the commission felt the place was a time bomb, and that when it blew it would blow into a major scandal. The track had opened in 1959 in what seemed to be a heady mixture of politics and skulduggery, complete with such mystery and intrigue as a Berkshire Downs certificate placed under the rug in the home of Governor Foster Furcolo's father. Remarkable! If there hadn't been any skulduggery, how did anyone imagine a rundown track with a seating capacity of 2970 had managed to corral those 24 valuable dates? There were broad hints of Mafia influence in the original ownership. Frank Sinatra's name was inevitably bandied about. If so, the Mafia was losing its touch. Given the location and the meager facilities, the original owners went broke and the track was taken over by a couple of Rhode Island guys, Santi Campanella, a well-connected contractor, and B. A. Dario, the owner of Lincoln Downs. It was not the best investment that those estimable gentlemen had ever made, either. They had been losing nothing but money for four years. The place was being shopped around, and there were no takers.

The track I wasn't interested in. The 24 dates I was. In that regard there was one interesting historical footnote. In 1966 the new owners of Berkshire had made a technical mistake. They had failed to perform the paperwork necessary to revalidate their status as a licensee, and Suffolk Downs had leaped into the breach and applied for the full 90 days. For Suffolk, that was a most uncharacteristic action. Right from the beginning, Suffolk Downs could have applied for the full 90 days if it had wanted to. Instead, it had contented itself with anywhere from 47 to 66. With Suffolk running those 24 dates instead of Berkshire, everybody had profited. The Commonwealth had profited to the tune of $1.5 million. Suffolk's stockholders had profited to whatever extent an additional 212,000 customers profited them. The commission had been presented with a glorious opportunity to defuse the time bomb at Berkshire once and for all by continuing to award Suffolk Downs the full 90 days. Dave Haber assured the commission that he would apply for them again. The commission assured Haber he'd get them. And then, at the last minute, Haber changed his mind and asked for only the usual 66. Joe Linsey apparently stepped into the picture with the appropriate words of wisdom.

Tradition being where you find it, I saw no reason why we shouldn't return to the 90 days of racing that had been traditionally ours in the year of '66.

In my first weeks in Boston, I took the temperature of each of the commissioners. The obvious one to start with was the commissioner whose term was coming to an end, Elmer Nelson. Nelson had been the campaign manager for the former Governor, John A. Volpe. The new Governor was no great admirer of Volpe's and everybody knew he wasn't going to be reappointed. If I wasn't going to get an honest count from Nelson, I wasn't going to get one from anybody.

Nick and I met him for dinner at the Red Coach Inn on a rainy night, within days after I had been introduced to the press. Nelson's advice was to apply for the full 90 days and then try to buy Berkshire Downs. He confirmed that the track was eminently purchasable, and he could tell us that the asking price seemed to be $550,000. He also confided that we didn't have the slightest chance of getting the dates without buying the track, because the commission was not going to allow itself to be placed in the position of putting anybody out of business.

This being a free country, we could interpret that any way we wanted to, depending on whether we wanted to think in terms of administrative policy or political realities. If you happened to have a naturally suspicious mind you might come to the conclusion that the political realities in Massachusetts were such that nobody was going to allow the boys from Rhode Island to be put out of business until they were adequately recompensed for their losing operation.

Peter Consiglio was, as usual, sympathetic and, as always, noncommittal.

Tom Beedem held a lot of conversations back and forth with Dr. Walsh, and I finally got on the horn with him a few times myself. The chairman left me with the distinct impression that, happy as he would be to see that boil excised, he didn't view the commission as the proper agency to perform the operation. His advice, like Nelson's, was to buy the track. The only thing wrong with that, I told him, was that I wasn't interested in real estate at the other corner of the state, and the price that had been quoted to me was far beyond what I was willing to pay for the dates alone.

Within a couple of days, who should drop by the office to try to peddle the track to me but Santi Campanella himself. Unhappily, he didn't quote any new price to me. Or, for that matter, any price at all. For some reason, he seemed to be operating on the premise that I already knew what it was. His whole pitch was geared toward relieving me of any misgivings I might have on whether the commission would award us the dates if we did buy it from him.

Another day or two, and yet another voice was heard from. E. M. Loew's. The word sure was getting around. Loew's proposition was that we join forces and buy Berkshire together. We would get all the flat racing for our half of the money, and he would get all the harness racing for his. I laughed and I laughed. I mean, he didn't have the idea at all. "I don't only want more flat dates," I told him. "I'm out to get more harness dates too."

At pretty much the last minute, I decided to apply for 76 dates, a figure I arrived at through a not particularly complicated formula by which I counted back to the first Saturday we would be able to run within the statutory framework and then added one at the other end. My over-all strategy was a variation of the burnt-earth policy. Let Berkshire continue to lose money, let the commission meditate upon the fact that the taxpayers were not realizing anything like the potential return on those 24 dates, and sooner or later maybe one of them would give up.

The man who finally came to me with a practical deal was our contractor, Martin DeMatteo. Martin had been doing the general contracting for Suffolk Downs for years, and although Nate Dolin had come in with a friend from out of town, Martin's bid was as good as Nate's guy's, and I felt he was entitled to hold on to it. I also thought I was entitled to hold on to Martin DeMatteo, and for the same reason, quite frankly, I had wanted to hold on to Sonny McDonough, who was also a good contractor. Contractors are deeply involved in politics. Not all of them. Only the ones who stay in business. It might even be said that if anybody could figure out a way for contractors to make money out of solving the pollution problem, the air of America would be shining with cleanliness.

As far as Martin's interest in Berkshire was concerned, there was also the customary interplay of tracks. Along with his other interests, Martin owned Green Mountain, a little racetrack just over the Vermont border from Berkshire Downs, and he was not at all averse to eliminating a competitor. Martin's proposition was that each of us would put up $275,000. We would get the dates. He would get the real estate plus the six-day fair.

Sounds simple. Sounds eminently fair. Forget it. Absolutely nothing was simple in my pursuit after those 24 dates. In Martin's deal—which we will call Deal No. 1—he would end up with solid real estate and we could very well end up with a fistful of air. Everybody was always guaranteeing us he could deliver the Racing Commission, but in the final analysis nobody could deliver the commission except the commission. Or the Attorney General. Or the Governor. What followed was a long afternoon of give-and-take, with both sides jockeying for position.

Joel moved in with Deal No. 2 to protect us if we didn't get the 24 days. DeMatteo would buy the track and inform the commission that he was not going to have any racing there. We would then apply for the 24 days, and after they had been granted by the commission we would pay him our $275,000.

With DeMatteo and his lawyer arguing that their promise to surrender the dates was all the protection we needed, I came back with

Deal No. 3: If we were each going to put up 50 per cent of the money, we would each own 50 per cent of the deal. Until we were sure of the dates, we'd be partners in Berkshire. Once we had them, we'd sign over the real estate and everything else.

Deal No. 4 was his lawyer's counterproposal. We would put up the money and own Berkshire Downs outright until we got the dates. At which time we would convey the real estate and the rest of the assets to him, and he'd pay us the $275,000.

Deal No. 5, Joel's counterproposal to their counterproposal, was that if we were going to put up all the money we would also retain a permanent 50-per-cent interest in the fair.

That was only the beginning. The number of variations we were able to play on so simple a theme was truly breathtaking. Martin was always a hard businessman in the sense that he wanted to get everything there was to be got out of any deal. But once he shook your hand on it, his word was good. Minor difficulties had a way of arising before the contracts were signed as his lawyers came up with those little alterations so dear to their profession, but whenever things got sticky, he and I would get together, profess our honor to each other, and very quickly come to an understanding on what our original agreement had been.

The next day, DeMatteo and his lawyer obtained a seven-day option from Campanella and called back with Deal No. 6. The latest goody was that Berkshire had a $300,000 loss carryover, which meant that whoever bought the corporate shell would also own a tax loss. The way it went this time, we would put up all the money and inherit the tax write-off. He would immediately buy a half-interest in Berkshire, and we would agree to sell him the other half on September 1 (just in time for the fair), when presumably we would have cleared up the little matter of the 24 dates.

Through all this, I should say, his lawyer, Herman Snyder, had been implying that if we didn't want to be good sports about it, he had somebody else who would be only too happy to. We got some hint who it might be later in the day, when E. M. Loew popped up in the New York offices of Realty Equities to warn them that if Suffolk Downs got 24 additional days of flat racing by buying Berkshire Downs, he would fight to get all the harness dates—which was such an admirable attempt to put himself into the game that I had to look upon him with new eyes. However he had learned about our negotiations—and it could have been from Campanella as easily as from DeMatteo—he was there to inform Realty that anybody with the slightest knowledge of Massachusetts politics could tell them the commission would most certainly rule in his favor.

Having brandished the stick with one hand, Loew held out a carrot in the other. His new proposition, detoured through New York, was that we buy Berkshire together for $500,000, with each of us putting up $100,000 in cash and raising the rest of the money by means of a bank loan. Beautiful. By deftly inserting the idea that Campanella was willing to sell for $500,000, he was attempting to make us think twice—I surmised—before we closed the deal we already had and maybe foul it up completely.

That wasn't all. Being the warm and compassionate human being that he was, he was willing to let me save face by not having to accept the same deal I had laughed off a couple of months earlier. He was now willing to let us have the 24 days of flat racing for only half of our harness dates. Once that basic formula had been agreed upon, he was confident a fair and equitable deal could be worked out for the other half. What he seemed to be saying was that since we all knew it wouldn't be worth our while to convert the track from flat to harness for 15 days, he might be willing to give us a percentage of the profits on those 15 other days every year. Or something. It's always hard to figure out what E. M. Loew means, and if I had been there to ask him about it I'm sure I'd have been able to become even more confused. E. M. Loew has come a long way for a man who does what he does to the English language.

On June 3 (the same day we learned we had won the suit on the kids) Herman Snyder called back to inform us that he had just made an appointment with Santi Campanella to close the deal on the morning of Friday, June 6. If we wanted to stay in it, we were going to have to buy DeMatteo's option before it ran out at 5:00 p.m. on Thursday. He was now willing to offer us Deal No. 7 on a take-it-or-leave-it basis.

We were still putting up all the money, but he was now willing to pay the full $275,000 on or before September 1 (at his discretion) for half the real estate and half the fair. When we got *any part of the 24 dates*, we would sell him the other half interest for $1.00. In return, he volunteered to write in a restriction against Berkshire ever being used for flat or harness racing except as part of the fair.

We met with them in the afternoon and were told by Snyder that they were under extreme pressure to go elsewhere. Sorely as he was tempted to accept the offer that had been made by our unnamed competitor, he was going to give us a chance to match it. Deal No. 8. He was going to buy Berkshire himself as a straight real-estate deal, and then sell us the corporate shell after we saw how things were going with the commission. We hit Deal No. 8 head on by ignoring it. If there was one impression that had come through stronger and clearer than any other during our financial shadow-boxing it was that DeMatteo was out to put up as little front money as possible. Joel started by taking them two giant steps backward to Deal No. 6, in which DeMatteo would put up half the money immediately. When they showed little appetite to go even that far, we threw in the towel and agreed to accept the take-it-or-leave-it Deal No. 7. With one modification. They'd put up their $275,000 by September 1, regardless, but we weren't going to sell them the other half for $1.00 unless we were awarded at least 13 of the 24 dates.

What we were saying in effect was: Okay, we'll get up the money and find out if we can transfer the dates. If we can, you own all the physical premises and you will give us the $275,000. If we can't, you will give us the same $275,000 but we will own 50 per cent of Berkshire Downs until we are able to get at least 13 dates. That was Deal No. 9.

On the morning of June 5 we gathered in the room off the Paddock Club that I eventually converted into an apartment for myself and typed up a single-page contract, full of handwritten notations along the margins. Snyder had already arranged for us to meet with the Berkshire people in his office so that we could get something on paper before the option expired. We signed an agreement with them, put up a $50,000 binder, and put the closing off for another week. That done, I headed right for the airport. My son Michael was graduating from high school the next day, and, track or no track, I was going to be there.

The following Thursday we met in Joel's office for a routine closing. Ha! I should have known better. We had a half-million dollars' worth of certified checks when the meeting started, and we were still sitting on them when it ended. It didn't turn out to be routine; it turned out to be hilarious.

Also crowded. Rudie Schaffer was there for our side. Joel's father, Frank Kozol, knew Dario quite well from his years around the racing scene and he had decided to sit in on it too. Realty Equities, showing its first wisp of interest, had sent down an accountant from New York, possibly to wave good-by as the half a million dollars faded slowly into the sunset. In addition to Dario, the sellers were represented by a dazzlement of Campanellas: Santi, the father; Santi P., the son; and Amerigo Campanella, who was Santi's uncle and lawyer. Plus a couple of other people I never knew or can't remember.

I had seen Dario at the racetrack the previous day. Dario has a racing stable, and one of his horses was running at Suffolk. As a matter of fact, the horse had won. As a matter of fact, every time Dario brought a horse to Suffolk the horse won. "I'll be seeing you tomorrow," he had said, with effusion. "I guess the thing's all set, huh?"

It didn't seem to be set any more. "I never saw this agreement before," he shouted twenty-four hours later. "I would never agree to sell to these people! I don't know nothing about this. It's all off!"

Well, he had an excellent technical point there, but no legal point at all. He hadn't been present when the agreement was signed; it had been signed in his name by Amerigo Campanella. We happened to have the telegram he had sent to Snyder, under his legal name of Dario Bacchiocchi, informing him that he was authorizing "my attorney, Amerigo Campanella, to execute all instruments in order to sell my 33 1/3 share interest in Berkshire Downs."

Dario had apparently been doing some thinking. And the more he thought, the less ecstatic he had become about finally bailing his money out of Berkshire. His real wheel, after all, was at Lincoln Downs. Had it suddenly occurred to him that if we were able to move the 24 days to Suffolk Downs—and why would we be buying them if we couldn't?—any or all of them could very well be run in direct competition with him?

Or maybe E. M. Loew had got to him. All kinds of wheels are running around within wheels in this thing. Here is Dario, there is Martin De-Matteo, and off on the horizon sits E. M. Loew. There are five tracks involved here, and such machinations as can only be imagined. Fortunately, I didn't know that much about it yet, and even more fortunately, I didn't care. All I knew was that the 24 days were within my grasp, and that cut through everything.

Well, maybe not quite everything. There is a paragraph in the agreement which obligates the seller to secure a waiver from the Berkshire concessionaire, and since we have an exclusive ten-year concession contract with Ogden Foods at Suffolk, it is absolutely essential that he get it. Berkshire's concessionaire happens to be Sportservice, now being run by Louis Jacobs' son, Jerry. Campanella had assured us that Jerry would do that little thing for him. No problem at all. I hadn't anticipated any problem there, either. Maybe Jerry wouldn't have done it for Santi Campanella in your ordinary run-of-the-mill business deal, but when Jerry heard that good ol' Will was on the other end of the deal, there'd be no trouble at all.

There was trouble. Campanella hadn't been able to get the waiver.

Up jumps Dario. "See! We can't do it, that's all! The deal's off! It's off! Everything's off!"

Whoa there, Dario. Not so fast. We didn't put that paragraph in there to protect you; we put it in to protect us. If the concept that a man can call off a deal because *he* can't deliver on a promise were ever accepted, broken contracts would be strewn across the landscape from here to San Diego. Well, telling Dario that is one thing. Deciding what to do about it is something else. I bring up the possibility of pushing the closing back to Monday to give me a chance to see what I can do with Jerry Jacobs.

Dario is up again. "You don't want it? The deal's off! Give us the check right now or you can forget the whole thing! The deal's off!"

Throughout Dario's whole delightful performance, Joel and I have been sneaking glances at each other from under our eyelids, doing our best not to laugh. The looks Santi Campanella has been sending at Dario are something else again. Santi owns two-thirds of the thing, remember. They've dropped a quarter of a million dollars in four years, and they're $400,000 in debt. He's been shopping the thing around for a couple of years and he's finally come up with a lamb. He has come to this meeting hoping desperately to find some way of keeping the deal from falling apart. Campanella says something sharp and abrupt to Dario, which can be freely translated as, *Will you for once in your life shut your big mouth!* Dario, who doesn't care who he's mad at by this time, responds in kind. When they finally pause for breath, Amerigo Campanella jumps in to inform Dario he hasn't appreciated the slur on his professional ethics that was implied in the wholly uncalled-for accusation that he had signed Dario's name without authorization. Dario finally explodes completely and goes storming out the door, shouting, "It's off! There's going to be no extensions here! It's off, it's off, it's off!"

Fortunately, Frank Kozol has known him for years and he goes running out into the corridor after him to calm him down and coax him back into the office. By the time Dario is gentled and sat back down again, Joel and I excuse ourselves and go out into the corridor to decide whether we want to go through with our deal if it means risking a lawsuit with the concessionaire.

"One slight correction," Joel says. "We're not *risking* a lawsuit. We're *buying* a lawsuit. I can guarantee it."

It had not exactly come as a complete surprise to us, you see, that Jacobs wasn't giving up any of his concession rights. The day after we had signed the agreement with Campanella—which means an hour after Campanella had told him about it—Jacobs had sent me a "Dear Bill" letter which read:

> I just learned today the good news that you are purchasing Berkshire Downs. Congratulations. We will be looking forward to renewing our relationship and working with you as concessionaire. For your information, if you don't already have it, I am enclosing herewith a certified copy of our twenty-five-year concessions agreement dated January 17, 1964, with Berkshire Downs. I understand that you are contemplating moving the Berkshire meet to Suffolk. Our contract provides that in that case the contracts would also apply to Suffolk Downs, and you will be assuming all the obligations thereof. If you have any questions please telephone me.

The letter had arrived Air Mail Special Delivery, Certified, return receipt requested.

"Nothing like having friends in this business," Joel had said then.

"Your friend thinks he has you by the short hairs and he isn't going to let go," Joel says now.

Well, we have no obligation unless they can come up with the waiver. By the same token, we have no deal. And I want those 24 dates. "Just for the sake of argument," I say, "suppose Jerry does sue. What are our chances?"

"I see a way. Any client who is guaranteed he's going to win a lawsuit has a fool or a charlatan for a lawyer. So I'll only say this: I'll win it."

We went back in and asked for an extension over the weekend to give me a chance to take a whack at Jerry Jacobs.

I took my whack. I got nowhere.

Come Monday, we bought it anyway. It would have been worth it just to see the look of utter astonishment on Dario's face.

We were the proud owners of a racetrack I had never seen and, from everything I had heard about it, never wanted to see. We didn't know if we could get the 24 dates. We didn't know if we were facing a lawsuit.

But the way I looked at it, we had bought ourselves 24 dates a year for $275,000, and that was one heckuva buy. If we didn't get the dates this year . . . well, we could always apply for them again the next.

Jerry Jacobs? Aw, Jerry was just making noise. Jerry was never going to sue good ol' Will.

10

It Couldn't Be Done, and We Did It

Now that we had the 24 dates, all we had to do was get them. Two possible ways had suggested themselves.

Route 1 was to transfer the license from Berkshire to Suffolk.

Route 2 was to surrender the dates that had been granted to Berkshire and apply for them on behalf of Suffolk Downs.

Now this may seem like a lot of nonsense, but it is the stuff on which lawsuits are won and lost. The course we chose wasn't dictated by our reading of either the commission or the Attorney General but by the vexing problem of the Sportservice contract. In that contract, it was clear that the whole protective clause was geared to the transfer of the license. If the operation was transferred—and it wouldn't be easy to argue that the transfer of a license was anything else—the concession agreement was to go along with it.

We had closed the purchase of Berkshire on Monday, June 16. On June 23 we put on our Berkshire hat and went through the charade of electing our own officers at Berkshire Downs and immediately held a meeting and voted to shut the track down. A week later we informed the commission that "due to the extensive and persistent losses" which Berkshire had experienced, we were canceling our applications for the dates that had been awarded to Berkshire. The licenses, we pointed out, had never been issued "and will not be requested or accepted by us."

The question we were posing was: When do you become a licensee? When the dates are granted or when the license is issued? No ruling had ever been made on this nitpicking legal point before for the very good reason that there had never been a reason for anybody to care. Although the commission must award the dates by January 30, the license isn't actually issued until—well, until the commission gets around to it. This may not seem important, but it is, once again, the vital link on which everything hung. The licenses are actual licenses. Like a license to practice medicine. The commission prints them up and mails them to you, and you are entitled to hang them on the wall as proof of your legitimacy or stuff them into a drawer or make such other use of them as might seem good to you.

Immediately after we had signed our one-page contract with Martin DeMatteo, we had called the secretary of the Racing Commission to tell him what we were doing and request an informal meeting with the commission. Our motives were pure; that is, purely practical. Having just rapped the commission so decisively in the courtroom, we felt it an excellent idea to show it that we were not out to embarrass it further by confronting it with a *fait accompli*. Not an act of contrition, but of genuflection. To put it another way, we were out to protect ourselves by putting the burden of proof on the commission. If there was any reason why it didn't want us to acquire the track or why it didn't want to shut the dates down there or—to get to the crux of the matter—why it didn't want us to run the dates at Suffolk, it could tell us about it right at the outset, and we could decide whether we wanted to blow the $50,000 down payment and walk away.

We didn't get our meeting with the commission until June 12, only a couple of hours before we were scheduled to meet with Dario and Campanella in Joel's office. The commissioners listened to us, they seemed relieved, they didn't commit themselves. Nobody had ever filed a Supplementary Application before. Their attitude was that they would have to hold a hearing and then make their decision on the basis of whatever legal opinion came out of the Attorney General's office.

Good enough. Joel had already met with Barry Corn, the Assistant Attorney General in charge of the Racing Commission and all other administrative agencies. If Corn were going to take the position that the license had been issued at the time the dates were granted, we were going to have to find another way. Corn was the lawyer Joel had beat in the kids suit. Fortunately for us, he had adopted a purely professional attitude about it. He had been given a bad case, he had fought hard, he had lost. So what else is new? On July 3, the day before our 66-day meet was ending , Joel delivered a Memorandum on the Law to Barry Corn, along with the notation that we felt the commission "unquestionably" had the power and authority to grant the Supplementary Applications we intended to file at the conclusion of the holiday weekend.

We anticipated no real difficulty. Berkshire Downs was dead. All that was involved really was whether or not the Commonwealth wanted to pick up something between $1.5 million and $2 million in tax revenue. Even when Berkshire was alive, it had never turned over more than $350,000 for those same 24 days.

When Joel returned to his office after the Fourth of July weekend, he found another memorandum from his father.

Re: Realty Equities–Suffolk Downs application for 24 additional days.

Joel:
I met Barry Corn in our building downstairs at 1:30 p.m. today. We had a discussion and he said as follows:
1) He has read your Memorandum on the Law and he agrees with it 100%. He can't conceive of any other answer.
2) He's going to check the statute and cases but is certain you are completely right because he came to the same conclusion himself independent of us.
3) There is no need of you wasting any time to discuss it with him. As he thinks of the matter further, should he have the slightest doubt he will call you immediately to discuss it with you. He can't conceive that this could happen.
4) Unless he calls you in advance for further discussion, he gave me his firm assurance that when the Racing Commission asks for an opinion he will tell them bluntly, directly and unequivocally that the Racing Commission has a complete legal right to grant the supplementary applications of Suffolk Downs for 24 supplementary dates to be raced at Suffolk Downs in 1969. Barry assures me that this is the formal Attorney General opinion that he will give to the Racing Commission and concurs with me that the only question was whether we had a right to file a supplementary application. And concurs with me that any other judgment or opinion would be nonsensical and stultifying.

"Bluntly, directly and unequivocally." That would seem to have been that.

We filed our Supplementary Application with the commission two days later. Two applications, actually. A license is granted for consecutive days, which only means that any time you break up the pattern by asking for a "dark day" you have to start all over again with a new license.

The problem we were confronted with was that the statutory strait-jacket had us hemmed in on all sides. In the best of all worlds, we would have simply tacked the new days onto the old ones and run 90 straight days. The ship had already sailed on us there. The summer meet had ended, and our horses were running at Rockingham. That left us squeezed rather tightly between the end of the fair hiatus on September 15 and the opening of our harness season October 24. To look on the sunny side of the street, the one break we did get from the calendar was that Labor Day was falling on September 1. If it had fallen on September 7, we'd have been left with only six days to pull the harness track out and get the flat track into reasonably good condition. As it was, we were going to be able to indulge ourselves with our one dark Tuesday—Tuesday is always the worst day in the week—and still have eleven whole days to work with.

As expected, the commission shot our Supplementary Application right up to the Attorney General's office for an opinion on whether it had the legal power to act upon it. And I must say that Barry Corn was every bit as good as his word. "A vital distinction exists between the granting of a license and its issuance," he wrote in the course of a terse three-page memorandum. "In my opinion, Suffolk Downs clearly has the right to file the Supplementary Application and hearings must be held thereon. . . ."

There was only one small shadow across our horizon. A shadow, I must admit, we were slow in spotting. Barry Corn, it seemed, was leaving the AG's office. His memorandum hadn't been sent to the Racing Commission, it had been sent to his successor as Chief of the Administrative Division. We had a copy only because Corn had instructed Quinn's secretary to send us one. Joel whipped it right over to me with the prophetic note: "I'm hopeful that the formal opinion will follow fast upon the memorandum."

It didn't. It started the most dramatic fight I've ever been involved in.

We had filed on July 8. The commission had thirty days in which to rule. If it had followed its usual procedure it would have published the notice for a public meeting immediately. Two weeks passed by without a whisper. That alone was enough to make us nervous. The word that filtered in from other sources was even more worrisome. Joe Linsey didn't like the idea that we would be running in the fall, which he had always looked upon as his private preserve. Not that we would be competing against him. Our horses would be running during the day; his dogs would be running at night. He had been running against the Rhode Island tracks on that basis for years. And right there, you had what he *was* so upset about. He was afraid that Narragansett, unable to take the competition from us, would go to nights as Dario had. And Narragansett was less than twenty miles from Taunton.

The word also reached Tom Beedem that Wonderland was very unhappy about the way we were rocking the boat. And that was ominous. When Wonderland sneezes, thirty-six legislators wipe their noses. When Clarence King sneezed, Robert Quinn called a doctor. Taunton's opposition was worrisome in quite another way. Not so much to me as to the lawyer's office. Joel was the moving factor for us, and his father was the driving force for Taunton. Frank Kozol was not only Taunton's legal counsel, he was one of its directors. He had literally acquired the track for Joe Linsey, and they were close personal friends. In my own office I was being warned that as the new kid in town I was going to be whipsawed between the old friendships and loyalties. If it wasn't put to me like that in so many words, it was certainly implicit in Tom Beedem's attitude when he came running in to tell me that Linsey was going to fight us. "Take it easy, Tom," I told him. "I already know about that from Joel. I don't hear things last from him, I hear them first."

What it amounted to in the beginning was extra pressure on Joel. And yet, the whole thing redounded to our benefit in a curious way when the Honorable Mr. Quinn so infuriated Frank Kozol that he ended up working with us.

On July 30, three weeks after we had filed our application, we came into the hearing room and discovered that the Attorney General still hadn't got around to rendering an opinion on the simple question of whether the commission had a right to entertain it.

Everybody else seemed to have an idea of what the ruling should be if it did. The whole racing community had come out, in full cry, to oppose us. Everybody except George Carney. Taunton expressed its fears that we would do irreparable damage to it by way of Narragansett. Wonderland's attorney, Robert T. Capeless, made his opposition to any more racing in the county more emphatic by vowing that Wonderland would never accept any increase in its own dates even if everybody else got them. (Let us pause here for a peek into the future. As I was leaving the Great Commonwealth with the situation broken wide open, Capeless was accepting 25 more dates for Wonderland. Not too happily, I must admit. He had asked for 50. An increase of 75 dates for the dogs had been rushed through the commission as an emergency measure—now that it knew the way—and signed under emergency authorization by the Governor.)

E. M. Loew was there in person to make a long-winded speech—irrelevant even if it had been true—about how DeMatteo and I had perfidiously expropriated his plan to buy Berkshire. The pay-off of his speech came somewhere near the end, when he informed the commission that if we were given the extra flat dates, he should be given our 30 harness dates. Since we weren't there to talk about harness dates, he was not only irrelevant; he was out of order. Joel, who is never quite able to resist an opportunity to have some fun with E. M. Loew, put him on the stand. Joel can just stand with one hand in his pocket and an absolutely straight face and get E. M. Loew so infuriated that he twists himself into knots.

A former racing commissioner named Amos Wasgate was there to urge the commission to hold those 24 days in escrow for a track he was planning to build in Worcester some day when he got around to it.

Our own case, impeccably presented, was based on the benefits that would accrue to the Commonwealth in the form of taxes. To the racing public and to sportsmen everywhere. And to us.

All of their huffing and our puffing meant not a thing, of course, until the AG unleashed an opinion. Two days after the hearing, Larry Lane called Tom Beedem to ask what the deadline was. "Tell him it's August seventh," I said, gritting my teeth. "You can also tell him it wouldn't make us mad it they got the word to us tomorrow."

The continuing delay was becoming more ominous by the hour. Quinn had to know we had Barry Corn's memorandum on the crucial question of the license. He wouldn't dare overrule his own administrative assistant on something like that. What could the delay mean except that he was trying desperately to find some other justification for ruling against us?

We had gone over the statute word by word. Nothing. The law was clear. "A Supplementary Application by a license for a subsequent license in that calendar year relating to the same premises and the original application . . . may be filed with the commission at any time prior to the expiration of said year."

We couldn't see how even Clarence King could advise-and-consent the AG out of that. And, mind you, he had to come up with a legal bar, not a philosophical one. Nobody at the hearing had even attempted to go into the legalities. For that matter, nobody who had opposed us could even lay claim to a legal standing; all had been allowed to address the commission only as "interested persons." In the entire Commonwealth, there were only two parties with a valid legal interest in the proceedings. We and the Attorney General.

I was, at least, discovering another fascinating side to human nature. Mine, anyway. There is nothing really frightening about anything, just so long as you know what you're fighting. But as the delay mounted, and the mystery deepened, it was becoming increasingly frightening in my mind. It's one thing to say, "The so-and-sos are trying to pull *that* on me, are they? Wellll, I'll show them!" It's quite another to be continually asking yourself, "What in the world are they trying to *do* to me?"

I'll say this for them. They didn't wait until the last possible day. Not quite. Three days before the deadline, the Honorable Robert H. Quinn delivered himself of the opinion that the commission had no authority to act on our application. And here's how he did it.

The statute, you will remember, said that a Supplementary Application must relate to the same premises and the original application. Obviously, these were the same premises. What he did was to take the five words, "relating to the original application" and interpret them to mean that we could ask only for *the same dates we had asked for in the original application.* I defy anyone to take us to task for not having had the wit to anticipate that he could have come up with anything as ludicrous as that! Since you would hardly be applying for the same dates unless they had been rejected the first time, he was saying that the legislature had used the word *supplementary* (Webster: that which supplies a want or makes an addition) when it had really meant *appeal* or *rehearing* or *reapplication.*

It had, of course, used the word *supplementary* because it meant supplementary. The phrase "relating to the same application" meant that you didn't have to burden the commission with all the massive detail that goes into the original application, which is about the size of a small encyclopedia. Our original application had contained seventeen exhibits, running into hundreds of pages. The list of Realty Equities stockholders alone had run into hundreds of pages. The Supplementary Application "relates to the original application" even more directly in that the original form runs thirty-five pages and asks some fifty-odd questions. The Supplementary Application asks only twelve questions, one of which specifically asks for information to identify the original application.

And yet, even with so strained an interpretation he hadn't been able to close us out completely. We hadn't applied for 66 days originally, we had applied for 76. And because the commission isn't bound by the dates the track asks for, we had added, with no malice aforethought, "or such dates as the commission might see fit to assign."

Now, if he was going to hold so rigidly to what had been asked for in the original application, how could he wheedle his way out of that? Easy. All you have to do, students, is say that it doesn't mean anything. It's "alternative language," see, and "the alternative language in Suffolk's original application is surplusage." *Surplusage* is a legal term meaning forget it. "Any language in the application that purposes to leave it to the commission to determine for what dates the applicant is applying is not properly part of the answer and may be disregarded."

See how easy it can be if you're really trying?

Or is it? In closing the door that completely on us, he was also closing it, in complete disregard for all precedent, on the commission. And that he didn't want to do. No problem. Nothing is a problem, students, if you have the power—and the *chutzpah*—to say it's no problem. "This does not mean, however, that the commission is bound by dates specified in an original application." In an original application, the commission was still perfectly free to award "such number of days of racing (up to 90) as the commission's judgment indicates."

Nothing was left to dispose of after that except the 10 days we had applied for and had not been granted. No problem there, either. We were not only limited by the number of days we had asked for; we were also limited to the specific dates that had been asked for. "On the facts, therefore, the commission is not authorized to approve Suffolk's Supplementary Applications since the period April 9 through July 5 has expired."

But why? Why was he going to all that trouble to deprive the Commonwealth of all that tax revenue? That is the allegedly unanswered question that was allegedly perplexing us. All right, we had been a little slick in the way we had transferred the dates from Berkshire. No argument. But that was a private matter between Jerry Jacobs and me. Berkshire was stone-cold dead. If we didn't run those 24 days, nobody was going to run them. You'd think the Attorney General of the Great Commonwealth would have been leaning over backward to find some way to rule in our favor. Even if—yes—he had to cut a few corners in the other direction. Instead, he was standing the language on its head to rule against us even though it was going to cost the taxpayers, who had by electing him placed their legal business in his hands, almost $2 million.

Dedicated public servant that he is, the Honorable Robert H. may very well have anticipated that someone would pose that embarrassing question. He might have even anticipated that it would be me. Lord only knows he didn't have anything to worry about from the Boston newspapers. An expression of piety was clearly called for; a moment of quiet meditation. "I am not unaware of the commission's concern that maximum use be made of the racing days provided for by the statute," he murmured piously. "It is only as a result of Berkshire's surrender of their twenty-four days that all ninety days of racing will not be used this year."

It was, fellow taxpayers, all my fault.

I'll say this for the Honorable Attorney General. His anticipation was faultless. "I am shocked and amazed," I said. "Although I suppose there's no reason I should be. Having read the Attorney General's opinion several times, I still find that the gentleman's logic completely escapes me.

"It does seem strange," I commented thoughtfully, "that as a public servant working in the best interest of the taxpayer, the Attorney General should have dug so deep to justify depriving the citizens of the Commonwealth of $1.7 million of badly needed funds."

Indignation, always a perishable item, was quickly swallowed up by the descending gloom. Joel had absolutely no doubt that he could destroy an opinion as absurd as that one in any court of law in the land. He was equally confident that it would be impossible to move through the courts fast enough so that it would mean anything. Horsemen don't make their plans overnight; we'd have to give them at least three weeks' notice to have any hope of filling our stables. We didn't have the full forty days to work with; we had something much closer to twenty. Even under normal conditions, that was hopeless. When you were up against the Attorney General with his unlimited funds and his diverse methods for legal foot-dragging, it was doubly hopeless. And if through some miracle of justice we were able to get a verdict in time, he just might be able to kill us anyway by dragging it into the appeals courts.

Oh, we'd win eventually. No question. We'd win the right to run 24 days *last year*.

"Joel," I said, "you told me once that you had a strong judiciary in this state. Let's just find out how strong."

"You want to go to court?"

"I want to go to court."

On August 5, the commission dismissed our application. On August 27, the same commission awarded us the 24 dates.

I cannot tell you why I was so sure we could do it. I am no starry-eyed idealist when it comes to the law, to the rectitude of judges, or to the triumph of right over wrong. Maybe it was this: You can't keep these bums from taking their shots at you, but there's nothing that says you have to take it lying down. If the Honorable Mr. Quinn would stoop to such a low and shabby subterfuge to help his friends, the least I could do was make him walk into a courtroom and spread it across the record.

You have to be a little bit lucky, sure. We were a whole lot lucky. We lived in luck. I am going to show you skeptics how with a few good breaks—the right judges sitting on the original moves and the right trial judge sensing what was going on and getting angry—it is still possible to move through the courts with lightning speed. We zipped through even faster than I have indicated. We didn't file suit until August 12, and we had our verdict on August 21. The chronology at the end of the chapter can serve as a road map on how it was done.

Let me begin by giving credit where credit is due. The decision to sue was mine. Once it had been made, Joel Kozol sat down and planned the entire strategy step by step. Right there in the office. Right off the top of his head. We never wavered from that blueprint by one agate line, and we never had so much as a momentary setback. I mean, he really showed me something.

The first day was unquestionably the key to the whole thing. Although the case was going to have to end up in the Superior Court, Joel came up with the idea that we might be able to place a stamp of urgency upon the case by having it sent down from the Supreme Judicial Court, the highest court in the state. To impress the urgency of our plight upon Judge Paul C. Reardon of the Supreme Court, he brought our motion in the form of a Petition for Determination of Rights. Judge Reardon rose beautifully to the occasion. He promptly transferred the petition itself to the Superior Court and *authorized us to state to the presiding judge of the Motion Session that in view of the heavy work load that was on the full Supreme Court, the disposition of our case could be more speedily (speedily!) handled downstairs.*

We went racing to the Superior Court and presented the petitions to Judge Walter H. McLaughlin. An excellent judge, Joel told me. You bet he was. Judge McLaughlin listened intently to the words of Judge Reardon, carrying as they did the imprimatur of the Supreme Court, and ordered that the preliminary hearing be held on Friday, only three days later.

The first phase of the psychological campaign had come off faultlessly. Phase No. 2 was to keep the heat on the Attorney General. Toward that noble end, Joel delivered Judge McLaughlin's order to the AG's office in person, along with a letter in which he expressed his confidence that the Attorney General was every bit as interested as we were in resolving the matter speedily so that if the court should decide he was in error the Commonwealth would not be needlessly penalized by the loss of such a significant amount of revenue. To wrap it up neatly, he reminded Mr. Quinn that since he had already studied the matter for a full month in order to render his formal opinion, he would hardly require any more time to study it.

We knew Quinn would try to stall, and of course he did. On Friday it was represented to the court that the Attorney General's office would need two weeks to prepare an answer. Judge McLaughlin gave it only until the following Wednesday. And then Judge McLaughlin put us on the glory road by not only ordering that the case would go to trial on the very next day, Thursday, August 21, but placing us at the top of the calendar as "first case out."

From there, Joel went to work on the Attorney General's office to make it as difficult as possible for it to drag out the trial. In dismissing our application, the commission had stated that it was acting solely upon the AG's interpretation of the statute. Since no *facts* were in dispute, Joel had drawn up a stipulation on what the facts of the case were and delivered it to the Attorney General's office for his signature. Although lawyers, as officers of the court, are charged with agreeing to just such stipulations wherever possible, as a courtesy to busy judges, the Assistant Attorney General balked. Joel was right back at him on Monday, demanding that he sign it. Hammering away. Demanding that he be told what the Attorney General's office was objecting to. Forcing the AG to decide how obstructionist he dared to be. All right! What fact or facts do you find fault with? Come on! If you won't tell me, I'm going to inform the judge you find nothing wrong with it but contumaciously refuse to sign it!

He kept the pressure on, never letting up, and on the third go-around, on the day the AG had to file his answer, they signed the stipulation. This eliminated the need to take testimony.

And then we got our third straight break on the judges. We were the first case out on Thursday, and Judge Harry Kalus was the first judge open. We liked that. He had already ruled in our favor in throwing out a temporary restraining order Sportservice had come up with that would have prevented us from running the 24 days with any concessionaire except it. A very tough, very able, very straight judge. An alert judge who liked to ask questions. "He's a good lawyer," Joel told me. "And best of all, he's fast."

And sharp. Joel had barely begun his opening presentation when Judge Kalus broke in. "Excuse me. Is this matter going to become moot? I'm not saying that this court will not give you a speedy trial, but . . ." Immediately, he ordered the court reporter to strike out that remark and ordered Joel to go ahead.

Marvelous. The Judge had gone out of his way within the first couple of minutes to let us know that he had smelled out the real issue. As the proceedings continued, you could see that he didn't like what he smelled.

Now, the Attorney General's ruling may have been an absurdity by all known rules of logic and semantics, but you do have to say this for it: It was even more ludicrous historically. The original statute hadn't said anything about Supplementary Applications. As it had originally been written, an applicant could file for additional dates at any time during the year within ten days of the period he was asking for. The change had come about after one of the fairs, in a truly remarkable display of poor judgment, had closed Wonderland down for six days. The Racing Commission, needless to say, had fallen all over itself to vote Wonderland six additional days, along with, we can assume, profuse apologies. For the next three years, the commission had pleaded with the legislature to amend the statute on the grounds that it needed *more flexibility in administering the racing statute so as to maximize the revenue that would be obtained.*

In 1950 the statute had finally been amended and, as part of the same package, the supplementary rule had come into being. To give the commission more flexibility and to maximize the tax revenue.

The Assistant AG who had to stand up and argue his noncase, hedged in as he was on all sides by his boss's airy opinion, was James P. Kiernan. I must say for him that he did his best under the kind of questioning that was withering in its very archness.

"What do you say as a plain matter of ordinary dictionary English?" the judge asked him. "How can the words 'supplementary application' relate to a preliminary, a previous application?"

Since he was unable to argue that words didn't mean what they meant, Kiernan based his whole argument on the total effect of the amended rules. For it had been in that series of amendments of 1950 that the legislature had written in the straitjacket, front and rear, including the restriction that forced the commission to assign the dates by January 30. Since that part of the amended statute was clearly restrictive, Kiernan's argument went, it had been the intent of the legislature to make the whole thing as restrictive as possible.

The truth of the matter is that he did have an argument of sorts, if only he had been able to make it. But just how is an assistant AG supposed to get up in court and say, "Your Honor, I know and you know and everybody knows that the legislature seized upon the commission's request for flexibility and for a maximization of income and used it as a smokescreen to reduce its flexibility and minimize the income for the greater gain of out-of-state interests." Why, if he had said anything like that, the judge might have been moved to ask him whose interests the Attorney General had been trying to serve in making the ruling that was now before his court. (Stick around. He gets to it in the next go-around.)

No matter how you looked at it, it was a self-defeating argument. The rule on the Supplementary Applications was the one part of the amended statute that was not written to be restrictive. It was the sop that had been thrown to Suffolk Downs to keep the thing from looking too lousy, and the first time anybody had tried to use it, the Attorney General had interpreted it away.

Judge Kalus's questioning forced Kiernan to deal with that question over and over again.

JUDGE KALUS: "In summary, then, it is the Attorney General's position that the amendment has curtailed the authority of the Racing Commission to give 'additional racing days not in excess of ninety.' That it?"

KIERNAN: "Yes, Your Honor. In effect the opinion says that the commission cannot grant a subsequent license unless—to state it affirmatively—a—"

JUDGE KALUS: "You started to say *unless* there."

KIERNAN: "Unless all the days in the original applications haven't been used, and it must be limited to the dates specified."

JUDGE KALUS: "Then I ask you, can you tell me what is there left if he has asked for eighty days and got eighty?"

KIERNAN: "There would be nothing left in that situation, Your Honor."

JUDGE KALUS: "Gentlemen, I have considered this matter as you were arguing it, and I am ready to make findings and rulings and order for decree."

He didn't leave the bench, you understand. There was not the slightest break in the rhythm and tempo of the exchange. Joel had said he was fast; he hadn't said he was faster than the speed of light. Without pausing for as much as a deep breath, Judge Kalus ruled that the Racing Commission did have the authority to consider our Supplementary Application, and then, incredibly, he directed them to grant it.

Joel and I looked at each other in utter astonishment.

"Let a decree be entered accordingly," the court ruled.

He was giving us the dates himself!

But then he realized that he had been somewhat carried away. "Now, I want to ask counsel," he said, turning to Joel, "was it not represented to me that the State Racing Commission has or is ready to approve the Supplementary Application as a matter of discretion?"

Joel, who had already been savoring his victory, had to tell him that he could only state that the commissioners had indicated to him, individually, that the application would have been approved. Which was almost the same thing, but not quite. The court thereupon pulled back a bit and contented itself with directing the commission to "consider and act upon" the application.

He had gone just as far as he could go. The Attorney General had told the commission it couldn't consider it. The judge was ordering it, by interlocutory decree, to act upon it. And we did know that the commissioners wanted to give us the dates and be done with it. Because, just as Joel had said, they had told us so.

We had done the impossible. We had filed our suit, and nine days later we had our verdict. By law, it is not possible to get an interlocutory decree stayed by appealing. The best they could do was stall for another week by delaying the finalizing of the decree. To save that week, Joel went right down to the AG's office with a proposed decree to see whether he just might be able to get the Assistant AG to assent to it while he was still reeling. And the Assistant AG signed everything Joel put in front of him, and the decree was entered.

From there, we went back to Joel's office and called the commissioners to request that they set up a special meeting on Friday to award the dates.

On Friday, all hell broke loose.

To a man, the commissioners had told Joel that they took their instructions from the Attorney General, not from the judge. Okay. On Friday morning Joel was back in Quinn's office with a copy of Judge Kalus's decree, the edict the judge puts into writing after he has delivered his findings from the bench. "I trust," Joel said as he handed it to him, "that you will immediately give the Racing Commission appropriate instructions." That's how naïve we were about what was going on.

On Friday afternoon Quinn appealed. He had, it seemed, assented to the decree under the misconception that he could still file an appeal and keep us from running the 24 days. Even more incredibly, he sent out a news release over his signature on the official stationery of the Office of the Attorney General. The operative sentence ran: "Attorney General Quinn has advised the State Racing Commission that it should not take any action on the two applications pending the appeal to the Supreme Judicial Court."

He was instructing the commission to ignore the order of the court! In writing! (On sober second thought, we could only conclude that the commissioners had protected themselves by insisting that he put those instructions in writing.)

It was unbelievable. Either he wasn't a good enough lawyer to know that the mere filing of an appeal did not stay an interlocutory decree, or he had been convinced that doing something was better than doing nothing.

We were doing something too. We were hopping up and down in

rage. We had won over impossible odds, and we were being cheated out of our victory.

Joel was incredulous. "He's in contempt of court," he kept saying. "I don't know what he thinks he's doing. He is in contempt as of the moment he told the commission to ignore Judge Kalus's order." I couldn't believe it either. He had given a patently wrong opinion to the commission. The judge had reversed him without leaving the bench. Joel had outmaneuvered and outplayed him at every turn. I couldn't believe that he would place himself in the position of being lacerated further in the Supreme Judicial Court.

Frank Kozol wasn't incredulous, though. Frank Kozol, who is normally a cheery, cherubic man, went wild. And when the Attorney General refused to accept his phone call, he went right into orbit. He went bombing up to the State House—it's only a few blocks from his office—and I suspect that he flew there under his own steam. From everything we heard later, he went storming into Quinn's office to inform him that he had just done the most stupid, arrogant thing he'd ever seen in a presumed law-enforcement official . . . And then, you know, he got a little personal. I wouldn't be at all surprised if he was moved to proffer a few philosophical observations concerning the Attorney General's motives.

And then, Quinn made his second brilliant move of the day. "If you're supposed to be such a big man in this town," he said, or words to similar effect, "let's see what you think you can do about it!"

Good going, Quinn. That put Frank and Joel Kozol side by side to show Quinn what they thought they could do about it.

In the meantime, Joel and I had been roughing out a press release of my very own. It was in the form of a letter addressed to the Honorable Robert H. Quinn, and, to make sure it got to the proper news desks in time to make the evening papers, Nick hand-carried it to the papers.

In that letter I had written (with some help):

> I made no public comment following Judge Kalus's decision that your opinion to the State Racing Commission was wrong as a matter of law because I did not want to further embarrass the Attorney General's office. I can no longer remain silent because for some curious reason you seem intent on depriving Suffolk Downs of 24 days of racing and the Commonwealth of more than 1½ million dollars.
>
> My attorneys tell me that your advice to the Racing Commission is incor-

rect and in contempt of court. Accordingly, I have instructed our attorneys to take whatever steps they deem necessary to implement Judge Kalus's decision.

I hereby request that you let the Racing Commission decide our applications on the merits, as Judge Kalus said they had the power to do.

On Monday morning, we were right back in court to file our petitions to force him to comply with the court's decree. We also filed two petitions to hold Quinn personally in contempt. Judge Kalus docketed the hearing for the very next day.

Frank Kozol came into court to represent us, and perhaps even to show Quinn what he thought he could do about it. Quinn showed what he was made of by not showing up to find out. Instead, he sent his administrative assistant, Joseph Hurley, to argue the case along with Kiernan. The Attorney General had apparently been checking the law over the weekend, though, because Hurley came in with a motion to suspend operation of the decree. Now, get this: The Attorney General was asking Judge Kalus to suspend the operation of his decree, which Quinn had already defied.

If you think Judge Kalus had been outraged before . . . !

Hurley put his foot into it the first time he opened his mouth, by asking the judge to hear his motion before he heard ours.

"Who marked this matter for hearing today?" Kalus asked him frostily.

We had, of course.

"Is there any reason why you should be heard before the petitioner?" Kalus asked, and the air was turning to gelatin.

Frank Kozol was all heart. "I have no objection," he said. Of course he didn't. He was quite willing to let the Attorney General's man be lacerated.

Judge Kalus nodded his head. Once. Grimly. "I *want* to hear from him."

Hurley informed the court that while he knew that he wasn't entitled to be heard first, "the Attorney General has instructed me to advise Your Honor that if the motions are denied we intend to file in the Supreme Judicial Court for a stay of Your Honor's decree."

They could do anything they wanted to. They might even get the decision overturned, although the odds were, conservatively, a million to one against it. The one thing they could not do was to disobey the decree while they were appealing.

When Hurley responded by arguing that the court's decree hadn't technically been an interlocutory one, Kalus interrupted him. 'There was in your case an adjudication by me that the Attorney General's opinion was erroneous as a matter of law."

And then, Hurley—incredibly!—argued that the question was one not so much of law but of conflicting interpretations. "The Attorney General advised the Racing Commission that the commission had no jurisdiction, so to speak."

He sure had. And the court had instructed him that the commission did have jurisdiction. Kalus wanted to know when it had become the AG's function to advise state agencies about the jurisdiction of his court. "The function of the Attorney General, as I see it, is that if an agency requests his opinion concerning its power that he will give it. It is not the law. It has no standing in law. The petitioners saw fit to seek a review of the opinion of the Attorney General, and the court made a ruling. *That* is the law. Under the *law*, there is no right for you to advise a state agency to disregard the decree of this court."

Hurley argued his motion anyway. He began by stating that he was not going to reargue the case that had been made in the trial, and promptly proceeded to reargue it. Some effect had to be given to the "real meaning" of the words *relating to the original application,* he said. "The opinion that was rendered by the Attorney General gives such effect. A contrary interpretation, with respect, does not give effect to those words."

Would you believe that he was questioning the right of the court to overrule the Attorney General?

Judge Kalus looked down on him as if he were a creature from outer space. "What do you mean, 'a contrary interpretation'? *Do you mean my ruling?* I am not an interpreter of the law as the Attorney General is. I act in behalf of the court and *rule.*"

When Hurley, unfazed, continued to argue that a serious question of jurisdiction was involved, Kalus asked him icily whether by virtue of having filed the motion to suspend his decree he was at least recognizing that it wouldn't be suspended unless the court suspended it. Kalus was so angry, in fact, that he deliberately brought the AG's true motivations into focus.

KALUS: "Do you have in mind the calendar in connection with these events? Do you have in mind what the probable duration would be of the hearing of this case by the Supreme Court on its merits?"

HURLEY: "I do, Your Honor."

KALUS: "What do you estimate it to be?"

HURLEY: "I think the case would not make any list prior to December or January."

FRANK KOZOL: "February. I have checked it."

KALUS: "And by that time the whole issue would be moot, wouldn't it?"

Presumably, the judge would have let it go at that if Hurley hadn't turned his attention to the terrible consequences that could ensue if it should develop that the decree was appealable (and, of course, the judge had never said that it wasn't) and the verdict was overturned. "I estimate that [the appeal will be heard] some time in the month of September," Hurley said, in flat contradiction to his flat statement of a few moments earlier. "The meet which the petitioners are seeking will be in progress. Where would that leave the status of that meeting once Your Honor's decree is vacated? It would seem to me that there would be a serious doubt as to the legality of the meeting at that point."

JUDGE KALUS *(with a lift of the eyebrows):* "Who would raise that?"

HURLEY: "There may be private interests involved that I have no knowledge of."

"Does the Attorney General represent the private interest?"

"No, Your Honor. I am not suggesting that the Attorney General is going to raise that question."

"You are raising it now as his assistant."

After a couple more exchanges, the judge cut Hurley off in midsentence. "What would be so calamitous from the point of view of public interest, leaving competitors out for a while—"

HURLEY: "I didn't mention competitors."

KALUS: "You said 'private interests.' "

HURLEY: "I was thinking of, maybe, people with contracts involved . . ."

The judge knew what he meant. He had wanted to let him know that he knew what he *really* meant.

Frank Kozol was quite brief. "I find the position, the legal arguments, and the attitude of the Attorney General absolutely incomprehensible. . . . I don't find any justification for his posture because it is so totally against the interest of the Commonwealth whose interests he has sworn to represent and defend, which he certainly is not doing here. And what other motivation there may be, I do not know. I will simply say this. It is apparent beyond a shadow of a doubt that, having lost on the merits, he is trying procedural activities, knowing full well that in any circumstances, if he blocks compliance with your decree, the case becomes moot and dead because, by checking with the Supreme Court clerk this morning, no case is enterable until next February. I make this specific representation to the court."

And, do you know, we still hadn't appreciated the full extent to which the Attorney General had been willing to go to use procedural technicalities to block us. When Frank Kozol sat down, the court made it known that it had received a letter in the previous day's mail asking for a report of the material facts in the case, a preliminary move that is made in order to challenge those facts in an appeals court. That's right. Having stipulated the facts, having become the co-sponsors and co-guarantors of those facts, Quinn was now fully prepared to challenge them.

Judge Kalus demanded to know who had been responsible for sending that letter to him.

HURLEY: "I think it was a joint responsibility, Your Honor."

KALUS (*firmly*): "Who and whom?"

Oh, he wanted to know who had actually written the letter?

Yes, he wanted to know who had actually written it.

It wasn't really such a mystery. The letter had been written by James P. Kiernan, seated right there beside Hurley. The very same James P. Kiernan who had argued the case under the stipulation.

Put on the griddle, Kiernan admitted that the case had been heard on a stipulation of undisputed facts. Yes, it was true that the sole issue had been a question of law involving the interpretation of the statute. It was Alice-in-Wonderland time.

"What facts are you looking for from this court?" asked the judge.

Kiernan answered, rather vaguely, that he had stipulated the facts "pertaining to the particular issues involved." Whatever that meant.

KALUS: "Didn't that stipulation, then, resolve all factual questions? Didn't you so agree?"

KIERNAN: "I agreed at that time, Your Honor . . ."

Apparently, he didn't want to agree any more.

Judge Kalus gave up and asked him rather wearily whether he wanted to make any further argument "before we decide the question of contempt."

I am calling that quotation to your attention because it was right at that point that Frank Kozol broke in to bring a further fact before him. We were asking that the court direct the commission to act on our application at its regularly scheduled meeting the following day, and Hurley had informed the court that there were such "a large number of items" on the agenda that the commission probably wouldn't be able to comply with such an order. Frank Kozol wanted the court to know that the commissioners had told him personally that if the bar which had been imposed upon them by the Attorney General were removed, they were ready and willing to pass on the application.

Judge Kalus apparently took the interruption as a signal that we weren't interested so much in a contempt citation as in the dates, and if his interpretation was wrong, his conclusion wasn't. He gave us every ruling we had asked for, including an order that the commission was to act and render its decision the next day. "It is further ordered," he said, in a gratuitous swipe at Quinn, "that the State Racing Commission shall abide by and comply with this order, *notwithstanding any contrary advices from the Attorney General.*"

He was leaving it to us to tell him whether we wanted him to rule on the contempt citations then and there, or whether we'd just as soon keep them hanging over Quinn's head until we had the dates in our hands.

It took us no time at all to decide to leave them hanging.

Either the Honorable Robert Quinn still hadn't had enough, or that King is a glutton for punishment. Before the day was over, Quinn filed a petition in the Supreme Judicial Court to have Kalus's order stayed before the commission could act on it. Why was he fighting so hard? Why was $1.5 million in tax revenue—minimum—so offensive to him? Why did he care so much about our affairs? How could he possibly think he was going to win? Did he really think he was going to win, or was he just trying to show somebody that he was doing everything he could to stop us? If any of you think you can answer these insincere and quite fathomable questions, don't bother to write me.

The commission meeting was scheduled for 10:30 a.m. We were in the Supreme Court at 9:30. And whom did we draw but Justice Paul C. Reardon, the man who had started it all. Justice Reardon listened to the Assistant AG's plea and turned him down, and then we were racing out to Nick's station wagon and heading for the commission offices. The funny thing was that we made it on time and then had to wait patiently for Dr. Walsh. Dr. Walsh had been caught in traffic, coming in from

New Bedford, and he was half an hour late. Mike Holovak wasn't there at all. He was back in San Francisco. Despite Hurley's representation to the court about the backbreaking agenda the commission was faced with, it had no other business at all. Absolutely none. The meeting was clocked, from beginning to end, at eighty seconds.

At 11:10, Dr. Walsh called the meeting to order. Peter Consiglio said, "The commission moves that the dates be granted to Suffolk Downs."

Dr. Walsh said, "I second the motion."

Fifteen days after we had filed our suit, we had the dates. In those fifteen days, we had been in court eight times and survived two appeals. It couldn't be done, and we did it.

I was magnificent in victory. "I'm delighted and elated," I said. "Right now," I said. "I'm concentrating on one thing. To put together the finest racing program possible." I apologized to the fans and horsemen for whatever confusion or inconvenience might have been occasioned by the delay. I all but strained myself taking the commission off the hook. The commission had been the very model of fairness, I purred. "The commissioners maintained perfect decorum throughout and showed great intelligence in their decision." I mended every fence in sight. I said not a word about the Attorney General. I was so humble that I couldn't stand myself.

So one of the local papers headlined the story: VEECK GLOATS AFTER NEWS OF VICTORY.

Oh boy. They ought to see me when I'm trying.

We were back in action. Larry Howley, our racing secretary, had already gone up to Canada to try to line up some stables. Tom Beedem announced that we were ready to accept applications for stalls.

On our opening day, our handle was $846,632. Narragansett's was only $396,759. In the face of that kind of financial disaster, and despite all Linsey's fears, Narragansett went to nights only on Fridays. It almost makes you wonder whom Linsey had been working for, himself or Narragansett. But no, men of that stature don't get together and say things like: *Well, I'll do my best for you, and if I don't succeed you'll restrict yourself to (X) number of nights.* Naw. Why would they say anything like that when they had no reason to doubt that they were going to succeed?

Conflict or not, I had estimated that the state would benefit by between $1.7 million and $2 million. I was hoping for the larger figure. It was closer to the smaller one. The final figure was $1,783,784.

As the meet opened, the contempt citations against Robert H. Quinn were still hanging. So for that matter, not that it mattered, was Quinn's third appeal. Immediately after Justice Reardon had turned down his petition to stay Judge Kalus's decree, the Attorney General had appealed the decree itself. What was he appealing? Beats me. By the time it got to the Supreme Judicial Court, we'd have run the 24 days and quite probably be into the next year's meeting. Perhaps he was showing somebody that he was still with them all the way. Or perhaps he was squirreling away some chestnuts for a trade-off.

With nine days down, and fifteen to go, I suddenly had to make a decision. For that was when Quinn made the call to Joel in which he told him, as his opening gambit, that he was dropping the appeal on the kids suit. And then he said he was abandoning the appeal on the twenty-four dates, too, and asked if I wouldn't drop the two petitions for contempt that were pending against him.

I hope you understand what was happening here. We had him. The law of the Commonwealth was that anyone who "counsels or aids" another party in disobeying a decree of the court is punishable by both criminal and civil contempt. Perhaps we could have sued him personally for damages. "Bill," Joel said, "we can cause him a lot of embarrassment, because the contempt was final when he ordered the commission to ignore the court. He was in contempt then, he made no effort to purge himself, and there is no way for him to come up with a new order now, but do you really want to bother?" It wasn't worth going after damages; we had everything we wanted. The only question was whether I wanted to force Mr. Quinn to stand up in open court and say, "I'm sorry, Your Honor. I didn't know what the law was." Because that was the only defense he had.

Well, I may not be on the all-time list of good losers, but I'm not in the sore winners' Hall of Fame, either. He seemed to be asking for peace. A new start all around. And, as Joel had said, we had everything we wanted. "Naw," I said. "Drop it."

If the Honorable Robert H. Quinn wanted to extend the olive branch, why not pick it up? All I really wanted from the man was that he go away and leave us alone.

He didn't. He wasn't done with us, and that meant we weren't done with him. We had trounced him on the kids. We had humiliated him on the supplementary dates. We didn't know it yet, but we had an appointment to take him on a third time and force him to run for cover.

The one other thing that had been hanging as we were preparing for our 24-day meet was Sportservice's breach of contract suit against us on the Berkshire concessions. By another of those coincidences, the trial was docketed for September 15, the opening day. "Joel," I said. "You've shown me how it's possible to cut through the law's delays. I now want you to show me how to use the quiddities and cupidities of the law and push that thing back a day. Because I promise you that if you're not there at my table with a load of guests, I'm going to cancel the whole thing out."

He was there. He argued the case in the morning and informed the court that he was turning the afternoon session over to his father.

Yeah. We won that one too.

CHRONOLOGY 1969

June
5— Agreement executed with shareholders of Berkshire Downs, Inc. ($50,000 deposit)

10— Meeting with Bary Corn

12— Informal meeting at commission, at which chairman stated that upon receipt of Supplementary Applications it would seek opinion of Attorney General

12— Meeting with Berkshire stockholders; closing scheduled for this date continued until June 16

16— Closing of purchase of stock of Berkshire Downs, Inc.

23— Meeting of Berkshire stockholders to vote in own officers

July
2— Advise Racing Commission that Berkshire Downs to be closed down because of extensive and persistent losses

3— Memorandum of Law delivered to Assistant Attorney General Barry R. Corn

8— Two Supplementary Applications filed

9— Commission requested Attorney General's opinion

11— Date of Corn memorandum to Joseph J. Hurley, Assistant Attorney General, Chief of Administrative Division, stating Suffolk "clearly has the right to file"

17— Notification of hearings on Supplementary Applications

30— Commission hearings

August 5— 9:55 a.m., Attorney General opinion delivered to commission

5— 10:00 a.m., commission dismissed Supplementary Applications

12— Petition for Determination of Rights filed in Supreme Judicial Court

12— Justice Reardon transferred petitions to Superior Court, where "speedier" trial could be had

12— Judge McLaughlin issued short order of notice returnable August 15

12— Letter to Attorney General, requesting he complete pleadings before August 15, enter into stipulation, and join request for trial on August 18

13— Proposed stipulation delivered to Attorney General

15— Hearing before Judge McLaughlin; Assistant Attorney General requested two weeks to file answers; ordered to file answers by August 20; case to be tried August 21, "first case out"

20— Attorney General filed answer and demurrer; agreed to stipulation

21— Trial before Judge Kalus

21— Judge Kalus entered findings, rulings, and order for decree

21— Final decrees entered.

21— Certified copy of final decrees delivered to Attorney General with request that he give commission "appropriate instructions"

22— Attorney General filed claim of appeal and request for report of material facts

22— Attorney General advised commission to take no action pending appeal

22— Attorney General issued press release

22— Bill Veeck wrote letter to Attorney General

25— Motion for an order to commission to comply with decrees; motion to strike appeal; and two petitions for contempt filed

26— Attorney General filed motion to suspend operation of decree

26— Hearing before Judge Kalus

26— Judge Kalus entered supplementary and amended interlocutory decree ordering commission to pass on Supplementary Applications "notwithstanding any contrary advices from the Attorney General"

26— Attorney General filed petition for stay with Supreme Judicial Court

27— Hearing before Justice Reardon and entry of final decree denying petition

27— Racing Commission granted dates

27— Attorney General filed claim of appeal

September 15— Opening Day

11

Fathers and Sons

Joel Kozol was not our original lawyer. In the negotiations to buy Suffolk Downs he had represented the other side, and I have a vague recollection of him at the first press conference: a small, dark young man sitting with Dave Haber at the other side of the room. His firm had handled various facets of the Suffolk operation from the Judge Pappas days, after Frank Kozol had figured out a way to save a track which was in such bad shape that for a while it didn't seem as if it were going to be able to open.

A month after I had taken over, I was in New York to go over the complicated business of finding a new concessionaire. I preferred the Jacobs boys, of course, but they pulled out when Realty tied the concession contract into a package deal that was going to permit the lucky winner to pay part of the purchase price for them—a chapter we shall develop later, when things begin to fall apart for us.

Jerry Deutch, the Realty vice president who was running the meeting, informed me that Realty was going to hire a new Boston lawyer to handle the situation, and that was just fine with me. I had been far from happy with the performance of the lawyer it had come up with to take us through the first series of hearings on the dates. It was a miserable rainy day, though, the kind of weather that somehow seeps into the bones of a building. I remember thinking that it must be some great lawyer whom Realty could get to fly in at five o'clock on such a lousy day.

In he came, right on time, a young man, rather short, wearing glasses and moderately long hair—just long enough, I thought, to qualify as a mod without really committing himself. I was sitting on a couch at the side of the room, and, since all the chairs were occupied, he sat down alongside me.

And Jerry Deutch began to put him through the jumps. Setting him up. He liked Joel's firm very much, he said, because it had a lot of experience with the Racing Commission and racing in general. He liked Joel personally. He liked the way he operated. "The only thing that has us worried is that we know your firm represents a couple of other tracks around the state, and we're wondering whether there might not be a conflict here." (I reminded Joel of that meeting at a time when we were both wondering how we were going to get the money that was due us, and he said, "If I was really the smart young Boston lawyer I'm cracked up to be, and you were really the hustler you're cracked up to be, we'd have both jumped up right there and hollered, 'Boy oh boy, will there ever be a conflict!' ")

Joel gave us a workmanlike outline of the way racing operated in New England and then said, "So there's two ways of looking at it. The other way is that it might help to have somebody who was in a position to speak to everybody."

Now that he had him on the defensive, Jerry proceeded to talk about the fee. The books we had inherited showed that Suffolk's $40,000 legal fee had been split between Joel's firm, which had represented Linsey in the previous sale of Suffolk, and the New York firm which had represented Haber.

The only reason I'm bringing up all this background on legal fees is that Jerry Deutch didn't see why Joel shouldn't go right on doing all the work for the same fee he had been getting or, to put it another way, one-half the fee Suffolk had been paying. Joel entered a mild demurrer that he thought $40,000 was the right figure for representing a track of our size. "But, all right," he said amiably enough. "Let's try it for a year. If at the end of that time it's been unfair to either of us we can talk about it some more and—"

And then, just like that, he wasn't amiable any more. I could feel the bristles go out alongside me. Two small flames hardened in his eyes.

"Hey, wait a minute!" he snapped. "I didn't come down here to solicit this business. You guys called me down here. And at a very strange hour. We work twenty-four hours a day in our office if we want to. We don't need another client."

I was beginning to change my mind about him.

"Lookit," he said, "I wouldn't sit here this long except there's something special about the track to me. Our office has been with Suffolk from way back. There's something sporty about going to the Paddock Club. And with this new man here, Bill Veeck, I think there's a chance for it to become the pre-eminent track in New England that it always should have been. But don't you think you can call me down here and start interrogating me. We don't need your $40,000 or your $20,000 or your $100,000."

I slapped him on the leg and said, "You're my lawyer, Joel. Let's leave these creeps and go out for a drink."

It turned into quite a night. Nate Dolin caught us in the street along with a guy named Arthur Puro, who hung around the Realty office and had come in just in time to catch Joel's explosion. We went across the street to Longchamps for dinner, and then we were on the town. Like most good trial lawyers, Joel throws himself completely into his work when he's working, and goes all out when he plays. A real goer. As the night wore on, we wandered around from one joint to another, adding to our merry band as we went. Always it was a battle when it came time to pay the check because there wasn't a man there who wasn't a fast-draw out of his pocket. I must have been having a real good time myself, because when I'm really enjoying myself—and after enough bottles of beer have passed in review—I will signal every oncoming voyage to the men's room by performing my inimitable, patented, world-famous peg-leg high kick in the general direction of the men's room.

One of the more valued additions, I remember as through a haze, was a young lady who was introduced to me as "the Doctor" and never referred to as anything else. In addition to being blond and beautiful, she was a doctor of philosophy or something like that and engaged in writing a book on, of all things, logic. Blond and beautiful and intelligent, and impervious to my pleas that she give up her wastrel life of books and glamour and become a lady jockey. I thought I made a very strong case myself, but I guess the logic of it escaped her.

Arthur Puro was having quite a time too. If hearing "The Impossible Dream" played over and over and over is your idea of a good time. All through dinner, he kept slipping the violinist a few bucks so that he would keep playing it. Every time we hit a new joint, he'd send some money up to the bandstand with the instructions to just keep playing "The Impossible Dream" until we left.

At the end of the night, Puro insisted that we repair to his favorite nightclub. A club, he assured us, where he was a beloved and valued customer. His home away from home. We were barely through the door, need I say, before he sent his money and compliments to the band leader, along with the request that he play that cursed song until closing. The band played it once. And only once. When the welcome strains of something else came sounding forth, Puro sent the waiter over to renew his request. When that didn't work, he went running over himself. The band leader smiled, nodded, and kept right on not playing it.

At closing time, Puro reminds us that this is his personal club and we are his personal guests and he will take it as a personal insult to his personal honor if any of us so much as looks as if he is going to try to fight him for the check. So he gets the check and begins to reach for his wallet. And then his eyes bug out and he looks at it again. It is an outsize check. It is a check all out of reason. He runs his eyes down the charges, turns absolutely purple, and sends for the manager.

There is a $150 charge for six bottles of champagne, and nobody at our table has been drinking champagne. Puro is furious. He reminds the manager that he has been coming to his club for years and has spent lavishly and freely. He never thought they'd try to pad a check on him like this as if he were some tourist from out of Ohio.

Well, you can see that the manager is terribly upset. He calls the waiter over. They bend over the check. They exchange a few rapid, soft-spoken words. The waiter straightens up and points—right at me! At me, your humble, smirking servant, sitting there looking so very well pleased with himself.

Who else do you think had sent six bottles of champagne over to the bandstand with instructions not to, under any circumstances, play "The Impossible Dream" again.

That was the night I met Joel, and the social and professional sides of our relationship were always so intertwined that I got to know a great deal about him. He was, at the time, thirty-nine years old and he looked about ten years younger. His father had been brought over from Russia at the age of two years, carried in his grandmother's arms, and they were one of the very few Jewish families to settle in South Boston, the rough-and-ready Irish section of the city.

His grandfather had opened a tailor shop, got to know everybody, and in his final years, after he had stopped working, fallen in love with the law. By then, the bench of the Commonwealth was filled with Irish judges who had grown up in South Boston, and when the old tailor would come into their courtroom they would stop the proceedings to greet him.

Frank Kozol, the oldest son of immigrant parents, went to Harvard on a scholarship in the days when Harvard imposed a strict quota on Jews, zipped through college in three years, took his master's in English, and had an appointment as an assistant professor of English at Cornell when, for no reason anybody can explain, he changed his course completely and enrolled in Harvard Law School. To the practice of the law he brings the literary grace of an English professor.

And his son is better. Joel would never admit it. He will take it as a personal affront when he reads this. But the father knows that his son is a better lawyer than he is, and he wouldn't have it any other way. The relationship is one of those things you feel privileged to observe. When the father and son come upon each other, even if one only walks into the other's office, they beam at each other. They glow. It's not too difficult for a father and a son to love each other. It happens every day. These two men admire each other. The son knows that the father climbed out of poverty to set a standard of accomplishment for the whole family. The father knows that he has sired the best damn lawyer in the country.

Joel was an editor of the *Harvard Law Review* for two years. He graduated *magna cum laude*. In his final year he was research assistant to Dean Griswold. Upon graduation he went to Washington to become law clerk to Supreme Court Justice Stanley Reed, and when he came out of the Army he passed the Massachusetts bar examination at the top of the list. Number one. But that only tells you that he has a superior brain. The irreducible qualification for becoming a trial lawyer is the love of battle. One of Joel's uncles, who was a much-decorated Marine in World War II, says that the reason the Kozols are fighters is that when you're a member of the only Jewish family in South Boston, you have to learn how to fight in order to survive.

Joel won every case he tried for us, and none was any tougher than the suit brought against us by Sportservice. It was a tough case to begin with, unlike the suits we brought against the state, because he could not bring the hot white flame of righteous indignation to it. Let's not kid anybody. We bought the track to close it, and we told the concessionaire to go take a walk. Sportservice was the injured party, not us. What made it a lawyer's nightmare was that he had an absolute minimum of help from his client. I could not bring myself to believe that Jerry Jacobs, whom I had known since he was a boy, would sue me. Which really means, I suppose, that I couldn't believe that Louie Jacobs' son would sue me. Oh, he'd go through the motions maybe; he'd file all the necessary papers and make all the right noises. But he would never really take me into court under circumstances where he could hurt me that badly. All right, I've admitted that we had played it pretty slick. But, at the same time, Sportservice is the largest racetrack concessionaire in the country, with about a thousand concessions in the United States and Canada. It does a business of well over $100 million a year. Berkshire Downs must have been the tiniest of its operations, no more than a flyspeck in its financial report.

The fix we were in—and this was why I couldn't bring myself to believe Jerry would push me to the wall on it—was that we already had a ten-year contract with Ogden Corporation which gave it the exclusive rights to all food and beverage concessions for any event held at Suffolk Downs. There wasn't anything I could have done about it if I had wanted to. To complicate it beyond all hope of extrication, the law forbids you to have more than one liquor license on the same premises.

It never occurred to me that maybe Jerry was being so tenacious because he had never thought I'd do that to him. Or maybe it did. Maybe that's what made me so incapable of fighting back. I do know that every time Joel had to prepare something, I would tell him blithely that there was nothing to worry about, the case was going to be dropped.

The day after we signed the agreement to buy Berkshire, Jerry sent me the "Congratulations, partner" letter. The day after Dario tried to call the deal off, Jerry sent a letter to both Campanella and me reiterating that he did not intend to waive his rights or privileges. The only reason there was a week's delay between the time we voted ourselves in as officers of Berkshire and the time we informed the Racing Commission that we weren't going to accept the dates was that I had received a telegram from Jerry's Boston lawyer advising me that he had a couple of temporary restraining orders against us. At the same time Joel was putting together his Memorandum of Law for Barry Corn, he was also working feverishly to prepare our defense against Sportservice and sending me reams of documents to try to make me appreciate that it was going to be necessary to take this thing seriously.

When the commission hearing came up on July 30, Sportservice was right there with Wonderland, Loew, Linsey, *et al.* to tell the commission that it should refuse to give us the dates unless we made Sportservice our concessionaire. The commissioners practically laughed Sportservice out of the room. I was chuckling softly too, until Joel, who never lost an opportunity to remind me of the inconstancy of my friends, snorted, "Well, there's your friend Jacobs again. Always right in there trying to make this a better world for you to live in."

I can only imagine how maddening my unshakable confidence must have been to Joel. There was one restraining order we hadn't been able to throw out, an order to prevent us from disposing of any of the assets of Berkshire. When the day of reckoning on the contract with Martin DeMatteo came around, we asked Sportservice to dissolve the restraining order so that we could turn the real estate over and get our $275,-000. The trial, after all, was only two weeks off and we were offering to have both Suffolk Downs and Realty Equities guarantee any judgment Sportservice might win in court. The concessionaire wouldn't do it. Joel then offered to put the $275,000 in escrow pending the outcome. The concessionaire turned us down on even that. "How many more times are they going to have to hit you in the mouth to make you understand that this is not a friendly litigation?" Joel demanded. "This is nothing less than a total arm's-length fight. If your friend wins this, he's going to take it and twist it off!"

If somebody can discover a formula for telling a man something he doesn't want to believe, he will become either the new Albert Einstein or the new Joan of Arc. In the face of all that evidence, I believed to the end that we would come to some kind of settlement. And we almost did. Sportservice had always been quite cognizant of the fact that our contract with Ogden did not include the parking, the programs, and the souvenirs. On the morning of the trial, we got together with the other side in the corridor and offered to give Sportservice the parking concession, which was easily worth whatever it might be losing from the whole Berkshire operation. Instead of jumping at it, as we had expected it to, it demanded that we also give it the food and beverage concessions for fifteen years after the expiration of Ogden's contract.

There I was, back in court again.

I was called to the stand immediately so that I could give my testimony and get back to Suffolk for our opening. And I was worthless. They must have had me under cross-examination for a couple of hours, and I just gave it to them the way it was, without making the slightest attempt to equivocate or palter. Yes, we had bought the track to close it down and transfer the dates. Yes, I knew who had the concession contract. Yes, I had been informed before the closing that Sportservice was not going to waive any of its rights. Yes, yes, yes. Have it your way. Yes, everything.

As I was taking my leave, I told Joel rather haplessly, "You don't have to say a word. I was no help at all. I'm afraid you're going to have to do it alone."

What won it for us, I think, was that although Sportservice's case against us as Suffolk Downs was appealing, its case against Berkshire, as Berkshire, wasn't. It had written a contract that was so harsh and so one-sided that it gave Sportservice a right to handle any of the concessions it pleased "in its sole discretion," while binding the track hand and hoof. It had then made the mistake of admitting what a one-sided contract it was by inserting a clause that forced Berkshire to agree that a legal contract existed "even though there is no mutuality."

Joel was able to argue that you can't take an illegality and make it legal by saying that it is, and although the judge didn't find for us on that basis I am convinced that it more than balanced out whatever distaste he might otherwise have felt for our own fancy footwork.

What killed Sportservice in the end was that it over-reached itself. It had put another clause in there which read that if Berkshire "for any reason fails to operate during any year . . . this agreement will automatically be extended" into future years. By turning that clause around, Joel was able to argue that Sportservice had conceded that the track had the right not to run "for any reason," and if persistent losses weren't a compelling reason, what in the world was? In other words, we hadn't breached the contract. It still ran "into future years." If we ever ran at Berkshire again, Sportservice's contract would still be in force. Only don't call us, huh? We'll call you.

Fancy footwork, indeed. A veritable twinkling of toes. Because we had to put forth this fragile exercise in distorted mirror-imagery in the face of that meaningless little clause DeMatteo's lawyer had been good enough to throw into our contract—remember it now?—guaranteeing that Berkshire Downs would never be used for racing again. Well, that didn't mean us, Judge. It had been put in there for our protection. I mean, if you want us to waive it, heh-heh-heh, we'd be only too glad to.

The real defense was always unspoken. The real defense was: Look, this gigantic corporation stuck this little track with a lousy contract, and now it's trying to keep us there and make us continue to lose money so it can continue to bleed the place dry. Are you going to let them get away with that, Judge?

The judge wasn't. His ruling was that one year's abstention did not a breach of contract make. In other words, we won the untried case.

It was a long time before that verdict came down, though. Four months. I guaranteed Joel that Jerry wouldn't appeal. Three weeks later, Jerry appealed. Sometimes I wonder if there is anybody left in this country who doesn't appeal.

Two weeks after the appeal had been filed, Jerry asked me to testify for him down in Little Rock before the Arkansas State Racing Commission, which was investigating Jacobs' enterprises. It came at a bad time. I had been asked to be one of the judges for the Junior Chamber of Commerce in selecting the ten outstanding young men in the area, and I had to cut out from the awards dinner to catch a plane and then get back again the following night in time to make a dinner speaking engagement in Kirkland House at Harvard. They invite a small, select group of—ahem—distinguished citizens to speak to the students and answer whatever questions they choose to flatter or flog you with.

So I flew down, took the stand, eulogized Louie, uttered some kind words for Sportservice, and while I was about it gave Jerry three depositions to be used in other states. Not one word about Berkshire or the lawsuit was ever mentioned. Just between us, though, I had every confidence that Jerry was going to rush back home shouting, "Drop the appeal! Kill the suit! Fire the man who talked me into filing a lawsuit against Good Ol' Will!"

Step by step, Sportservice proceeded through every preliminary move attendant on an appeal. Including the printing of the trial transcript, which runs into a couple of thousand dollars. It was just trying to see if it could panic us into offering it the parking concession again, I told Joel. Sportservice was never going to take it all the way.

In July, I received a letter from Joel informing me that Sportservice had entered the case in the Supreme Judicial Court. "If they have any idea of making their peace with you," he wrote, "this is a strange way to show it. Should they decide to drop this appeal (which I doubt they will do), well and good. But if they pursue it we will be there in full strength."

In the first week of January 1971, a hectic week in which we were filing our dates and trying to save our creditors and negotiating new deals with Ogden by the day, Joel had to go up to the Supreme Court to argue the appeal. By that time, the only part of it that interested me was that Jerry Jacobs had really carried it all the way through. It took me that long to try to understand how I could have misjudged our relationship that badly.

It is not by accident that I have coupled Joel and Jerry together under a chapter heading of "Fathers and Sons." Jerry was his father's son too, don't you see? It was a harsh contract written by hard businessmen with their lawyers at their sides, and Jerry was going to defend it as his father would have defended it. Whether he has his father's saving virtue, his loyalty to his friends, I really have no way of knowing. That's where I was so unrealistic. You can't transfer friendship, because you can't transfer experience. That wasn't Jerry Jacobs on the other end of the phone in 1941, and I wasn't any fresh twenty-eight-year-old kid hanging onto a shoestring with one hand and spurning a magnanimous gesture with the other. Quite the contrary. *Quite* the contrary. The mistake I had made was in assuming a relationship that didn't exist, and because I am my father's son too, in my own fashion, I cannot really fault myself for it. Through all my early years, I was the beneficiary of my father's friendships. He literally never had a friend who did not remain his friend throughout his life and after his death. The world of baseball was filled with men who were anxious to go out of their way to pay one last tribute to William Veeck by helping his crazy son Bill.

I had assumed that Jerry would do for me what I would have been only too happy to have done for him—not because Jerry Jacobs meant so much to me but because it would give me a chance to pay one last tribute to Louie. I had the generations mixed up, that's all. That kind of favor doesn't flow upward through the years, it flows downward.

When you're down to the last throw of the dice, you are dealing with the sons of your own generation, not with their fathers.

Oh yeah, the final disposition of the appeal. Well into July, long after I was gone, the Supreme Judicial Court finally handed down its ruling. By then, Ogden (or an approximate facsimile thereof) owned the track complete with the 24 days we had fought so hard to get, and I must say I had mixed feelings about it. On the one hand, I knew by then that I was going to have to sue Ogden for welshing on the $250,000 it had contracted to pay me. On the other hand, I didn't want to see Joel lose his case after all the work he had put into it.

He didn't.

12

Horses and People

In considering the romance of horseracing, I had never anticipated that I was going to find myself so intimately involved with the end product. Thoroughbred horses eat well and work hard, and, in the countless years and effort that have gone into the improving of the breed, their digestive tracts have been brought to a truly magnificent pitch of efficiency. Would that the United Nations functioned half so well.

Under normal conditions, we had 1350 horses stalled in the stable area. Their normal output was 30 tons a day. Not to give them undue credit, it wasn't entirely the pure unadulterated product. The floors of the stalls are covered with straw, and what you end up with is a sort of thatchy mixture. Until recent years, the operator of a racetrack could close his eyes, contemplate all those beautiful animals straining in their stalls, and smile. For decades upon decades the mushroom industry bought all the horse manure it could get its hands on. Came and got it and left their money behind. By the time I came onto the scene, the formerly eager mushroom-growers were in the process of converting, en masse, to commercial fertilizer, which they are able to control with a far greater degree of precision. I could tell you how the horse manure was processed but I have a feeling you don't want to know.

The year before I came to Suffolk, the mushroom interests were in the final phase of their retooling and they were still willing to come out and take the manure off the track's hands. When I got there, they were willing to take it if we shipped it to them. Freight costs, like everything else, have been on the rise. In my second year, it cost us $100,000 to ship it.

It's a problem. It really is. The grooms muck out the stalls and pile it out front and that's where the obligation of the horsemen ends. The track has the responsibility of collecting it and delivering it to the flat cars lined up on the railroad siding, a job we contracted out. Theoretically, the flat cars pull out as soon as they're loaded. In practice, we had small control over the railroad schedules, and there were times when they sat there with their fly-drawing cargo for days. Since the siding was right by the bay, we tried to get permission to load the stuff on barges and dump it out beyond the three-mile limit. The way things are, with the ocean more polluted than the air, we might as well have asked for a shuttle rocket to the moon. We made inquiries about buying a piece of land so that we could dig a big pit and fill it. No chance. The Revere City Council was always moaning about the situation for hygienic as well as aesthetic reasons; unfortunately it couldn't do anything to help us because, like all other city councils, it had what was fast becoming an insoluble garbage disposal problem of its own.

For the sake of accuracy, to say nothing of family harmony, I had better add right now that there was one phase of the operation that wasn't contracted out. After my son Mike had completed his freshman year at Loyola College, he came to work at the track, and I could think of no better way to teach him that nobody had ever promised him a rose garden than to hand him a shovel and point him in the general direction of the paddock. The Thoroughbred is a high-strung animal, and once he is led into the paddock he does seem to understand that something is about to happen. On that alone, he's brighter than 83.7 percent of your elected officials. The boss's son should always start at the bottom, and I couldn't think of anything more bottom than that. Mike's job was to stand there with his shovel and watch carefully. It made for a very active twenty minutes, nine or ten times a day.

As a result, Mike seems to think that, given the title of this book, it should be dedicated to him. "What do you know about thirty tons?" he has been screaming around the house. "You were sitting up there in a big dining room behind glass being the big celebrity. I can tell you about the thirty tons! Wheeeeeewwwww!" You see what I mean about the younger generation? They don't appreciate their opportunities. He can't seem to understand the favor I did him in permitting him to discover both the joy of physical labor and the uses of humility at one fell scoop—I mean swoop.

We spent a lot of time trying to prepare ourselves for the inevitable day when the mushroom industry began to charge us for taking it off our hands or, more thought-provoking, refused to take it off our hands at any price. The two acceptable methods we came across were incinerators and pressers. As a result of our complete and comprehensive investigation I am able to report that Japan, which had to face up to the problem earlier than we did, solves it the best. Not recycling but transformation. In Japan they press all their waste material into cement-like blocks which they are able to use as either building material or fill. In this country there were a few relatively small companies working on this, but none that were anything close to operational.

The only practical method, Tom Beedem, our expert on manure disposal, discovered, was to lease incinerating equipment that would be big enough to handle thirty tons a day and would burn fast enought to discharge a minimal amount of ash into the air. The difficulty we ran into there was that the manufacturers didn't rent equipment out. You had to buy it, and since we were only going to be using it a hundred days out of the year, there was a very real question of whether we could amortize it out. Not that it mattered. By the time we found the kind of incinerator we were looking for, we didn't have the money to build a decent fireplace.

I don't think the horsemen knew what to make of me in the beginning. I was coming in with a reputation as a guy who liked to shake things up, and horseracing is as hidebound, as encrusted with taboos, as baseball. In one way their suspicion was understandable. I was some kind of strange creature who had been dropped down upon them from another world; they felt I didn't know as much about horseracing as they did, which happened to be true, or know as much about horses as they did, which also happened to be true. Who was I to come barging in, shooting my mouth off from both barrels?

I will say for myself that I made every reasonable effort from the beginning to be on good terms with them. While I was down in Florida to meet with Nick Jemas about the girl jockeys, I was contacted by Gerry Colella, the president of the New England Horsemen's Benevolent Protective Association. There was a minor item in our contract that had to be ironed out, and Colella (no relation to the Revere mayor) thought that Miami was an excellent place to start the wrestling. He turned out to be a white-haired man, short and dapper. A rather nice-looking man, actually. The first words out of his mouth were, "I don't get paid for this job, you know."

Anytime I ran into Colella, even if it was only on the way to the men's room, the first words out of his mouth were, "I don't get paid for this job, you know." I can't imagine why he was eager to flaunt his altruism at me, but I always listened with interest. With friendly interest, even. You might even say that every time he put his hand out, I shook it.

The minor item was that the horsemen owed the track some money. The way the purse structure is set up, you have to estimate what the total handle is going to be and make whatever adjustments are necessary the following year. We had something like $50,000 coming back to us, and Colella wasn't anxious to have me assert my rights. For that matter, neither was I. Cutting the purses was not quite the best way to generate a feeling that I was out to bring quality racing to New England. He wasn't at all happy, though, when I let him know that as part of the same grand design we were going to be running a $200,000 turf race, the richest stake ever run in the country, with the money being put up by the track above and beyond the percentage called for in the contract. My thinking was that taking over a run-down track was like taking over a lousy ball club. The one thing you have to do is *something*. You can't buy a winner, but you can buy respectability.

Colella, no man for the Grand Design, thought it would be a far better idea to take the $200,000 and spread it over a lot of races. Keep it in the family, so to speak. "If I was going to do that," I told him. "I wouldn't be putting up any extra money at all." But Colella went right back to Boston and stirred everybody up. The increase in purses and the willingness to forget the past debt for the time being weren't good enough. Almost to a man, the owners and the trainers resented the fact that we were putting up $200,000 for horses that would undoubtedly be coming in from the outside.

I don't know; I suppose Colella thought it would look as if he were doing something for his people. And maybe he thought he could work it so there might be something in it for him. After all, he wasn't getting paid for the job. All I know for sure is that we had problems with him on anything we wanted to do. For one thing, he was extremely friendly with Dario at Lincoln Downs. At the time of our first conflict with Lincoln, when they ran 18 racing dates into our meet, Colella was right there backing Dario's position that any horse that was shipped from Lincoln to Suffolk couldn't be shipped back. The kind of thing, you know, that would make an overly suspicious fellow like me wonder who he was working for.

It may not have been completely coincidental that we were running against Lincoln Downs again in our second year when a struggle between the HBPA and the Jockey Guild over the jockeys' pay scale almost closed us down. Under the existing agreement, the jockeys were paid $50 for a winning mount, $40 for finishing second, $35 for third, and $30 for fourth. A $10 differential between winning a race and not winning it would have been patently unfair if it weren't that by long tradition the winning jockey was actually paid 10 percent of the purse. The Jockey Guild wanted what was traditional to be made obligatory. It also wanted an increase of $5 in each of the other categories. When the horsemen balked, the Jockey Guild asked the Racing Commission for it and, being good fellows, the commissioners granted it.

The horsemen decided that the commission didn't have the right to impersonate a Labor Relations Board. Your little boy would have decided the same thing. We thought we had instructed it that it was supposed to interpret the laws, not make them. Or maybe it was that the commission hadn't been chastised by a judge for something like five full months, and it was growing nostalgic for the good old days.

How I got into the middle of it, I still couldn't tell you. The HBPA sued the commission, which seemed about par for the course. But then Colella called a meeting and the horsemen voted to withhold their entries. A kind of strike. Flattered as I was by the suggestion that we had any influence with the commission, I held a meeting with Colella and his executive committee and blew my top. Why make me the patsy? The horsemen had given the jockeys the same raise at Narragansett over the winter without any trouble at all. Why were they making such a big issue about it now? The answer to that and many other intriguing questions may have come when I accused Colella of agitating the whole thing so that he could help his friend, Dario, by closing us down. That wasn't sheer guesswork, either. Two members of his committee, who were very much against the strike, had told me as much. To sweeten my temper not at all, Dario had brought his horse into Suffolk only two days earlier and waltzed off with the $15,000 Lou Smith Memorial Stakes.

Colella, who had a nice little talent for insult-to-injury himself, suggested that the track could bring the dispute to a speedy end by underwriting the pay raise itself. I suggested right back that if worst came to worst I had a pretty good idea whom to sue. We did accomplish one thing. The horsemen agreed to a ten-day cooling-off period, and the first threat of a boycott was overcome.

Ten days later, it was right back at our throat again. For two weeks after that we were in constant turmoil. The entries, which were supposed to be in forty-eight hours before post time, seldom trickled in before twenty-four. I had three or four more meetings with Colella, all equally silly. One of his more brilliant solutions was that we resolve the situation by taking the horsemen's side. I wasn't taking anybody's side but my own. The role of the innocent bystander might not be a very appetizing one, but it was heck of a lot better than anything else on the horizon.

The strike was called for Wednesday, May 13. I must say they picked a beautiful day for it. The city had gone wild over the Boston Bruins, who had just won their first Stanley Cup in something like thirty years, and I had moved nimbly to get myself a piece of the action by designating guess-what-day as—guess what?—Stanley Cup Day. The entire Bruin squad had been invited to attend as our honored guests. Anybody who sported the name of Stanley anywhere in his signature—fore, aft, or dead center—had been invited to join in the festivities.

At four o'clock on Tuesday, we had twenty-six entries for a ten-race card instead of the eighty-to-a hundred horses we'd have normally had. A sudden plague seemed to have hit the stable area. An influx of nasty head colds, tendonitis, and melancholia. I'll tell you something. I wasn't going to be shut down. We had issued a short, terse press release which read, in full:

> Bill Veeck in commenting on the reported boycott said today: "There will be racing on Wednesday, on Thursday, on Friday, on Saturday, and on every scheduled race day through July 18."

That would show them. Now, how were we going to show them? Rudie and Nick and I got together and asked ourselves where there might be an untapped supply of horses. The police academy seemed to be a likely source. And riding academies. We could always run some quarter-horse races if we could find any quarter horses anybody would be willing to ship in overnight. We could gag it up a little by running a special "Milk-Wagon Stakes" for a field of swaybacks. If it had four legs and a tail, we were definitely interested. Just so long as it was smaller than an elephant and bigger than a team of ballroom dancers.

And then, just as we were getting ready to start calling around, the whole thing was settled over our heads. There was a third party of interest, you see. The Great Commonwealth. If the races weren't run, the state treasury was going to be out a minimum of $80,000 a day. All of a sudden somebody seemed to remember that Gerry Colella was also a member of Governor Sargent's Economic Advisory Board, a job, I might add, for which he *was* getting paid. I'm not sure exactly what the board does. I'm not even sure whether it meets. But it's there, and the checks go out regularly. Now what kind of a way is that for an economic adviser to earn his salary?

In rapid succession, everybody proceeded to get himself off the hook. Dr. Walsh came through with a letter promising to expedite the court proceedings. The Attorney General's office agreed to take the burden off the HBPA's hands by filing a suit of its own. (I'm not sure what the legal phraseology is, but Quinn now seemed to be suing either the Racing Commission or himself.) And, finally, the HBPA agreed to abide by whatever decision the court should hand down, an unprecedented display of generosity and civic obedience.

A wave of miracle cures swept through the barns, and the entries came pouring in. It was too late for them to be published in the papers, of course, but who wanted to quibble. Somehow or other, 10,459 unregenerate horseplayers found their way to old Suffering Downs, less than average for a Wednesday but, all things considered, not bad.

Legal footnote: In due time, the court ruled that the commission had exceeded its authority. Again.

We didn't have another full-fledged crisis for almost two months. The Great Fireworks Caper. In that bifurcated, bi-city setup we had, with our track in East Boston and our stable area in Revere, Boston got the white meat and Revere got the stable odors. We owed Revere. More to the point, I owed Mayor George Colella (no relation to "I-don't-get-paid-for-this" Colella). Revere's Fourth of July celebration had been a fiasco the previous year because a sparsity of open space had forced the city to spread the thing all over town. Well, if there was one thing we had, it was space. And if there is one thing I love, it is fireworks. Since we were going to be closing on the Fourth of July anyway, I had offered to hold a Monster Fireworks Display at the track as a kind of Last Hurrah. Unfortunately, my kind offer had come along too late. The plans were too far along to be changed.

Another year, another chance. Even though, with the 90-day meet, we weren't going to be closing on the Fourth. Tony Cartalano, the genius who had put together all my firework shows for me in baseball, had already come in to case the joint. He had, as a matter of fact, come in on the day the strike threat came to a head, just as Dr. Walsh was coming through with his expediting letter. I hadn't seen a real no-holds-barred fireworks display for a couple of years and, to make it perfect, by holding it on the Revere side I wasn't going to have to wrestle with the city of Boston for a permit.

Instead, I had to wrestle with Gerry Colella and his horsemen. They knew the fireworks would panic their horses, see? They weren't sure how they knew it, but they sure did know it. It was ultimatum time again. The first ladyfinger that was sighted within the holy precincts of the stable area, they were going to pull out every horse in sight. As ultimatums went—and they came and went on a tight bi-weekly schedule—that was a pretty good one. There were still three weeks left to the meet, and a racing meet without horses can leave an embarrassing gap in the program. When I asked whether any of them had ever seen horses panic at the sight or sound of fireworks, they looked at me as if I had gone stark raving mad. Of course they hadn't! That wasn't a point for me, you understand; it was a point for them. I didn't think anybody had ever been crazy enough to shoot off fireworks in a stable area before, did I?

To see it from their side, I would suppose they were making an automatic, and not unnatural, association in their minds between firecrackers and fire. And fire is the nightmare vision all horsemen have to live with. Training a Thoroughbred is a schizophrenic business, anyway. On the one hand you're trying to train a fragile and flighty animal to such a fine edge that he'll be ready to run his hindquarters off when he hears the bell. On the other hand, you're trying to keep him in as quiet and relaxed a mood as possible whenever you have him back in the stall.

I was able to persuade them, at length, to let me make a test, if for no other reason than to expand the horizons of man's knowledge. Our regular fireworks guy came in and made me every kind of bomb, at every graduation of decibel from a BIG BOOM to a noiseless boom. Don't ask me what purpose is served by an un-boom. Or how it's possible to do it. All I know is that we did do it, and it kind of broke my heart.

Bristling with bombs and uncertain intentions, we marched to the stable area in the cool of the evening, in solemn delegation. Once we were there, we reconnoitered the area, crouching to show how observant we were all being and also, I suspect, because we were afraid we wouldn't be getting a true reaction from the horses if they saw what we were up to. And then we began to throw our samples around. It was kind of fun. A couple of horses turned around long enough to send brief, bored stares in our general direction and went right back to munching their oats or scratching their fetlocks.

On the evening of July 4, we had thirty thousand inhabitants of Revere on the grounds. We gave them a spectacular, glorious Fourth of July show, and the horses took it with such equanimity that their daily thirty-ton output remained spectacularly, gloriously unchanged.

In fairness to the horsemen, we rarely had any trouble with the top trainers. Most of the trouble came from the guy who had two horses, neither of them any good. If you didn't happen to be in a position where you had to deal with him, you might even be able to sympathize with him. Nobody ever set out to end up scuffling for a living with two broken-down horses. These were soured and crabby men who could only let you see, whenever the opportunity presented itself, that they were still men who had to be contended with. Being of such a saintly and forgiving nature myself, I had firmly resolved that, come another season, I was going to allocate stalls with exquisite care toward letting somebody else contend with them.

The better the trainer, the easier he was to deal with. Jack Van Berg, who had been the national leader in total victories for two straight years, came to Suffolk in our second year and took over as the top trainer on the grounds with no trouble at all. Van Berg ran a public stable with something like forty horses under his charge, and his operating theory was that if we were running ten races and his horses were only entered in nine of them, he had slipped up somewhere. To keep himself busy, he was commuting back and forth during our first few weeks to a track in Ohio where he was also the leading trainer. Now, a guy like that isn't looking to shut you down. He's too busy taking your money.

Needless to say, he was also a very nice guy. And a very interesting one. His daddy and his mother had been trainers before him, and Jack had been a licensed trainer from the time he was sixteen. From time to time, he'd drop by the office and if I was smart enough to keep my mouth shut I could pick up some fascinating theories about training horses. Some trainers, for instance, put sawdust down on the stable floor and change it maybe twice a week. Jack uses nothing but straw and cleans the stable out every day. His theory, which was really far more than a theory by then because he had been testing it out scientifically, was that if you take two horses of equal ability and put one in a clean stall and the other in a stall that is cleaned only a couple of times a week, the first horse will improve steadily and the second horse will go straight downhill. "It's like putting him between clean sheets," is the way Jack puts it. The reason he uses the straw is that it smells cleaner and affords the horse a somewhat better footing. Once again, the horse *feels* classier.

Before I leave the horsemen here, I do want to say that by the time I left them there, their resentment and distrust had pretty well been dissipated. I began to hear from a not inconsiderable number of them who had decided, in retrospect, that they never would have gone through with the strike because "horsemen are basically fair-minded, and we realized we were doing you an injustice." My irresistible charm had nothing to do with it. Neither did the weekly luncheons I had initiated to permit them to come in, in small groups, and air their beefs. What turned them around more than anything else was that the first returns on the over-all promotional campaign were beginning to come in. Suffolk Downs was being talked about. The horsemen were walking into restaurants and bars and finding that they weren't part of something that was considered slightly disreputable any more. Quite the opposite. As soon as they were introduced, they became the center of a delighted and spirited conversation which left them with the sense that they were participating in a quasi-public venture whose fortunes were on the rise. The same kind of freshening breeze had begun to stir that stirs when a ball club is incontrovertibly on the improve.

And now a final footnote on Gerry Colella. As I was leaving, Colella was in trouble with the horsemen, and it was his friendship with Dario that was doing him in. Even with his sweetheart contract, Dario had ended up owing the horsemen money at the end of their 1970 meet, and the deal Colella worked out with him left Dario owing them about $100,000. There was an insurrection in the ranks, and Dario was forced to get up the money. Colella then made the mistake of suspending a couple of dozen of the leading dissidents, and that brought on another fight which very well might have forced Colella out when his contract came up for renewal. But I don't know. An unpaid job isn't that attractive to active horsemen. As nimble—as ring-wise—as Colella had always been he'd probably have found a way to save himself. We'll never know. A month before the the contract ran out, Gerry Colella died.

Jockeys are a special breed. I hadn't thought of them, if I had thought of them at all, as anything except little people. They are, I discovered to my amazement, amazing athletes. Horses are powerful animals. They are not very smart. They jump at shadows. Once you get below a high grade of claiming horse, they are either habitually sore or simply not very interested in running. The jockey has to force them to run and keep them at it by pushing and shoving and whipping. And to do it all in heavy traffic at a considerable speed. Timing, coordination, and a healthy competitive instinct are the basic requirements for the job, and what does that add up to except the basic attributes of any athlete?

As people, they are even more interesting because they are men whose options in life have been so severely limited by their physical size. With some of them, and usually the most intelligent, a minority psychology comes very strongly into play. A top jockey can be among the highest-paid athletes in the world, but if he hasn't been able to come to terms with his size, the racetrack can become a sort of torture chamber for him. Every time he puts on the silks he is reminded of the dirty trick life has played on him. Every time he looks around at the other jocks he is looking into a mirror. The psychology of latent self-hatred can be seen all too frequently in the enmity and distrust jockeys display toward each other. It comes to the surface, even more conspicuously, in their penchant for big blondes and big cars and big motor boats.

The relationship between a jockey and his agent is the closest relationship extant. Even husbands and wives say "we." A jockey's agent, in hustling around to get mounts, never uses any word except "I." ("I'm riding Big Bertha in the fifth, and if I can get her out of the gate . . .") In some curious way, which I haven't quite been able to isolate, I have a feeling that the pre-emptive "I" is associated with the jockey's size, too. It's as if the jockey doesn't exist as a separate entity but only as an appendage, totally dependent upon the agent's contacts and the agent's ability to handicap the card. Because that is just what the agent does. He is handicapping the card a couple of days ahead of time and trying to get his jock up on the most likely winner. One jockey is all an agent is allowed to handle. At the most, one full-fledged jock and one apprentice. And so again you have this pure symbiotic relationship, two people living as one. The jock is utterly dependent upon the agent to get him live horses, and the agent is just as dependent upon the jock to win often enough with them to keep them both in style or, at least, alive. It is a love-hate relationship in which the opportunities to hurl recriminations back and forth are endless.

The jockeys themselves are such notoriously poor handicappers that the gag around any track is that the easiest way to get rich is to book the jockeys' bets. They are suckers for the "inside information" which abounds around the back side and which, like most inside information, is compounded of nine parts optimism and one part fact. It isn't that the trainers are lying when they pass the word around that their horses are ready. If they're lying to anybody, they're probably lying to themselves. Trainers are like everybody else. They overrate their horses and they overrate their own ability. And even if the horse is legitimately "ready," there can very easily be, and all too frequently are, other horses in the race who may be "readier."

One of the real breaks I got at Suffolk was in falling heir to a hot apprentice jockey, a jockey who was more than ready. To backtrack for a moment, the first horseman of any kind I had met upon coming to Suffolk was Dick DeStasio, a former jockey who was one of the leading trainers around New England. A marvelous guy, very bright and extraordinarily articulate. He and Nick Del Ninno were friends from way back, and they had been going around making appearances on a small scale to try to make people aware that there was a racetrack out in East Boston. Dick had mentioned, in passing, that he had a promising young kid from Italy who certainly had the desire and intelligence and seemed to have the touch. In this instance, the trainer most definitely wasn't being over-optimistic. Charlie Maffeo (pronounced Ma-FAY-o) was a nineteen-year-old kid who had come over from Italy only a year or two earlier. He had quit school in the little farming community of Avellino when he was fourteen to become an automobile mechanic, and he was a good one. Better than good. But Charlie stood only five feet tall and he didn't weigh more than a hundred pounds, and so even though he had never been on a horse in his life, after he came to the United States he was brought to DeStasio by a relative he had come to live with. Dick kept him working around the stable for another full year before he let him get on one. The boy rode a few races in our summer meet without any notable success and then went up to Rockingham and absolutely exploded, winning 72 races to tie the track record. He came back to Suffolk, hot as a pistol, and won 38 races in 18 days to become the leading jockey in our 24-day meet. When racing shut down in New England, he went to Tropical Park in Florida and won 67 races, an all-time record at a track which had quartered all the great jockeys of our time. It was nothing for Maffeo to win five or six races a day. Charlie was so remarkable that although he hadn't won his first race until July 15, which meant he had to pack his whole year into a little over five months, he was still the leading apprentice jockey in the country with 211 wins. On the night he broke the record at Tropical I sent him a telegram, with considerable help from Nick Del Ninno, which read, TUTTO AVELLINO E SIERO DEL SUA SUCCESSO E ANCHE NOIL QUI A SUFFOLK DOWNS. Which, Nick assured me, meant, "All Avellino is proud of your success and so are we here at Suffolk Downs."

Not that Maffeo had any trouble with English. Although he spoke with a slight accent, he had picked up English with the same ease with which he seemed to pick up everything else. Including the exotic habits of the natives. When the New England Breeders Association named him as the Jockey of the Year, he asked Dick DeStasio what he was supposed to do. "Well," DeStasio said, "I don't think they'd take it amiss if you bought a table at their dinner."

"What?" Maffeo gasped. "I get an award, and so I have to pay money for it?"

"Don't worry," Destasio told him. "You're showing them you appreciate it. And, besides, it's deductible."

A couple of days later, a friend of Charlie's was complaining about being hit with a $50 fine for a motor violation. "Don't worry about it," Maffeo told him, airily. "It's deductible."

The people I got along best with were the fans, whom I found to be uniformly friendly and endlessly fascinating. Racegoers have to rank among the most considerate, well-behaved people I have ever encountered. A tremendous number of them, to cite only one example, have favorite seats. They arrive early, drop their programs or *Racing Forms* on the seat, and that's all it takes. It's theirs. Do the same thing in a ball yard and you'd come back to find both the seat and the scorecard gone. There are very few drunks to contend with and I can't recall having to deal with a single serious fight. Now, when you consider that we're selling alcoholic beverages as well as beer, that's really remarkable. Until you realize that their money is involved, and then it isn't remarkable at all. They are not merely spectators; they are participants. They are pitting their own acumen against the event.

Roughly speaking, the fans break down into two basic types, the racing aficionados and the general run of sport fan. The aficionado is interested exclusively in the relationship between the *Morning Telegraph*, the tote board, the betting window, and the horse. Basically, these are the people who set the odds, and when I tell you that almost 35 percent of the favorites win and almost 80 percent of the favorites finish in the money, you can see that they are extremely knowledgeable. The sport fan is the guy who will decide to come to the track under the same impulse which at other times makes him decide to take in a baseball, football, or hockey game.

Each type could then be broken down into several categories. At the very top of the aficionado list you have to place the winner. For, despite the popular mythology that all horseplayers die broke, it just ain't so. That's no more than the Puritan ethic coming to the surface again. I liked to wander around the stands and talk to the people I saw there every day, and I can tell you that there is a surprisingly large cadre who follow the races from track to track—following the sun, as it were—and make a very, very good living. They all do it the same way. With a cold, businesslike approach to betting. They have to be good handicappers, that goes without saying. Not exceptional, but good. Well, the track is filled with good handicappers who find themselves ground down by the end of the meet by the 16 percent which is taken from the money bet on every race by the state and the track. And right there is what separates the winners from the losers. The winner has two qualities which are not often found in combination. Patience and nerve. He may go the whole day without betting. He may go two or three days. He may also bet as many as three races in a single day. But he won't go to the window until he has found exactly what he is looking for, and when he does go he loads it in good.

What he is looking for is more than just the horse he has handicapped as the stickout in the race. That's only where he begins. The winner understands, on a far more sophisticated level than the average bettor, that bettors are betting against each other, not against the track. He will not bet until *the other bettors* have set the odds on the horse he likes high enough to make up the 16-per-cent take-out *plus* whatever arbitrary percentage he has, in his personal formula, set on top of that. Forty per cent. Fifty per cent. A hundred per cent. In other words, if he has handicapped the horse at 3–1, he won't bet unless it is going off at 9–2, 5–1, or 6–1. And the higher the odds, the *more* he will bet. He is quite literally pitting his intelligence against the combined intelligence of all the other bettors in the track and taking advantage of their mistakes. And in so doing, he is turning the game around so that the percentages are working for him instead of against him. If he knows what he's doing —and if he didn't he'd have departed the scene a long time ago—he won't lose.

According to the mythology again, system bettors are supposed to be the surest of losers. Well, that depends on the system. The most successful one I ran across was the "key horse" system. As soon as the basic theory behind it was explained to me I knew they were on to something. Horseracing has a rigid class structure in the sense that the horses seek their own level of ability. From what I have already written about claiming races it should be perfectly evident that no owner would be so amiable as to enter his horse in a race where it could be claimed away from him for $3000 if it had the ability to compete in a race where it would take $3500 to claim it. But here again, it isn't even so much a matter of ability as of some mysterious element of class that runs through the bloodstream. For reasons that it would take a Linus Pauling to uncover, there are horses who can usually win in a $3000 claimer but will never win at $3500 even if the time of the classier race is lower than the times they have been consistently winning in down lower. Okay, racing fans. That's your key horse.

The basic concept involved here is that the horses in any given race are running against nobody except each other and that what you must therefore be looking for is a meaningful basis for comparison. Now, there are no more than two or three key horses in each classification, and obviously one of them is not going to be in every race. If it were as simple as that, no handicapping would be involved. On the other hand, you will find that most of the horses in a $3000 claiming race have run against one or the other of the key horses at various time, or have run against horses which *have* run against the key horses.And that is where the key-horse bettors can begin to make their comparisons. From there it is a matter of balancing the almost infinite variables of class, speed, pace, jockey, shift of weights, condition of track, and, if the horse is a front-runner, the wind . And oh yes, one other thing. Memory.

The aficionados are there every day. They can remember how those races were run. Stocked in their heads are a great many small but significant details that are not necessarily shown in the charts.

Since the key-horse bettors are every bit as aware as the traveling cadre that they are betting against the other customers, they will also wait until the last minute to catch the last possible flash of the odds in order to take advantage of any significant overlay. That's the one constant that separates the winner from the loser. The loser will decrease his bet as the odds rise, on the theory that he's going to be getting a big enough return to make up for it. He is, as a result, making his big bets on favorites or near-favorites. The key-horse bettor, who is dealing in claiming races where there are generally full fields and therefore generally bigger and wider fluctuating odds, is not only winning more often, he is cashing his biggest bets at healthy odds.

And right there, incidentally, is one of the edges the bookie has over the average bettor. He has the pyschology of the average gambler going for him. When the average horseplayer is losing he will tend to increase his bets to try to get even; when he is winning he will tend to decrease his bets to make sure he comes out ahead. Over the long haul, he is losing big and winning small. The winner is used to coming out ahead. When he's losing, he's more likely to decide it isn't his day and take a walk. When he's ahead, that's when he figures it's time to throw it in good and make a killing. He's winning big and losing small.

But if many of the aficionados are winners, most of them are losers. Why do they keep trudging back, then? Day after day? The psychology of the loser is far more fascinating than the psychology of the winner. The first thing I did, you will remember, was to tear down the barbed-wire fence. In wandering around town making my speeches, I kept using that gag about not knowing whether it had been put there to keep the people in or to keep them out. Lies. All lies. I had discovered soon enough that I could have set machine-gun emplacements at strategic places around the perimeter, and the regulars would have attacked in waves, to fight their way in. There is a psychology to the aficionado-loser that has to do with his view of his own life. To these people, there is a symbolic meaning to winning and losing that goes far beyond the money that is involved. Not that money has no importance in their scheme. In a money society, money has a meaning that goes to the very worth of a man. Without the money to keep score by, how would you know how you're doing?

The *Racing Form* is a mass of arcane figures, meaningless to the uninitiated but crammed full of information for the aficionado. To a greater or lesser degree, the regular horseplayer believes that somewhere in those figures lies the secret of success. Never mind that the variables in each race are endless; never mind that the horses below a certain class are so inconsistent as to turn past form into the chanciest of guides; never mind that racing luck is a factor which overhangs it all. That's the lure of it. That's the terrible grip it has over him. Luck itself is the most important sign of all, don't you see? It is a sign delivered on a direct line from heaven, telling him whether he has been chosen to be one of the winners or doomed to be a perennial loser. For to a greater or lesser degree, the aficionado-loser believes—subconsciously, to be sure—that there is only one possible outcome to every race, and that he has only to search the figures deeply enough and read them wisely enough for them to give up their secret to him.

The tragedy is that he doesn't believe it. He is a supplicant and supplicants are, by definition, losers. When his horse loses by a dirty nose—again!—after the worst kind of racing luck and he is moaning about the bad luck that continues to plague him ("Who else could that happen to?") he is really saying that it was in the cards that it should have ended that way. He is saying that by the act of placing his money on the best horse in the race he turned it into a loser. There was only one possible outcome, and he has changed it. The two sides of the coin again. He is not only a supplicant, pleading for a sign, he is a Grand Inquisitor seeking confirmation that it isn't his fault. He picked the right horse, *he found the answer*, and still he lost. Lady Luck is against him. Why?

Well, why is it Lady Luck when Lord Luck would be so much more appropriate? Aha! Maybe—just maybe—the key to his problem can be found right there. Luck is a woman. Whether it is some displacement of the sexual drive (it's not his fault that women find him unworthy) or whether he is confirming over and over that if Mama hadn't always turned her back on him things would have been different, I am not going to presume to say. Different strokes for different folks. I would suggest, however, that the betting drive can be an offset for the sexual drive.

"Who else could have such bad luck?" he asks. But if there is a complaint in that question, there is also a boast. He is not only unlucky, he is the King of Unluck. He is so unlucky that he has the power to influence the outcome of future events.

And what is that, I ask you, except a return, however perverted, to the child's fond belief that he has the power to control everything around him? Back to the days when Mama—all women—was no more than a tool to do his bidding and respond to his needs. A new start, pre-sexual—but in reverse! And maybe that's what keeps him coming back to the racetrack, day after day. To seek a sign that Lady Luck, well known for her fickleness, is going to change her ways again . . . and to find the answer to where everything has gone wrong. And though nothing is going to change, and he knows that it isn't, where else is he given the opportunity to woo his fate and to ask his question every twenty-seven minutes, ten times a day?

On an average day the aficionados and the sports fans are split just about fifty-fifty. Running in the afternoon as we are, we have a large percentage of night workers. Printers, post-office workers, bartenders, entertainers, club-owners. And people like salesmen and cab-drivers, whose time is their own. The cabbies will take a couple of loads out, stay for the races, and take another load or two back. And then there is the Wednesday Factor. The attendance on a Wednesday is always higher than on any other weekday. Not just at Suffolk Downs; at any track in the country. Since you're never going to guess why, I'll give you a hint. You know all those jokes about calling the nearest golf course if you're bleeding to death on a Wednesday? Don't believe them. If it's really an emergency, all you have to do is call the nearest racetrack. If your man didn't happen to be at Suffolk, we could have offered you a wide selection, and they come in all ages, sizes, and specialties. Better yet, if you're thinking of having a mild heart attack, Wednesday's the time and the Paddock Club is the place. It's doing it the hard way, to be sure, but believe me it's the closest you are ever going to come to a good old-fashioned house call.

The other regulars come in every age group too, although, as I have indicated earlier, they are weighted heavily toward the middle-aged. And older. They're into their fifties and sixties; their children have married and the horses give them a continuing interest and a form of mental stimulation. They're $2 bettors for the most part, and since they always sit in the same place the track serves the added purpose of providing them with a whole new set of friends.

I liked the old people. One of the traditional events we had inherited was something called the Hannah Dustin Stakes, named after a Revolutionary heroine, I guess (if she wasn't, she should have been). I changed the name to the Fair Lady Stakes, because it gave me the opportunity to officially anoint a marvelous ninety-year-old regular, named Annie Guay (prounced, most fittingly, Annie Gay) as our Fair Lady and invite her to make the presentation. A remarkably vivacious lady. I had seen her every day as I made my rounds through the grandstand. She had told me she had been there when the track opened in 1935 and, to prove it, she brought me the Opening Day program the next day. She was so thrilled at being called down to the track and allowed to mingle with the horse people in the winner's circle that it made the whole year worth while for me. A delightful woman. Just delightful.

To encourage more old people to come out, I set a policy of admitting senior citizens for half-price, and while I won't say that the prospects for swelling our coffers never entered my mind, I made it a point to emphasize that I made my money off their attendance and consumption of hot dogs and couldn't care less whether they bet or not.

There is another kind of regular, the people who work at the track. The mutuel clerks follow the races from track to track. The extras, the people who are put on when we expect a big day, are mostly night workers who would be at the track anyway and look upon the work as a pleasant way to pick up some betting money while they're there. Like the other regulars, the clerks are quite superstitious about working the same window every day. The same obsessive quality that you find in the make-up of all gamblers. It is as if they are building up to some great moment that will come only if they disturb the environment as little as possible. Or maybe it's an offer of faith to Lady Luck that they know she has something great in store for them if they continue to exhibit the same unswerving, if hitherto unrewarded, faith.

Most of the waitresses and concession people follow the races from track to track too. The waitresses can do very well for themselves. The winners, being in an expansive mood, are inclined to do a little drinking, and the tips to the waitresses can be large. On a real, real good day, a waitress will make $250 to $300. Being young and fair of face and form, they might be expected to take the next day off and buy themselves new dresses. Not at the racetrack they don't. The absentee problem at a racetrack is zero. The one thing all the regulars have in common is that the racetrack has become a complete way of life for them. I had always thought that nobody could become more involved than a baseball fan with his team. I was wrong. Compared to racetrack people of any stripe . . . well, there just isn't any comparison.

And, finally, there are the chiselers. The creeps who are forever working angles to give themselves an edge. I'll give you an example. When the horses leave the starting gate, there is a gap of two or three seconds before the bell rings and the mutuel machines lock. What can be done in a couple of seconds? Well, a lot. Especially if you can get the clerk at one of the $50 windows to work with you. In New England, the bums who work this dodge are called the Speed Boys. They work in teams. One of the partners stations himself in front of the mutuel window. The other stations himself in a spot where he can see the starting gate and his partner, at the window, can see him. They have already selected their horse. All they are concerned about is making sure that it gets a good jump out of the gate. If it does, the guy out front unclenches his raised fist, the accomplice at the window snaps his fingers, and the clerk starts punching. In those two or three seconds, he can punch out ten or twelve tickets. That's $500 to $600. A tiny edge, sure. But if you can save yourself one losing bet a day over a ninety-day meet you have made yourself a pretty good year's pay right there. It isn't illegal; it's right on the borderline. If you want to look at it the other way, the Speed Boys are pretty good bettors and we're taking our cut of every dollar. And that's just it. The people who are getting hurt are the ones who have bet the same horse and taken their chances. We're taking our cut from their money, too. When we solicited their patronage we assumed several responsibilities, foremost among them being that they would get an even shake. Either you run a good operation or you don't. Whenever the Speed Boys seemed to be in action, I would make a minute check of the mutuel windows and make certain that any clerk who had been at a window where a significant number of tickets on the indicated horse had been sold was moved.

If you stick around long enough, though, something will always happen to renew your faith in human beings. For every guy who's sitting up nights scheming for a way to clip you, there's a meticulously honest soul who wouldn't take a shady dollar if it was handed to him on a silver platter. No? All right. I was passing through the concourse after a day of racing—the same day, as it happened, we had met with DeMatteo about buying Berkshire—when I couldn't help but observe that there was unusual activity inside the mutuel windows along the main line.

One of the cashiers had come up $1000 short, and since every mutuel clerk is responsible for any shortage in his tabulation sheets, they were tearing the place apart.

The next day, which happened to be the day we were running the Joe Fan Handicap, a call came in to Bernie Loftus, our mutuel chief. "I'll bet you were short yesterday," the guy at the other end said.

"We sure were."

"I'll bet you were a thousand dollars short."

"That's right."

"I've got it."

The caller was a fellow named Bill Holiday, who owned a restaurant in Westerly, Rhode Island. What had happened was that he had been to the track and left early, leaving $20 at the track with a friend to buy two $10 tickets on the perfecto. The pay-off should have been $1350 and the clerk had somehow counted out an extra thousand. When his friend came into the restaurant that night, he had handed Holiday the money in a sealed envelope. Holiday had put the envelope in his pocket and gone on about his work. It hadn't been until the next day that he had opened the envelope, discovered the mistake, and immediately called the track. Bernie had him hold on while the call was shifted to me. "I can't make it out today," Holiday said. "Saturday is my busy day. But early next week. Tell the guy not to worry."

"Look," I said, "I'm sure the guy will be delighted to drive up and get it."

You bet he was. As soon as the races were over. Holiday not only refused to accept a reward, he sat the guy down and treated him to a free dinner.

For my own part, I had invited Holiday to come out to the track with his wife and kids. As my guest. Any time he wanted to. Permanently. He did come out with his wife a few days later, the same day, as it happened, that we signed the contract to buy Berkshire Downs. And he continued to drop up from time to time. Not every time he was at the track, I'm sure, and not as often as I'd have liked. He just happened to be the kind of guy who didn't want to even give the appearance that he was trying to take advantage of a situation.

13

Into the Minefield

With the wonderful year of 1969 coming to an end, George Carney got us together with the new management of Rockingham Park for a meeting that would break the log jam on racing dates wide open.

The chronology can be started, really, with the purchase of Berkshire Downs. Now that I had the 90 dates, I wanted to run them consecutively. Hemmed in as we were by the statutory straitjacket, the first eligible Saturday fell on April 4. And that meant we'd be running right through the traditional Rockingham opener on the backside of the July 4 weekend.

As far as I was concerned, the ability to avoid a conflict lay with Rockingham, not us. Rockingham, after all, was operating in a state which would give it whatever dates it asked for. We were hemmed in on all sides. What Carney had been able to see was that each of us had something to offer the other. We had the strength to clobber Rockingham in any conflict. It had the flexibility to avoid one. As the third party at the bargaining table, Carney was serving his own interests. With the death of Lou Smith, the reins of Rockingham had been taken over by Kenny Graf, his lawyer, and Mac O'Dowd, the track's longtime secretary and vice president. As trustees for the Smith estate, they were charged with operating the racetrack as profitably as possible, and that

196

meant they were out to get as many dates as could be run without bumping into us. Flat and harness both.

George Carney could see where a sudden increase in pari-mutuel racing in New Hampshire could be just the wedge he needed to pry more dog dates out of the legislature for Raynham. My interest in aiding and abetting Carney in his splendid ambition was that once the dates broke for the dogs, the horses would not be more than a length behind.

We put our steaming, scheming heads together and when the last dates had been written on the last slip of paper, we had agreed to set up whole new circuits for both flat and harness racing.

For flat racing, the schedule went like this:

Suffolk Downs: April 4–July 18 (90 days)

Rockingham: July 20–October 15 (75 days)

Rockingham was awarding itself an extra 25 days (which eventually became an extra 27). Together, we were able to offer the horsemen a circuit of at least 165 consecutive days, as against the 116 we had provided the year before.

Rockingham didn't need us in order to get its extra days. Nor had it wanted us to run the 90 days consecutively. It was losing its traditional day-after-the-Fourth-of-July opening, which was usually its biggest day of the year. Instead of ending on Labor Day, it was going to have to fight through the end-of-summer, going-back-to-school weeks, always considered the deadliest dates for any kind of racing. To complicate its situation further, its new flat season would now be running right through where its fall harness season used to be. In recompense, once the Rockingham people saw they weren't going to talk me into splitting up our meets again, they asked me to run our harness meet earlier than usual so as to permit them to come on, as always, the day after we closed down.

It was a sacrifice. No matter how you looked at it, the late harness dates were better. The way I had to look at it, we had set a record our first year with a 9-per-cent increase in harness revenue, despite two weeks of steady rain. By running early, we would be hitting head on into those deadly days of September and we would be also bucking Joe Linsey's dogs at Taunton. I don't think I have to tell you again what the dogs have always done to the trotters in Massachusetts. But if you want to do a deal, you've got to do a deal. For everything the other side giveth, the other side wanteth something in return.

The way we projected the new harness circuit, it went like this:

1970	*1969*
Rockingham: February 4–May 12 (84 days)	Rockingham: February 21–May 6 (64 days)
Foxboro: June 23–August 31 (60 days)	Foxboro: June 23–August 30 (60 days)
Suffolk: September 18–October 28 (30 days)	Rockingham:–September 5–October 23 (42 days)
Rockingham: October 29–December 15 (42 days)	Suffolk: October 24–November 29 (30 days)

Taken altogether, the owners of the standardbreds could come to New England for 84 days in the spring, rest their horses for 6 weeks, and then count upon 132 days with only a 2-week breather in between. I promised Ken Graf, who was clearly the power in the new setup, that I would use my best efforts to get our dates changed. They turned out to be exactly that. My best efforts over a period of seven months.

The first popgun came from Lincoln Downs. In drawing up the new Thoroughbred circuit we were leaving Rhode Island, with its cheaper races, to shift for itself. Dario girded his loins and beat on his chest and bellowed that if the Rhode Island commission would award him the dates, he was ready to run against both of us "day for day." You're darned right he was. That would have given him 165 days, and he was down for the fall phase of the Rhody schedule, where he would be running only the 70-plus.

It was all just talk, of course. Shrewd operator that he was, Dario was catching the headlines with his war-talk, but he was also sending up trial balloons for 200 days of flat racing in Rhode Island as the only way to turn back the threat from the north. I wasn't sure whether I was for him or against him. If it developed that Dario was able to create an atmosphere that would make it politically feasible for the Governor of Rhode Island to increase the racing dates by any significant amount—and we're talking exclusively about flat racing here, since Rhode Island has no harness racing—the Governor of Massachusetts was going to find it impossible to hold the line. On the other hand, we had learned that the Rhode Island conflict cut into our handle by about $100,000 per day. But why worry? Shrewd operator that he was, Dario wasn't going after new dates so that he could run them head on against us. The popgun was all popoff. Go, Dario, go.

The charade played on when Governor Frank Licht of Rhode Island, acting at the behest of the chairman of the Senate Finance Committee (who also happened to be the secretary of Lincoln Downs), invited the Governors of Massachusetts and New Hampshire to sit down together like their Colonial predecessors and settle the dispute among themselves. The Governors met in solemn conclave and promptly passed the buck back to their respective Racing Commissions by instructing them to get together and "avert conflicts wherever possible." The chairmen dutifully scheduled a meeting with the presidents of the four tracks which were deemed to be involved, a meeting at which I was presumably going to negotiate on whether I was entitled to apply for the dates I was entitled to apply for. I responded to Dr. Walsh's kind invitation by informing him that I had no intention of attending a meeting where nothing could be accomplished, and the meeting was just as promptly called off.

It was all pretty obvious. If Rhode Island could intimidate us into backing off, fine. If not, the Governor had alerted the citizenry of his beleaguered little fortress that fiscal disaster was so imminent that drastic measures might have to be taken. From there, it was just a matter of playing out the scenario. A month later, when the two Rhode Island tracks applied for 125 days each, Governor Licht expressed grave doubts that he would grant them. After another month had slipped by, he gave them each 90. Narragansett, which was running its winter-spring meet on one of those "temporary" licenses, was granted the dates with an open-ended closing time. Lincoln was given its 90 dates, without either an opening or closing time. Just run them whenever you're ready, Dario. Instead of opening in the fall, Lincoln ran two meets, one in the summer and one in the winter. The summer meet opened on July 3—that Dario sure does know how to hurt a guy—and his 90 days dribbled on into 98. For those of you who insist upon keeping score, I will have to report that we murdered him. Conflict and all, we broke every financial record at Suffolk, averaging well over $1 million a day. Lincoln had to go to nights except for Saturdays, and even on Saturday afternoons he was lucky if he broke $600,000.

But that was after the game was over. The only perceptible effect all that preliminary jockeying had on me was that I suddenly found myself in great demand by every Rhode Island group that wanted to take a whack at me. I accepted the invitations gracefully and met the attacks head on. "We're allowed ninety racing dates in Massachusetts," I would say, "and that number has never changed. Rhode Island has about as many dates as it wants. Last year, we operated with about two-thirds as many as you did, and this year it will be less than half. And I do believe that Massachusetts is a little bigger than Rhode Island. So why should I worry about you? Next question."

Next question: How old is Satchel Paige really?

Our own dates, of course, were awarded on January 30. The flat dates were awarded with no trouble at all. How could there be any? We were the only track in the Commonwealth that was either licensed to run flat racing or licensed to run during the day.

The balloon went up on the harness dates.

Instead of awarding us the late dates we had asked for, the commission gave us pretty much the same days we'd had the year before. And, in the process, destroyed the harness circuit! From the time Foxboro closed down after Labor Day until the time we opened up on October 16, there was going to be a 45-day gap in harness racing in New England. Rockingham couldn't fill that gap any more, you understand. Its new flat season extended over the entire period.

What a 45-day gap meant to the horsemen was that if they wanted to stay around New England, they would have to go hungry for while. What it meant to me was that we were faced with the prospect of losing a lot of hungry horsemen to New York and New Jersey. What it meant to Rockingham was that it wouldn't be able to open its winter harness meet until late November unless it wanted to conflict with us, which would, of course, have been disastrous to both of us.

It also posed another of those intriguing questions. We could understand the commission being nasty to us. But the Rockingham harness meet was pretty much owned by Wonderland, and when was the last time anybody had been nasty to Wonderland?

The Standardbred Owners Association, which is the organization of the harness owners, went running to the commission yelling: *Can't you see what you have done, you fools? You've given Suffolk the wrong dates!* Getting no satisfaction there, it came running to us. "Take it easy," we said, with the smugness of the veteran litigants we had become. "We will simply file a Supplementary Application and make them consider it all over again."

Kenny Graf was all for that too. Kenny came running down from New Hampshire to let me know that he was ready to support us to the hilt in anything we chose to do, either with the commission or with the Attorney General's office. What influence he could possibly have with either of those august bodies, I wouldn't know . . . I wouldn't know

... I wouldn't know ... But somehow he seemed very confident that once he swung into action things would begin to move along smoothly.

And do you know something? I was too.

And so here we are again, back in action. We file another application for the earlier days, taking care to emphasize that we are acting at the behest of the harness owners, upon whom the assigned dates are going to work a tremendous hardship. Right away, a technical problem arises. Although it is now early in March, the license certificates for the awarded dates haven't been issued. Larry Lane calls back to tell us that he has been advised by the Attorney General that a Supplementary Application can only be filed by a licensee. Okay. They're throwing it back at us, and I can't find it in my heart to blame them. But let's see what else the Attorney General was doing: After we had bought the Berkshire track, Campanella and Dario had asked us (as the new owners) to submit a formal request to the commission for a refund on the $14,400 they had put up as bond in the normal course of submitting their own earlier application for the 24 dates. Since the statute reads that a refund can be made only to a licensee, and we had informed the commission that Berkshire would never under any circumstances accept a license, their prospects for getting that money back would seem to have been nil.

When it comes to interpreting the statute on licenses, however, the Attorney General has been known to display a rare ingenuity. In the case of a liquor-license application, Mr. Quinn had pointed out with a remarkable irrelevancy, it worked precisely the opposite; the applicant wasn't barred from getting a refund until *after* the license was issued. By treating the matter as if it were a liquor license (which it wasn't) instead of a racing license (which it was), Quinn was then able to make an unaccustomed leap into common sense and say, "No license having been issued to Berkshire, it never had the privilege of conducting a racing meet in 1969. Accordingly, it is my opinion that the fee paid for that privilege may properly be refunded."

The gentlemen from Rhode Island had got their money back. We gentlemen from Massachusetts were in a somewhat less favored category. We would have to file an affidavit withdrawing our new applications. When the commission then got around to issuing the certificates for the dates it knew we didn't want, we would be entitled to submit our applications all over again.

But what did it matter? "Okay, Larry, if that's the way you want it.

When are you going to issue us the licenses?"

On March 6. A couple of days away.

Not quite. It wasn't until March 25, a mere 53 days after the dates had been awarded, that the licenses were finally sent to us. In due time, we filed for the new ones. The hearing was set for April 29. E. M. Loew and Joe Linsey were conspicuously in attendance, and we did not jump to the conclusion that they were there to support us.

Okay. The hearing opens with Dr. Walsh explaining, for the record, the circumstance that had brought us together. And then he turns to us. "I would ask Suffolk Downs at this particular time, are you ready to surrender the thirty days which were granted by this commission in your original application?"

He didn't even ask it, really. He suggested it (". . . are you ready to . . .") as a rather routine procedure. Have you ever had the feeling that something is going on, and everybody knows what it is except you?

Joel comes up very slowly, and with a look on his face which very clearly says, *What kind of patsies do you take us for?* "Only if the Supplementary Applications are granted," he says, in firm, distinct tones. As soon as the commission approved the change of dates, of course we would surrender the old ones. "If the commission doesn't see fit to change the dates, we will hold the licenses that have been issued to us and we will run the races on those dates."

A very clear, unambiguous answer, wouldn't you think?

THE CHAIRMAN: "So in answer to the question I asked, as of now are you willing to surrender those thirty days originally granted, your answer would be what?"

Joel tells him again. "Not unconditionally." We would surrender those dates only after the commission had granted us the new ones.

At this point, up hops who else but E. M. Loew's attorney, Austin Broadhurst. "I know this is a little out of order . . ." he begins. And here we go again. Only where are we going? "We have handed to Mr. Lane a Supplementary Application for thirty days of harness racing . . ."

That's where we're going. Do you understand what has been happening here? The commission is holding an application from Foxboro in its hands for those thirty dates, and it hasn't bothered to tell us about it. It had tried to mousetrap us into surrendering our license without letting us know that we stood an excellent chance of never getting it back.

Since that ploy hadn't worked, Mr. Broadhurst is arguing that since the commission has already awarded the full statutory limit of 90 dates, there is nothing to discuss unless we give some of them back. "The hearing would be a nullity because it is a hearing on an application for a license which the commission does not have a right to grant."

The pre-conditions which Joel Kozol had laid down for the surrender of the dates were totally improper, he contended, because they would allow only one applicant to be eligible to receive the dates *"where there are now known to be at least two."*

They have first told us that in order to file our Supplementary Application, we have to be a licensee. They are now telling us that in order to have the application acted upon, we have to stop being a licensee. The moment we stopped being a licensee, it seemed to us, the commission would be considering an application which, technically, we were ineligible to make. And would that not leave only one of the "at least two" applicants eligible to be awarded the dates?

After a certain amount of debate, in which Joel pointed out that we could not, by any stretch of the imagination, be asking for a *new* 30 days since we were as aware as anybody else that the commission couldn't give out more days than the statute permitted, Joel suggested that if the commission was willing to do it the other way around—to condition the granting of a new license on our guarantee to surrender the old one— that would be just fine and dandy. But under no condition were we going to surrender what we already had in the hope of being awarded what we were asking for. No, thank you. We'd just take the dates we had and go home. And not unhappily, either.

And that's what makes this dreary little exercise in perfidy so bewildering and, at the same time, so treacherous. All things being equal, we preferred the late dates. We had walked in there, loosy-goosy, to try to do Rockingham and the horsemen a favor. The last thing in the world we could have anticipated was this kind of whipsaw.

With the proceedings so clearly at a deadlock, the attorney for the Standardbred Owners Association, Jesse Moss, requested a recess so that he could try to persuade E. M. Loew to cut out the nonsense and go along with the date switch. Not to help Suffolk Downs but to help the horsemen. While Moss was making his pitch to Loew—unsuccessfully, as it turned out—we were buttonholing the Assistant Attorney General, who was sitting at the chairman's side, as always, to advise him on the—uh—law. He informed us that the Attorney General had indeed advised the commission—without bothering to let us know about it again—that if we didn't relinquish the dates, there would be nothing for them to act upon. Foxboro's position to the jot and tittle. Maybe we hadn't been let in on the secret, but somebody sure seemed to have been talking to somebody.

We had walked into a minefield. If Joel had made the wrong step back there on the first question, we'd have been blown right out of the harness business.

After the recess, the chairman felt it necessary to inform the world of the purity of his motives. The only reason the commission had refused to grant us the dates in the first instance, he announced, was that it didn't want to set up a conflict with Joe Linsey's dog track in Taunton. "We try, even though at times it doesn't seem that we do, we try to be fair to all of our tracks. As fair as we can." After the dates had been awarded, he went on, the horsemen had come to the commission to complain about the hardship that was being visited upon them by the interruption of the circuit. "And so," he said, with grave and melancholy mien, "our action has been unfair to them."

Well, that looks very conscientious and high-minded on the record. Particularly if you didn't happen to be aware that the horsemen had told the commission the same thing at the original hearing. Quite obviously, it hadn't troubled Dr. Walsh quite so much then. There was, it seemed, nothing he could do about it now. Having conceded that his original ruling had been unfair, the chairman declined the opportunity we were giving him to rectify it, "on the basis primarily that Suffolk Downs in not surrendering the days that we originally granted, the commission feels we cannot hold a hearing for the dates that were available."

It was, as anybody should be able to see, all our fault. And this was, as we now knew, what the Attorney General had told him. Incredible! (With the best will in the world, one cannot help wondering why it's necessary to have a Racing Commission at all. Each commissioner is paid $7700 a year. The commission itself has ten permanent employees and an annual budget in excess of $200,000. Wouldn't it be both cheaper and simpler to let a couple of assistant attorneys general do the work in their spare time?)

Having ruled out any relief for the horsemen, the chairman was finally willing to permit Jesse Moss to speak on their behalf. Moss came through with a truly impassioned plea, otherwise known as an exercise in futility.

By all rights, the hearing was over. Only it wasn't. Because Joel wouldn't let it be. This mysterious application of Foxboro's had been popping in and out of the proceedings like a groundhog, and the chairman had consistently refused to let us have a look at it. In mounting his concern for fairness and justice for all—meaning Joe Linsey—after the ball game was over, the chairman had, all unawares, opened up a very interesting question.

And, so before the meeting can be adjourned, Joel is up to demand that if the Foxboro application is indeed in the possession of the secretary of the commission, it be attached to the record as an exhibit.

The chairman refuses. And in refusing he once again uses the exact language that Mr. Broadhurst has used. "We consider this hearing, in its present form, a nullity. We cannot see any reason for attaching it to a nullity."

Joel sticks his hand in his pocket, looks out toward the corner of the room, and purses his lips, his characteristic posture when the wheels are spinning. Before he moves out toward the aisle, he whispers to me, "Don't look now, William, but in about thirty seconds Joe Linsey is going to be glaring daggers at E. M. Loew." Suffolk, you will remember, had asked to open its harness meeting two and a half weeks after Foxboro closed. Joel's bet is that if Foxboro is after those same days, they are pretty much going to attach them to the end of their regular 60-day meet, running them night-for-night against Linsey.

While he is about it, Joel is laying down the foundations for a possible lawsuit. "If we go into court to find out whether a license has to be relinquished before a Supplementary Application can be filed," he says, "I think it is very relevant to indicate what happens if a license is relinquished. If Suffolk relinquishes the license it holds presently for thirty days of harness racing, we obviously have a licensee called Bay State (Foxboro) which will ask, I presume, for the thirty days and run them in direct competition with Taunton, night for night, and back to back. I think that is what their application does. I think we should have it for the record so that the court can see the whole parameter of the situation."

The chairman looks briefly to the Assistant Attorney General and denies the request.

Mr. Broadhurst is on his feet now too. Austin Broadhurst is a soft-voiced man. He always seems to be wearing a scarf—you have the impression of a man who is constantly fighting off a head cold. He even moves in muffled cadence, on the balls of his feet. A very cautious man. A very solid lawyer. He may not have been sure in which of those two directions Joel was headed, but either way he is out to pull the teeth from it. "As long as Bay State has been mentioned, may I say that I was careful to say to Mr. Lane as I was handing him the application that in my own judgment the application is as full or absent of value as the application filed by Realty Equities until the dates became available."

Foxboro's application, he emphasizes, had been filed solely for the information of the commission. So that if it had elected to go on with the hearing, Foxboro would have standing as a participant. It had been his intention that it be acted upon only if the dates had been made available by the surrender of the existing licenses.

Verrrry interesting. In making his record, Mr. Broadhurst has also made it quite clear, if there had ever been any doubt about it, that he had been aware for a considerable length of time what the Attorney General's ruling on the crucial matter was going to be.

Joel has been interrupted, but he has not been diverted. "I don't want to debate with the commission, but since there is a document which has been presented to the commission by counsel for a person who is an applicant and has been recognized by the chair and has been allowed to speak, I think I should be allowed to see the document if it is here in this room. And at least have it marked for identification so that if it is relevant in a court proceeding it will be marked for identification even though it is not an exhibit. This is what is always done when the exhibit is offered and not admitted." He strides up to the commission table, holding his hand out confidently. "I request that I be permitted to see that document."

As the chairman turns in some bewilderment to the Assistant Attorney General, Mr. Broadhurst is on his feet again. There is a little smile on his face and his voice is a bit softer. A stranger walking into the room would recognize immediately who was in charge. "Mr. Chairman, perhaps I can assist the situation a little by saying as a part of the record that we have offered, as a basis for a standing in this proceeding, if it had gone into that point, a Supplementary Application for thirty additional dates, commencing September 11, and ending October whateveritis."

Day for day against Taunton. Just as Joel had suspected.

"I certainly have no objection to having Mr. Kozol view it," Mr. Broadhurst intones, cleaning up that sticky phase of the record for the commission. "In fact"—he smiles, with a little bow toward Joel—"I would be glad to give him a copy if he wants it."

Joel would like that just fine. "And," he adds briskly, "I'd also like it marked for identification if it is here in the room."

BROADHURST *(deferentially)*: "As to whether or not it should be marked, that's up to the commission."

WALSH *(adamantly)*: "The commission denies your request to mark this for identification."

The way it looks to us, Mr. Broadhurst would just as soon have his application be made part of the record, in line with the usual procedure, now that the dates have been revealed; and the chairmain is unwilling to back off his previous rulings, since it could not help appearing as if he were following Mr. Broadhurst through every twist and turn.

And that ends it. They had held a hearing that wasn't a hearing. They had thrown us out without even considering our application.

So it's no great tragedy. It's galling but no tragedy. We'll run the dates they gave us. We'll lose a certain number of the horsemen, sure; but one way or the other we'll dig up enough horses to get by. When you come right down to it, the commission has stuck us with the dates we really want.

The next day, the horsemen begin to call. Jesse Moss calls to say that if we bring a suit he wants to join us on behalf of his horsemen. Do we want affidavits? He'll bury us in affidavits. He and his organization are prepared to cooperate with us in any way we ask.

Kenny Graf calls from Rockingham. In shock. He doesn't know what he's going to do now. The way things stand, he's thinking about extending his flat meet a couple of weeks and maybe not having any winter harness meet at all.

I'm in a dilemma of sorts myself. I have to come to a decision on whether I want to sue Mr. Quinn on his ruling that we have to relinquish our dates in order to file a supplementary application. On the one hand, I wouldn't mind giving the Honorable Robert H. another bloody nose in court. On the other hand, I wouldn't mind holding on to the late dates now that they have been forced upon me. On the third hand, I have promised Ken Graf that I'd use my best efforts, and I can get adolescent about keeping my word. On the fourth hand, I've already put in enough courtroom time to last me for the next ten years or so, and we're in the middle of our flat meet and who ever said that "best efforts" included the weary, dreary trek back into court?

I have thirty days in which to make up my mind.

For thirty days, everything is in constant turmoil. Ken Graf assures us that Reynolds himself is going to bring his influence to bear where it will do the most good, which is everywhere. We are informed that Dario isn't going to object because the harness circuit isn't going to affect him anyhow. Which is very big of him and, of course, pleases me no end. Between Rhode Island and New Hampshire, we may get out of this yet. We hear that the horsemen are putting pressure on E. M. Loew. He had taken his best shot and it didn't work, they are telling him. All he's doing now is hurting them.

Soon enough, we get a glimpse of yet another arrow in E. M. Loew's quiver. Foxboro's contract with the horsemen is up for renegotiation, and E. M. Loew is a man who can see a bargaining point before it flies into his ear and stings him. All right, he tells Al Thomas, the president of the SOA. If Thomas will accept the same contract his horsemen have been working under, Loew is willing to withdraw his objection to the switch in our dates. Well, Thomas isn't just about to agree to anything like that, and the E. M. Loew Factor is looming over us again.

As always, Joel comes up with the best advice of all: "Hey, lookit," he says. "What are we knocking ourselves out for? There are enough wheels in motion here, enough other interests at work. Let's you and me sit back for a change and let the people who have something to gain work it out."

Sounds reasonable. Two days before the deadline on filing suit, Al Thomas calls to tell us that he and Jesse Moss have written a letter to E. M. Loew reminding him that there will be other contracts, in other years, when maybe the horsemen will be sitting tall in the saddle and he will be pleading with them to be reasonable. We are also informed that Thomas and Moss have met with Attorney General Quinn and found him just overrunning with the milk of kindness and expressing every willingness to see what could be done to help them out of their bind. Swell. I could have told the Honorable One what he could do. He could change his ridiculous ruling.

Maybe the Attorney General had been talked to, but you know there was something about the idea of Mr. Quinn turning so all soft and cuddly right on the deadline that gnawed at my innards. On the last possible day, I called Joel and said, "Let's just protect ourselves by filing our suit, anyway. And then we can sit back again and let all those other wheels keep turning."

A month goes by, and then—look, kids, a miracle!—the word comes pouring in from all sides that the thing has been worked out. It's like somebody has blown a bugle and all the troops are falling into formation. The horsemen inform us that E. M. Loew has agreed to cooperate. And, sure enough, Loew's personal attorney, Bob Silvia, calls to pass the word that it's A-OK and all systems on go. Kenny Graf calls to say that Linsey has been brought into line. We hear from the commission that it will be receptive to a new application.

On July 7, with things getting very nervous among the horsemen, and many of them making arrangements to ship their horses to more stable climes, Frank Kozol and I meet with Kenny Graf at Suffolk over the luncheon table. Kenny assures me that Reynolds and Linsey have had their little talk, and that Linsey has absolutely agreed to the switch in the dates.

A week later, E. M. Loew writes a letter to Dr. Walsh stating: (1) that he will not seek those 30 dates, and (2) that any procedure the commission can work out with us will meet with his approval.

Well, yeah, the procedure is now the problem. We can't just go in and get the dates switched. That would be too easy. The Honorable Robert H. Quinn has ruled, in his wisdom, that we have to give up the licenses we already have, and he isn't going to admit publicly that . . . well, uh, maybe he was wrong again. We are not in any mood to surrender our licenses on anybody's word, because for some strange reason we have come to look upon the chairman with some misgivings and to view E. M. Loew—although you may not believe this—as a bit of a schemer.

To show how skittish we were, we insisted that E. M. Loew's lawyer send us a copy of his letter. The original letter to the commission wasn't good enough for us; we weren't going to make a move until we got it directly from the source. And thus it came to pass that on July 20 (the first working day after the close of our flat meet), we filed a new batch of—get this—preliminary Supplementary Applications. Supplementary Applications hadn't been used in thirty-four years of racing in the Commonwealth before we arrived on the scene, and we're whipping them in for the third time in ten months. Accompanying the applications was a letter in which I advised the commission that I was submitting them only on the understanding that it was going to either give us the new dates or return the old ones, but that one way or the other we were going to end up with thirty dates. And also on the understanding that E. M. Loew had committed himself not to contest us in any way. The last was no less important than the first. If anything had been impressed upon us through this whole mess it was that it was necessary to have E. M. Loew's permission to make any changes where harness racing was concerned. We had, after all, been waiting for three months for him to pass the word to the commission that it was all right to go ahead. Think about that. Everybody involved in New England harness racing had been forced to mark time for three months because E. M. Loew had filed a Supplementary Application for the dates which belonged to us; an application which was never made part of the record of a hearing that was officially a nullity. Cheers!

From there, Joel went into a series of meetings with the Assistant Attorney General to work out the mechanics for shifting the dates without exposing us to the remotest possibility of losing them. The device Joel eventually came up with was something resembling that old riddle where you start with a gallon container of water and an empty quart container and keep pouring them back and forth until you end up with the desired amount. I'm going to go through the procedure here to give you some idea of exactly how good we considered the word of the people we were dealing with.

We were sitting with three licenses: one for 9 days, one for 11 days, and one for 10 days. By a coincidence, most fortunate, the first license (the 9-day one) overlapped the final 9 days of the new dates we were asking for. In other words, we could surrender two licenses, retaining our 9-day license, and still have our full 30-day schedule intact as soon as the commission granted us the 21 days to replace them with.

(1) We would surrender the last two licenses (a total of 21 days) and hold on to the one for 9 days.

(2) We would then file four new applications, for 4,6,9, and 2 days repectively, a total of 21.

(3) At the same time we filed for the four new licenses, we would also file two alternate applications for the 21 days we had just surrendered. (If the commission didn't give us the new ones, it was to return the old ones.)

"Okay," I had said, when Joel first explained it to me. "What if after Step Number Two, the commission gives the twenty-one days to E. M. Loew?"

"Holy cow, Bill. We've got him in writing."

I still wasn't satisfied. I wanted the Attorney General pinned down as solidly as Loew was.

Immediately after we sent in the Supplementary Applications, we sent a letter to the Assistant Attorney General spelling out the whole procedure and advising him that as soon as he notified us of his approval we would dismiss the suit we had pending in court. The underlying threat there was that if he wasn't willing to give us an ironclad guarantee we were perfectly prepared to go after the dates the hard way.

Satisfied at last, I went right into the hospital for an operation on my ear. The same day. A long-standing infection that had held over, in varying degrees of virulence, from a bug I had picked up, would you believe it, in the Pacific during the war had flared up so badly that I had been staggering through the final month of the Thoroughbred meet. The headaches were killing me. My balance was precarious. I would go out to speak and find the hall floating around me. At times, it got so bad that I would have to reach back and take a good hold on the chair. I would get out of bed in the morning and find myself—this is the way it felt, anyway—blown across the room.

So I went into the hospital, and they operated on the inner ear and while they were about it they wheeled me back into the operating room a couple of days later and removed some polyps from my throat.

In on Monday, out on Saturday, that was the schedule. And then a long, well-earned, devoutly anticipated vacation with my family in Maryland. Just as soon as I put the finishing touches on that pesky little business about the harness dates. Mary Frances and I checked into the Parker House to wait for Joel, who was flying back from Majorca for a final progress report and strategy session before we filed our—get this —alternate Supplementary Application. Late Sunday night, with the legal talk long since disposed of, we were all sitting around sleepily when all of a sudden I could feel my face go lopsided. As casually as possible, I lifted myself out of the chair and strolled toward the bathroom. I could feel their eyes following me; I could feel them not saying a word. Holy mackerel! I stood in front of the mirror and watched one whole half of my face swelling up like a pumpkin. I had a donkey's ear, five times its normal size and turning a ghastly purple. "Just between you and me, fella," I murmured, "and just off the top of my head . . . but I've got a sneaking suspicion that the operation wasn't an unqualified success."

I struck a pose in the frame of the door. "Do you notice anything different about me?" I asked, smiling shyly out of one side of my mouth.

"Either you're wearing a crazy mask," Mary Frances said, "or you're auditioning for Bottom in the high-school play, or we'd better get you right back to the hospital." She was already heading for the phone.

"What difference does it make?" I said. "They can stop it just as well tomorrow as tonight." The pus and blood were beginning to run out of my ear and down the side of my face and neck, and I wouldn't hear of going back to the hospital. The only thing I could think of was that I had been lying there with tubes in my arm all week, and it can get pretty difficult trying to find a position to sleep when you're bristling all over with tubes. Here or there, I was in for an uncomfortable night. I'll take my discomfort without the tubes.

The next day I was back in the hospital. For two solid weeks I was in the hospital. For a solid month after that, I was recuperating at home. The only time I left was to fly back to Boston for the hearing on the dates.

And who was there to make the trip worth while but Joe Linsey, who we had been assured had been handled. This time, Linsey addressed the commission personally, pleading with them not to grant us the dates because they would be run in competition with him.

In the end, though, it wasn't our enemies we had to worry about. It was our friends. Jesse Moss was still so incensed that he insisted upon being heard. We had come to let the commissioners back off as gracefully as possible, and Moss was out to lecture them. When he got around to instructing them on what their true function as Commissioners was supposed to be, Consiglio broke in and barked, "Mr. Moss, we know our function. We will take care of our function."

Joe Arena was there on behalf of his Union, and he insisted upon being heard too. When it gets to the yelling, Joe is going to be heard above any din. All we had wanted was a nice quiet meeting, and it ended up with Moss, Linsey, and Arena screaming at each other while the Commissioners sat there and glowered. I just sat there and listened to the pain in my ear.

They switched the dates, though. A full seven months after we had filed and a scant five weeks before the meet was supposed to begin. Linsey's fears were completely unfounded. If he had any drop in his handle it was accountable for by the fact that the very worst of the recession bit into the economy in the fall of 1970. For us, it was a disaster. Not only did we catch the bottom of the economy, we were hit by what I had been most afraid of, a sucession of cold, drizzly autumn nights.

Sometimes I wonder if I'm too nice a guy. The only other possibility is that I'm a bit of an idiot, and I know that can't be.

On the over-all mission, though, we were a roaring success. During the course of two legislative hearings, where we once again submitted our bill to revise the statute and increase the dates, it became abundantly evident that the old barriers were about to fall. In another year they crumbled completely and Suffolk Downs was awarded an extra 60 days. The only drawback was that I was no longer around to accept the congratulations and express my appreciation. Another drawback was that I despised the new people who were.

14

Save Our Dump

Any association with Harvard is bound to be educational, and it was through my selfless efforts to bring some civic responsibility and possibly even humanity to the halls of Nathan Pusey and the shores of Harvard Square that I won myself a political education that you couldn't have bought for a million dollars or wanted to. I am talking, brethren, of the Great Stadium Caper, a feat of derring-do in which I set out to be a public benefactor and got no more than I deserved.

Put simply, the city was about to lose its professional football team, the Boston Patriots, not so much because of an unbroken history of non-support but because the Patriots didn't have a home to call their own. Through most of their ten-year history the Patriots had played at Fenway Park (seating capacity, 33,379) under terms which had required them to play their first seven games on the road. In 1969 they had moved to Boston College's little Alumni Field on a one-year deal which, while it might not sound like much, had been plenty long enough for ill feelings to develop on both sides. The solution was a municipal stadium. It was so clearly the solution that it had achieved the status of a political football—no joke intended, particularly to the Patriots. In ten years, something like seventy proposals for stadium sites had been put into the legislative hopper. Always the stadium had been voted down on the purely practical but highly charged political issue of whether the taxpayers should build a stadium for private interests.

Much as I hate to say it, the politicians were right. In order to have the best chance of breaking even, a municipal stadium has to have a major-league baseball team to pick up the bulk of the day-by-day expenses. In Boston, Tom Yawkey owned Fenway Park, free and clear, and he saw no great necessity of moving into somebody else's ball park so that he could find out what it was like to pay rent. No, that wasn't it, either. Yawkey could have made a good enough deal with a stadium commission, sold his land up off Kenmore Square at a very healthy figure, and got out from under the real-estate taxes. What was involved primarily was the special flavor of Fenway Park. Municipal stadiums are cooky-jar ball parks. They all look as if they've been built from the same spacious blueprint, and they all have been. Fenway Park is unique. It's a small, compact park. The spectators are close enough to the field to turn the game into a cozy gathering. The hulking left-field wall (the Green Monster) looms over the playing field like sudden doom and turns a 4-run lead in the ninth inning into a real nibbler. Under the right circumstances—which is exactly what Yawkey had—a limited seating capacity can make your tickets more valuable. With 35,000 people in the stands, you have a full house instead of a half-filled stadium. Full houses breed excitement. Excitement breeds happy memories. Happy memories breed return visits. With the smallest seating capacity in the American League, the Red Sox had been leading the league in attendance. Tom Yawkey has many good qualities and, I suppose, his duly allotted share of not-so-good ones, but nowhere in the mix will you find the slightest hint of stupidity.

As far as Fenway Park itself was concerned, the Red Sox had never wanted the Patriots as tenants, and the Patriots had no desire whatsoever to return. It didn't matter, anyway. Three years earlier, the league had passed a rule requiring all its teams—meaning that team in Boston —to produce a stadium or a reasonable blueprint thereof with a minimum seating capacity of 50,000. The year of reckoning had arrived. Come March, the owners were holding their annual meeting in Hawaii. (Where did you think they were going to hold it, in Gary, Indiana?) Billy Sullivan, the Patriots president, was under instructions to come to Honolulu prepared to tell them all about it. Since a NFL franchise was not a thing to be scorned in any civilized city in the world except Boston, Mass., offers to buy the team or build it a stadium of its very own had come in from Tampa, Memphis, Birmingham, Seattle, Toronto, Montreal, and, by combining their total resources, three little towns in North Carolina.

The Boston City Council met under the gun to decide, one last time, whether it was willing to build the stadium that would keep the Patriots in town. The overriding fact, overhanging all, was that "wolf" had been cried so often in the ten years previous that it was all but impossible for anybody to work up a sense of urgency. The attitudes were set. The political chips had been placed. There had been threats that Boston was going to lose the football team for years, and the team was still there. The worst team, as it happened, in professional football. If you had to lose a team, it would be hard to find a loss more bearable.

Once again, the stadium proposal was voted down.

There was, however, still one stadium within the city environs which did meet NFL requirements. Harvard's Soldiers Field. The only trouble there was that Harvard was conspicuously unwilling.

The Harvard-Veeck rivalry, which was not quite hallowed by tradition or sung about around the tables of whatever corresponds to Mory's was by then a good four weeks old. It began innocently enough—as these momentous affairs usually do—when I hired John Yovicsin, the Harvard football coach, as a promotion man of sorts. He had permission to work for us, but when the story broke, several old crocks gasped in horror. The Dean of Students had very little to say. I understand that he was tied up in his office at the time—or, wait a minute, maybe he was down at the Student Union helping to put out the fire.

But I digress. My dalliance with Harvard came about when a couple of fellow squash players down at the Harvard Club told me that John was looking for an off-season job to meet the imminent challenge of sending four teen-age children through college. That sounded good to me. I was looking for somebody to handle group parties, and John turned out to be an easy-going, low-pressure, somewhat naïve man who is likeable at first sight. I said he was naïve. He had been given permission to accept any part-time employment that wouldn't interfere with his primary job of teaching the massed flower of Harvard manhood how to trample the massed flower of Yale manhood, and he couldn't imagine how anyone could object to his working for a racetrack, which was, after all, perfectly legal, reasonably honest, and roughly within his field of sports. Being more conversant with the ways of the world, I cautioned him that he would do well to clear it at the highest levels before we made any announcement. And he did. That's the thing. He put the question to his three immediate superiors, including the Athletics Director, and they all gave their approval.

A considerable amount of time had elapsed, however, before our alliance was made public. I first had lunch with John during the early summer, the same day, I remember, that we were turning the checks over to Campanella and Dario. The announcement wasn't unfurled until the end of the football season six months later. Miraculously, we had managed to keep our little secret over all that time, causing Tim Horgan of the *Globe* to whistle. "Six months? That's a new record in this town. The old record was six minutes."

Sure I was out to have a little fun with Harvard. So what? Harvard may be sancrosanct to Harvard—that's the fun of going after it—but it's not sancrosanct to me. "John will give our operation that indefinable something called cla-a-a-ass," I said, giving it the Harvard Square pronunciation and intimating that if Aqueduct could call itself the Big A, we were now qualified to call ourselves the Broad A.

As soon as the first writer expressed the expected surprise that anybody connected with Harvard would work for a racetrack, I went into my commercial about how much we returned to the state in taxes as compared to Harvard, which had not paid a shilling in 320 years. All good clean fun. As an educational institution it wasn't required to pay taxes. If it's that sensitive about it, the remedy is in its hands.

The next day, the press somehow learned, I can't imagine how, that the Athletics Director, Dolph Samborski, and the chairman of the Harvard Faculty Committee on Athletic Sports (a neat redundancy, that), one Robert B. Watson, had closeted themselves in Samborski's office to discuss John's regrettable lack of discretion. When the question of prior clearance was put to them directly, they answered with a sly, meaningful "no comment," which developed soon enough—according to the press—into a flat statement that they hadn't.

John called me and said, "You know, I'm embarrassed. But I'm going to have to make a decision." And I said, "John, don't be. Listen, I understand perfectly, and if you have to make a choice . . . well, there's just no choice."

And that was almost that. One Harvard official was willing, under the cloak of anonymity, to let the snob in him hang out. "It is obviously not the proper area for a Harvard coach to be in," he sniffed. You have to give those Harvard officials all the credit in the world. Under the cloak of anonymity, they are sometimes willing to tell the truth.

It is possible that John's immediate superiors had misjudged the climate of upper-echelon opinion six months earlier. It is also possible that the climate had changed in the locker room. Although Yovvy was the winningest coach in Harvard history (71–40–5), he was now coming off a 3–6 season, his first losing season in eleven years and, horrible of horribles, he had lost, 7–0, to Yale. The morality of the overseers of collegiate sports is not that much different from the morality of the grasping professionals when the turnstiles are spinning. You are much better off when you're winning. A Harvard coach might be able to get away with working at a racetrack, and he might be able to get away with one consecutive losing season. But he sure couldn't get away with them both at once. Any doubt about that was dispelled when a couple of his players volunteered the information that Samborski had called in all the seniors after the loss to the Yales to ask them how they really felt about John Yovicsin anyway. The skids were being greased, it seemed, and they were trying to use the kids to help them compile a dossier. In Dickens' day they called a dastard a dastard, and this is dastardly. Samborski, legitimately embarrassed now, insisted that he had merely been following his standard procedure. Off the testimony of the captain of the '68 team, the only player who had ever been called in before had been the captain.

Fair Harvard had become fair game, and I went after it. I wanted the world to know that personal freedom stopped at the turnstiles as far as Harvard was concerned. Not its. Ours. Sheer snobbery, plastered over with ivy. I was out to demonstrate to the skeptics that liberalism and snobbery sleep together quite comfortably in Harvard Square. Harvard had broken its word to John Yovicsin and thrown the onus on him to break his word to me. It had done it openly and arrogantly, without, it seemed, a second thought. He was, after all, only an employee, and in the lexicon of privilege loyalty goes only one way. The typical aristocratic attitude of *Well, of course we're all equal and all that but we all really know that nobody is quite as equal as John Harvard.*

I had myself a field day. On my television show. During guest appearances on television and radio. In my speaking engagements. Harvard had opened the door for me, and it would not be unfair to say that if I was sorry for Yovvy's sake I was delighted for my own. "In all fairness," I would say, "I think I should have polled our alumni to see whether they approved of Harvard. Don't misunderstand me now, I think Harvard is as legitimate as we are. I don't know what they have against us, unless it's that they're afraid we're spoiling a good thing for everybody by paying our taxes."

"Listen," I'd say, "nothing is a total loss if you look at it right. We've finally been able to show the country that there is one thing, at least, which the president of Harvard University won't tolerate."

And: "My alumni didn't like it, either. They were coming up and telling me, 'After all, you can get into your office without an armed escort. And what college president can make that statement?' "

The more I needled Harvard, the more my audiences enjoyed it because I am a symbol in my small way of the impudent spirit which lies await in all of us. Promotionally, the issue gave me what I had been searching so hard for, audience identification. A common purpose. Harvard isn't very well liked in the streets of Boston, you know, which is a great improvement over twenty years ago, when it was absolutely despised. All their lives, my kind of people had wanted to take a whack at Harvard. When I whacked it, we were whacking it together.

I continued to have my fun with Harvard all the while I was there. The featured handicap on our second Saturday of the new season was called the Varsity Drag, a minor readjustment on what had previously been called the Varsity Handicap. Each of the races on the program was named in honor of one of the local colleges—no great feat of research in Boston—with Harvard being conspicuously honored in the absence. That wasn't because I wanted to slight my friends from across the river, though, it was because I wanted to be able to tell inquisitive writers, "I'm sorry you brought that up. I thought about having an eight-dollar-added handicap in honor of Fair Harvard, but the horses rioted. You know how horses are when they get to rioting, you just can't negotiate with them."

And then Nick came up with the brilliant idea of inviting the Harvard band out to provide the entertainment. "You're kidding," I said. "We can't even get Harvard's approval; how are we going to get their band?" There was nothing to be lost by taking a shot, though, and to my surprise the band accepted. Which was nice of it. It would have been nicer if the band had actually provided the entertainment. It was terrible. Just awful. Fortunately it was a very windy day, and the wind whipped into the microphone and drowned the band out. Unfortunately, when it stopped playing it went into its Funny Skits and Humor. It had concocted a series of hilarious skits for our edification and amusement, and if you happened to be a somewhat backward sophomore you might have thought they were hilarious too. I'll give you an example. We were running horseraces, so they put on—I blush to tell you—a whores' race with some of the bandsmen dressed up to fit the part. That's not the kind of humor I particularly enjoy, and it pleased me to think that my patrons weren't particularly enjoying it either. "Get rid of them," I growled at Nick. "Go down there and throw the bums out."

My favorite, though, was sending a plane over Harvard Stadium during the opening game of the football season. Our harness meet was on at the time, and I was able to greet John and shill the crowd at the same time by having the plane trail a huge streamer which read: "Hi, John. It's Even Better at Suffolk Downs." And back again with: "Your Stubs Will Entitle You to Admission at Suffolk Downs Any Time."

Sticking needles into Harvard can be a lot of fun—I recommend it highly for the young and old alike—but, you know, it's also like sticking needles into a bale of hay. Harvard has a rare talent for making an ass of itself, and it doesn't really matter. The institution is so big and powerful and devouring that it is beyond all earthly harm. Something like the Commissioner of Baseball.

John Yovicsin had a very successful final season, at the end of which Harvard, as expected, accepted his resignation. He had embarrassed the university by taking it at its word. What can you say about such people except that they are without truth, character, or honor? Well, you can also say that they are without civic responsibility, as they proved in the stadium controversy.

The final council vote rejecting the stadium had taken place while I was still getting all the mileage I could out of the Yovicsin affair. With that vote, all eyes had turned to Soldiers Field. First Billy Sullivan's, and then everybody else's who wanted to keep the Patriots in town. To hold onto my franchise as the foremost critic of all things Harvard and all things elitist, I picked up my trusty lance and smote at Harvard hip and thigh for not rushing forth with open arms to give the Patriots shelter, never failing to cast the Patriots as orphans of the storm and Harvard as the hardhearted landlord.

Dr. Pusey had never done anything for the city except take, take, take, I kept saying. His school had been off the tax rolls for 320 years and now when he was being given an opportunity to repay the city in some small way by keeping such an important civic and financial asset from leaving, he was dragging both feet.

I didn't believe for one minute that Dr. Pusey was going to be impressed by anthing a buffoon, troublemaker, and squalid racetrack operator like me might be saying. Nor anything the press or politicians were saying either. I was counting upon the population of his own tumultuous village to carry us in. With all the agitation about colleges assuming a role of responsibility in their own communities, I didn't think he'd dare to turn the Patriots away. What he did, in true institutional fashion, was to appoint a committee headed by the treasurer of the Harvard Corporation, George Bennett. Presumably, the committee was being impaneled to study the situation in all its aspects and report back with a recommendation. In fact, as was amply demonstrated when Billy Sullivan was summoned to Bennett's office, it was to draft a letter turning his request down. Weeks earlier, in the course of a joint appearance on a radio program, Barney Frank, the bright young executive assistant to Mayor Kevin White and a former member of the Harvard faculty himself, had told me that the Mayor had been writing to Pusey and paying personal calls upon him, always being careful to work behind the scenes so as not to give even the appearance of putting political pressure on him. "Pusey's answer," Barney said "is that it is inconsistent with the spirit of amateur athletes to have a professional team there. I can hardly say that with a straight face, but that's what the man keeps saying."

The main reason for Harvard's reluctance to share the stadium with the Patriots, the letter said in almost the same words, "is the fundamental incompatibility which results when professional and amateur athletic activities use the same facilities. Our first responsibility must be to amateur athletics and to our own program." A whiff of the old class structure there, a throwback to those more tranquil times when English gentlemen did not deign to mingle with their social inferiors. Who'd have thought the president of Harvard University would have proclaimed it so openly?

The myopia of college administrators as they peer through the bramble bushes of their unreal world never ceases to confuse and amuse me. But then, the remarkable thing about being snobs is that people don't know they're being snobs. If they did, one or two of them might not be. Although the letter was signed by Nathan Pusey, it was pretty well agreed that a letter so pathetic could only have been written by a full committee. A three-page single-spaced letter that was all excuses and no reasons. Let's understand one thing right away. There was no acceptable way that Harvard could have turned its back upon the citizens and taxpayers of the city. It chose to make the attempt with a mouthful of meal. It came out pompous and patronizing. Evasive and cavalier. Wholly transparent and wholly phony.

The bare assertion of the dangers of intermingling would not do. Even the framers of this particular Declaration of Nonintegration could see that. Each pitiful excuse sent back a snicker that had to be answered by another excuse. You could almost see the committee at work.

Who says there's any fundamental incompatibility?

"We have inquired of many, and are impressed by the reports we have received from institutions which had to face the issue."

Pennsylvania U. is the only Ivy college which rents out its facilities. I suppose you called Pittsburgh and Tulane too. The only thing that impresses me so far is that whatever the administrators of those institutions may have reported, they wouldn't allow you to use their names, would they?

"Even more telling is the fact that of those institutions consulted which have some sort of leasing arrangement with a professional team, none recommended this course."

Not that none had condemned it. Or had advised against it. Just that they hadn't recommended it. The weakest negative reaction possible. Come on, now. Is that the best you could get them to agree to?

"Those who had made good bargains admit a favorable effect from more athletic income, but all feel overwhelmed by the presence of a professional money-making organization on the campus."

We're supposed to read into that that Harvard is sacrificing plenty to protect its poor spindly students. Professional money-makers? I'll give you odds that if all the government grants to Harvard professors could be toted up at this very moment it would put the budget of the entire NFL to shame.

"Thus, the college people become second-class citizens on their own campuses. The college athletes come to resent the presence of the professionals, since the focus is no longer on student participation and amateur competition."

Athletes are, perforce, the most realistic of people. They have to know their strengths and, more important still, their weaknesses. Athletes don't resent talent or accomplishment, they have nothing but the greatest admiration for it. They stand in awe of it. To dismiss the possibility of learning by example is a remarkable position for any university to take. I always thought the pursuit of excellence was what colleges are supposed to be all about.

And, finally, as a kind of non sequitur, a last little candy-kiss thrown into the grab-bag for those who had found nothing else to please their palates: "Further, the demands made by the professional inevitab'y grow as they require more personnel, more activity, more and more games."

If I'm still not convinced, stick around for about five years, huh? All they're asking you for, for the luvva Pete, is seven Sundays for one year. Two years at the outside.

The only other excuse they could dredge up was the intolerable traffic problem that would be created. Although, frankly, that would seem to be a much stronger argument for calling off the Harvard-Yale game than anything the Patriots had in prospect.

To nip such negativistic thinking in the bud, they hastened to explain that on every Saturday and Sunday in the autumn the facilities and playing field were used for soccer, Rugby, football and touch football, tennis, skating, running, and volley ball. "The influx of Saturday football crowds always hampers these activities to some extent but is less severe at the time of our games than it would be for professional contests, because the Harvard crowds are to a significant extent local and pedestrian, while the crowds for professional games come characteristically by automobile." (I don't know, the use of the word *characteristically* there disturbs me, Dr. Pusey. It isn't exactly wrong but it isn't exactly right either. You can do better than that.)

What they are saying, it seems to me—although I don't believe it— is that the customers would be parking on the tennis courts and skating rinks and Rugby fields. Or do they mean that they'd be appropriating the parking spaces—which must number into the tens and twenties— of the students who come to play tennis or to skate. That can't be it because, as they continuously point out, those are their own people. They walk.

Whatever it was, Billy Sullivan could be assured that "these obstacles apply with equal force to short-term as well as long-term arrangements."

Which answers the question: Come off it, we're only asking for seven Sundays in the fall and winter.

And then, for all the world to see, they got down on their knees and begged: "During our consideration of your proposal you have been both patient and understanding—and particularly thoughtful in discouraging public and political pressure upon the university."

You don't want to spoil your record at this late date, do you?

And, in parting, a final little curtsy to their own enviable record of goodwill and charity: "As you know, we have been glad in the past to accommodate the Patriots for non-profit charity games in the stadium, just as we always welcome the chance to have the community use the stadium in other ways for responsibly managed non-profit activities in the public interest."

The wonderful thing about being a Brahmin is that it never seems to enter your mind that your word will not be taken as a command. Magnificently unaware that he had flunked the course in public relations, Mr. Bennett informed Billy Sullivan that the decision was irrevocable and to show that he was as tolerant as the next fellow invited him to come to Harvard Stadium as his guest for—holy of holies!—The Harvard-Yale game.

"I don't know what to do now," Billy Sullivan told his hastily assembled press conference. "I want to stay in Boston, but I'm barren of ideas. I am hoping," he said, turning to the gathered writers, "that maybe you men have something to suggest."

"Boy," said Timmy Horgan, "that's *really* barren."

The wasteland hadn't completely taken over yet. Sullivan still had that issue which I had been haranguing the populace with for a month. A tax-exempt stadium owned by a tax-exempt institution in a city with such a high concentration of college and church property that fully 51 per cent of the real estate was off the tax rolls. Was it not as a result of this situation that the city was not in a financial position to build a new stadium? Did not Harvard University, therefore, have a solemn obligation to keep a revenue-producing enterprise in town by letting it use its facility for seven lousy Sundays?

The one thing that was clear was that the Pusey letter had not settled anything. The press excoriated Harvard. The politicians, having tested the winds, were not far behind. A bill was introduced immediately to take the stadium by the right of eminent domain. Hearings were held the next day. Lungs were emptied and breasts were beaten. The politicians, now that they didn't have to do anything, were tigers. All political oratory. Whatever you thought of Harvard's attitude, it was Harvard's stadium to cuddle to itself as it wished. It was one thing to apply the pressure of public opinion; it was quite another to have the state seize the property because Harvard wouldn't do what the state wanted it to do.

The politicos went through their highly predictable ritual folk dances, as sanctioned by time and custom. If political choreography could bring on the rain, I'd have ordered a hammer and some nails and requested the Museum of Natural History to collect me all known living animals, two by two.

If you didn't know anything about the history of the past ten years, you'd have almost believed they cared.

The truth of the matter is that I had little time to worry about the fate of a football team during the time of the post-mortems which I have been recounting. On the day the Pusey letter was released, we were waiting for the Racing Commission to hand down the racing dates. Ted Williams was in town as the feature attraction in the Sportsmen's Show, and I spent the night with Ted, pontificating on the philosophy of baseball trades. ("What do you do," Ted wanted to know, "with an owner who wants to trade ballplayers you don't want to trade?" Scream loudly, I advised him, but scream in advance. Keep telling your writers you wouldn't trade the guy for anything and that you sure hope the owner doesn't get carried away. All the things, in short, I'd kill any manager of mine for doing.)

During the next couple of days I was wholly occupied in charting our course on the switch in the harness dates, and traveling to New York to meet with Phil Levin, who wanted me to operate the Arlington racetrack in Chicago for him.

When I returned, I sat down with Nick and Arthur over a cup of coffee and went through the stack of back papers. The front pages were still filled with the problems of the Patriots.

And I got to thinking: Gee, all this publicity. How do I get in on it?

And then: There must be some way to work this thing out so that a stadium can be built without government funds. Because once a stadium was in the works, don't you see, the pressure on Harvard to provide playing room until it was finished would become irresistible.

As easily and naturally as that, the two thoughts flowed together.

I said, "Nick, I think I've got an idea on how we can build a stadium for the Patriots, and I think it will work. Just off the top of my head, I can't see a flaw in it. Let's say the legislature gives us twelve extra dates—"

Nick's hand shot up like a traffic cop's. "Hold it right there," he said. "I think I've spotted the flaw."

"Let's say they give us permission to run twelve extra days, with all the money being set aside to retire the bond issue."

"What bond issue?"

"Nicodemus, you're not listening. The bond issue that has been floated to build the stadium."

We looked at each other across the table. "By George," he whispered in his best Higginsian accent, "I think you've got it."

The pencils started working. Over a twelve-day period—two weeks —we would normally be turning over about $1 million to the state. To that, we would add whatever remained of our own percentage above the actual out-of-pocket expenses; that is, the purses to the horsemen —we could hardly expect them to run their horses at Suffolk for the love of somebody else's game—and the salaries of the mutuel clerks and maintenance people. That's all. Everything else would be charged to overhead, and we'd take care of that. We would throw in all the admissions, the parking, the programs, everything that came into the coffers from any other source. And that would make it $1.5 million easy. (The only thing I wasn't throwing in was the concessions. For reasons I have already gone into, the concessions were out of my hands.)

I knew enough about stadium construction—well, I know a great deal about stadium construction—to know that to build a complex for all sports can cost from $50 million to the limits of imagination. A stadium built exclusively for football, though—just open stands without any frills —could still be built for about $10 million. After that, you were dealing with the cost of the land.

A simple, selfless plan. So selfless that the benedictions were already flashing through my brain. Suffolk Downs, the Racetrack with a Heart (only a few minutes from downtown Boston by car and easily accessible through all modes of public transportation). Good Ol' Will, riding in on his white charger, had saved the day. I saw myself being patted on the head by all right-thinking people. "I had been told that Boston was a cold city," I would say when the city fathers awarded me the plaque, "slow to accept outsiders and suspicious of strangers. Nothing could be further from the truth. I have lived in many cities in my somewhat checkered [devilish smile] career, but nowhere have I been greeted with more warmth and kindness than by the citizens of this great Commonwealth. If, in some small way, I have been able to repay . . ."

All kidding aside, the plan was a serious one, and a darn good one. I thought it important that Boston should not lose the Patriots. The city had lost the Boston Braves to Milwaukee. It had already lost two football teams. George Preston Marshall had taken the Boston Redskins to Washington the year he drafted Sammy Baugh. Ted Collins, the manager of Kate Smith, had brought in a team called the Boston Yanks which, after a brief stopover in Brooklyn, had become the Baltimore Colts. As a matter of principle, I am one of those people who does not believe public money should be used to build stadiums for private interests. As a matter of practicality, I had seen what happens when a major-league team leaves a city. Something goes with it. Something that goes beyond the financial loss, and the financial loss is considerable. Professional sports add something to the spirit and vitality of a city. They are a reflection of the city's image of itself. I don't simply believe that; I know it. A winning team can bring a city together, and even a losing team can provide a bond of common misery. It may be silly, in the grand scheme of things, to say that Pete Rozelle's imprimatur plays a meaningful part in a great city's existence. But realistically, in the way things are, it does. Major-league franchises flow inexorably toward vigor and vitality. The pervasive resignation with which Boston was accepting the loss of its fourth major-league franchise was, it seemed to me, just one more proof of the city's decline and decay.

I am perfectly aware that this is a view of human affairs which offends many earnest people whose interests run to nobler purposes and worthier pursuits. That doesn't make it any less a fact. The argument is made these days that in a time of crisis it is juvenile to think about sports, much less worry about them. If this be true I confess to an adolescence fast approaching puberty. There is more to life than grimness and—that word again—priorities. There is joy and gaiety and fun. There is the flash of personality and the clash of competition. John Lindsay has said that the incredible victory of the Mets in 1969 kept the city of New York from going up in flames or going down in a nervous breakdown. I wouldn't want to take it that far myself. But you would have to be a fool or a fanatic to keep insisting, so as not to confound your politics, that it did no good at all. People are what they are, God bless them, not what you'd like them to be. I am what I am, God save me, not what I'd like to be.

What am I apologizing for? To an extent—and I don't want to carry this any farther than it will go either—professional athletic teams as constituted today are the best examples we have of blacks and whites living together under circumstances where they are striving to achieve something that is larger than both of them. In this imperfect world, I'll take it the way I can get it.

And there was something else, too. Can you think of anything more exhilarating than to declare yourself in on somebody else's game, using nothing more than native wit as collateral, and then have the colossal gall to take the game over; by which I mean, in this instance, to put your own plan into action and—while the multitudes are cheering—ride it home.

On this tender of both my sincerity and the lack of it, I will now pick up the Great Stadium Caper.

Right away we were in luck. Jack Warner, the director of the Boston Redevelopment Authority, was a friend from way back. I had first met Jack in Pittsburgh during the 1960 World Series, and he was the first man I had called for lunch upon coming to Suffolk. At that time Jack was the Park Commissioner and he was always getting me involved in his projects, like converting the track into a playground so that we could hold a field day for a couple of thousand Boy Scouts and ghetto kids. I knew the facts of political life well enough to be aware that unless the plan was presented whole, with the site picked out and the financing impeccable, it was going to end up as just one more political football.

Immediately, I called Jack, told him briefly what I had in mind, and then hurried over to his office with Nick to spell it out in detail. As head of the BRA, Jack would be familiar with every available acre in the Boston area. "Where you put it I have no interest," I said. "I will have nothing to do with the selection of the site, because I don't want to get into that area of wrestling. All I'm saying is that this is the way to pay for it."

Before leaving, I took care to impress upon him how disastrous it would be for me if anything leaked out until we knew for certain that the mechanics of the thing could be worked out, financially and politically. If there is one thing I know something about, it's the uses and abuses of publicity, having chased as much of it as any one-legged man alive. From a public-relations angle, this thing came equipped with a built-in boomerang. If I were to announce that I had a plan to build the stadium and it didn't come off, I would look like a cheap bum who had seized upon the city's misfortune to make a grandstand publicity play.

Jack understood perfectly. In order to develop a working plan he was going to have to talk to some of his people. Beyond that, nobody.

Two days later, we were back again. Jack had done an enormous amount of work, and he was euphoric. The best possible site had already been picked out. In Neponset.

"I don't know where Neponset is, or what it is," I told him. "And I'd just as soon keep it that way."

He said, "It's a dump."

"A marriage made in heaven!" I chuckled. "That's what our track is built on too."

There was enough land. Not as much as we'd have liked because there was a river running through it. But enough. Fifty-seven acres. The way Jack had it figured, twenty-three acres would be used for the stadium and the rest of it for parking. The BRA owned some options to buy part of it. A bank had options on the rest. We were in luck there too. The bank was planning to build a mammoth processing center and apartment complex on the other side of the river, and since the elimination of the dump would enhance the value of the property in every way imaginable, it was more than willing to make the land available at a reasonable price. So willing that it had sent Warner copies of all the preliminary studies it had commissioned preparatory to laying the foundation.

Jack also had all the basic figures on costs and financing. An open, no-frills stadium seating 55,000 could be built for $10,620,000. The land was going to cost another $3 million, and the site preparation $1.5 million. Throw in another $1 million as a hedge against inflation, and the whole thing could be done for $16 million.

Depending upon whether the bond issue was floated over thirty or forty years, the annual cost of amortization would run from $1.7 million to $2.5 million.

A cinch. Although his financing wasn't completely pinned down, his estimates at that early stage were not much different from what they were at the end. They were, by design, ridiculously conservative.

Suffolk Downs $1,440,000

Rental of stadium to Patriots   700,000 (9 games)

Office rental to Patriots   40,000

To show how conservative he was, he was basing the income from the Patriots on an average attendance of 40,000. In view of the popularity of the game, and the lure of a new stadium, I'd have been willing to guarantee 50,000, and I wouldn't have bet against a total 9-game sellout. To my way of thinking, an estimate of $1 million would have been far more realistic.

And that was only the guaranteed, bedrock income. As the only decent stadium around Boston, there was every probability of renting it out for a college game every Saturday. (As soon as the story broke, Warner received inquiries from every college in the area with a football team except Harvard.)

Redevelopment man that he was, Jack was also thinking in terms of leasing the waterfront land for high-rise apartments, hotels, and restaurants. A marina complex was a sure thing. The marina had already been started; it had been discontinued because the city had reneged, for reasons I leave to your steaming imagination, on the sewer facilities. In addition to keeping the Patriots in town and upgrading the whole area, the city would eventually be profiting by $3 million in additional tax revenue. As the plan was later refined and developed, the state was also coming in for 15 per cent of the concessions and all the parking at $2 a car. Plus a 50-cent user's tax on every ticket.

Everything that could be done from his office, Jack had done. He had come to the point where he would be unable to take it any further without assistance from both the Mayor and the Governor. Or, for reasons of protocol, would care to. The Governor was going to have to send a bill to the legislature authorizing the extra racing days and the bond issue. The Mayor was going to have to ask the City Council to give us the land.

"The only thing I ask," I reminded him again, "is that you tell them to keep it quiet until we've got everything nailed down."

Jack saw the Governor and the Mayor that same day. They both took vows of silence and they both called press conferences within twenty-four hours.

Mayor Kevin White handed out a press release that very night promising that within forty-eight hours he would be revealing a plan— promptly labeled "the mystery plan"—to build a stadium. Governor Francis Sargent held a full-scale press conference the next morning to lay the whole plan before the public. Not that either of them was out to submarine the project, that wasn't it. We were in an election year, and the primaries were only four months off. Both of them were running for Governor. Sargent, who had come in as Lieutenant Governor, would be running for the first time on his own. White was facing a tough primary fight. Each of them might have been willing to permit a stadium to be built without getting credit for it, but neither of them was willing to take a chance that the other might get the credit.

To complicate the political scene even further, the City Council, though solidly Democratic, was bitterly hostile to White. Particularly Louise Day Hicks, the powerhouse of the council. Mrs. Hicks, a woman of imposing figure and mien, had been defeated by White in the previous go-around in one of the most bitter, most highly publicized elections in the country. The hostility between them went to the gut issue of the national debate, what was to be later known as the social question. On a personal level it went to the bitter intramural feelings between the working-class Irish and the lace-curtain Irish. Mr. White and Mrs. Hicks had only to look at each other to bridle.

And all I was trying to do was "create a philosophy for raising the money to build the stadium."

Although it was White who had bolted out of the gate first, it was Sargent who did the damage. His press release read in part: "If Suffolk Downs were granted 12 additional days per year, Suffolk Downs would agree to dedicate its share of the handle, an estimated $1.2 million *after payment of state taxes* [italics mine]." Unidentified aides of the Governor were quoted as revealing that I had presented the plan to the Governor "early in the week" and that private discussions had been going on continuously.

Exactly what I had been trying to avoid, and worse than I could have imagined. Either the Governor had inadvertently put me in the middle or he was deliberately setting me up as his fall guy if the time ever came when it was to his advantage to submarine the stadium. I hadn't presented anything to him, of course. I hadn't seen him or talked to him. Still, that part of it could be excused as a political gambit to prove that he had been on the scene before the Mayor. There was no way to explain away the mis-statement about the taxes. Jack Warner had, in fact, called me back to his office after the first meeting the previous day to meet with a couple of the Governor's representatives, and I had handed them a completely itemized breakdown on the potential sources of revenue from the track. Even without it, it was impossible for anyone with a rudimentary ability to count on his fingers to make that kind of a mistake.

From the meeting in Warner's office, I had gone directly to the airport to fly to New York for another meeting with Phil Levin. I was out of town while all those press conferences were taking place. The following afternoon I was strolling idly through the terminal at Logan Airport, and there it was, splashed across every headline in D-Day type. For once in my life I had nothing but publicity and, for once in my life, I didn't want it. I couldn't even get Warner on the horn. Jack had rushed over to City Hall to soothe Mayor White, whose nose was out of joint at being so deftly upstaged. In order to appreciate the extremely delicate position Jack Warner was in, all you have to be told is that the BRA is a state agency with a commission to rebuild the city. He was the Governor's man but he had to work with the Mayor. Inevitably, there was another hastily called press conference in which Warner tried to set the facts straight, and White tried to regain his position by explaining, in wounded tones, that he had been so secretive about the plan only because he needed the Governor's approval before he could proceed any further. The press conference ended with Warner stressing, in some desperation, "the nonpartisan approach" that was being taken.

And this, I want you to know, was still the honeymoon stage as far as I personally was concerned. The sportswriters were enthusiastic. I was being looked upon as a public benefactor, my fondest dream come true. I was "Beautiful Bill." The AP even called me "a battle-scarred Marine veteran," and I only get that in the early morning hours when the dew is on the grass. I have never had anything against sheer opportunism. As long as everybody else was getting in a blow for his side, I mentioned modestly that the idea had occurred to me months earlier when somebody had suggested that the toll for riding through the Sumner-Callahan tunnel, which connects East Boston to the city, be increased to pay for the cost of the stadium. If the politicos were going to lie for their favorite cause—themselves—why shouldn't the original proprietor fib just a little for his own favorite causes, himself and his customers? Why, after all, should the betting public be forced to spend money getting to the racetrack that they could just as easily spend after they were there? The only reason I hadn't come forward with the plan at that time, I said, seeing my opportunity and taking it, was that I had assumed that Harvard was going to let the Patriots use its stadium. "I was astonished when Harvard refused. I don't understand those people over there."

By exercising great restraint, I stopped just short of asking whether anyone could doubt the word of a battle-scarred Marine veteran who was the father of nine children.

I did not stop short, you should be happy to hear, of expressing my somewhat premature gratitude to Harvard for the action it was about to take in making the stadium available while the new one was being built. "I would hope,"—I smiled—"that Dr. Pusey will close his eyes while the pros are trodding upon his sanctified turf."

A representative of Dr. Pusey answered rather nervously that there had been no change in Harvard's policy.

The honeymoon lasted for almost two full days. Friday's front page had been filled with the news of how the Patriots were going to be saved. On Sunday the heading read: OPPOSITION BUILDS TO STADIUM PLAN.

One of the more compelling reasons for keeping the plan silent until the basic details had been ironed out was that the clubhouse politicians were being cut out of it. If business had been proceeding as usual, the ritual political wheeling would have taken place around the sale of the land and the attendant legal fee. If politics proceeded as usual, citizens' committees could now be expected to arise spontaneously to preserve the historic and aesthetic qualities of the unprofitable site. That's why the dump was so perfect. The whole area was an eyesore. It was in the backwaters of the city, cut off from the mainland by the Southeast Expressway, which is part of the system of overhead highways that rips through the city like a great green scar. I couldn't believe that even the Boston pols would have the gall to trot out any "save our dump" committees.

Do I have to tell you that the first thing to be knocked out of the box was the land?

The counterattack came from the most powerful legislative figures in both the state legislature and the City Council. It came from both parties. And it came immediately. For the most part, the opposition was pitched to the traffic problems that were going to be created for the people in the neighborhood. The leading opponents were the legislators representing the district itself. And they were both important men. The Senator was the chairman of the Joint Committee on Taxation, and the Representative was the House Whip. They were, indeed, going to save the dump for their constituents. The Senator, a Democrat, referred to the plan, as "White's elephant," illuminating both his beguiling wit and the disarray within the party.

The Speaker of the House had greeted the first announcement with enthusiasm. Reversing his field very nicely, he dismissed the plan as just another press release. "It's still fourth down," he said, "and the ball has been fumbled back to Boston."

Maybe not fumbled back. Passed back. A long 60-yard spiral.

Mayor White immediately announced that he would submit the enabling legislature to the City Council in about a week.

Mrs. Hicks, presented with a grand opportunity to hit a Republican governor and her arch Democratic enemy with the same swing of the bat (you take your sports imagery, and I'll take mine), demanded that action on the stadium be deferred until she and her colleagues had a chance to canvass the people of the affected neighborhood. "My mind is open," Mrs. Hicks proclaimed. "I am concerned with some of the details, especially the costs."

The questions and objections jumped up from everywhere. What about public transportation? What if the receipts from the twelve extra days weren't enough to meet the bond payments? What if they couldn't sell the bonds? All such good questions that Jack Warner had dealt with them days earlier in his press conference.

The Governor, along with other politicians, began to worry about the expense of building the ramps and access roads, and when a politician worries in public about voting money to construction men you know there are other fish on the line.

Word came to us that Wonderland was throwing its influence against us. They had been saying that more racing would be harmful for so long over there that they had apparently come to believe it. Gerry Colella moved nimbly to get his name into the paper. He was going to call a special meeting of his horsemen to consider the effect the extra racing dates would have on the purse structure. (That was easy. It would give his horsemen more money to run for.) B. A. Dario offered to build the Patriots a stadium in Rhode Island by guess what?—running extra days at Lincoln Downs. Before the thing had run its course, all the old familiar faces from the wonderful world of racing had been heard from. A column appeared in the Manchester *News* complaining that "there is reason for suspicion in New Hampshire that Veeck has his hand in the Granite State's collective pocket," an expression of concern that was followed, not entirely to my surprise, by a quote from Rockingham's publicity director. E. M. Loew offered to donate the land for a privately financed stadium near his track in Foxboro, and to loan the Patriots $2 million to get it started. Joe Linsey popped up as the big man in a syndicate that was going to build a stadium on some land of its own. The

Worcester *Telegram* came whipping out with an editorial admonishing caution and careful study. Anything coming out of Suffolk Downs was a gift horse that definitely needed examining, and who cared whether Billy Sullivan and his troupe departed for greener fields. If you are wondering what Worcester's great interest was, then you have forgotten it had a track in mind for some Great Come-and-Get-It-Day in the future. The more flat dates the legislature awarded to Suffolk, the less chance it was ever going to have of getting any.

From all corners there were remonstrances against "public money" being used for such a purpose. Well, sir, the Governor had gone to such lengths to protect himself on that score that you did not have to be a rip-roaring genius to suspect what was coming. No sooner had the first voices of opposition been raised than the State House swung into action to take the Governor out of the line of fire. It was done through that political equivalent of the prevent defense, otherwise known as "A spokesman for the Governor said today . . ." The Governor wasn't sure he was going to file the special legislation any more, it seemed. There were, it seemed, numerous legal questions that had to be studied by lawyers too numerous to mention. "As a matter of fact," one particularly high-placed spokesman said. "We've got nothing on paper. All we have is an idea proposed by Veeck which has been interpreted by Warner as reported in the press."

Hey, what about all those private conversations he was supposed to have had with me over a full week? None of the political reporters seemed to remember them. None of the voters would remember them either. All the voters would remember was that Sargent had shown every willingness to do anything to keep the Patriots in Boston as long as he didn't have to use public money to do it.

And, of course, it wasn't public money; it was betting money.

When it came time to pull the plug, the assignment went to his Commissioner of Administration and Finance, Donald R. Dwight. It now seemed that Dwight was awaiting Warner's presentation with skepticism. "Veeck told me there would be no state money involved," he reported. "Now it appears that they expect the state to give up its share of the take." If his suspicions were correct, said Dwight with an air of discovery, the state would be paying 85 per cent of the cost and the track only 15 per cent. "And that would have to change my attitude. My principal interest in this was that it did not involve state money."

So there it was. I was a fourflusher. Any spokesman, official or otherwise, who wanted to defend my purity of purpose was going to have to fight the *Herald Traveler*'s political columnist, Thomas C. Gallagher. Perfectly understandable. If politics is property, then the *Herald Traveler* was one of the largest property-holders in the Republican party. The paper didn't have anything against me, particularly. I just happened to be there. The game here, as in everything else, was to protect and preserve Governor Sargent and to savage Kevin White. It wasn't a prevent defense with Gallagher; it was a two-minute drill. Watch: "High sources in the Governor's office have stated that Sargent's staff believes that Veeck 'switched signals' after the initial presentation of the plan to the Governor. 'There was no reference to the involvement of any state money last Wednesday,' the Sargent aide states. 'The Governor intends to give the plan every consideration but if he is being given a fast shuffle, and state money gets involved, you can forget it.'

"Apparently, Boston's mayor Kevin White strongly favors the new stadium, which would be built by the BRA, and sees no problem with the constitutional provisions against using public funds for private purposes."

The *Christian Science Monitor* ripped a chunk out of my hide for entirely different, if equally praiseworthy, reasons. The *Monitor* was hewing to a religious dogma, and one of its severities was that gambling is sinful. The *Monitor* had never carried a line about Suffolk Downs before to my knowledge, any more than it had ever recognized the existence of any physical illness or disease. If gambling was evil, then anything offered by the proprietor of a gambling establishment was, by definition, "little more than a cruel hoax at the expense of the taxpayers and those sports fans who want a home for the Boston Patriots. Regardless of whether the 50,000-seat football facility is ever built, Suffolk Downs and its owners would be the big winners." Or, as my friend at the Worcester *Telegram* put it, "Bill Veeck isn't giving anything away." How do they know me so well in Worcester?

Even if the financing had been practicable—and he had made it clear that it wasn't—the *Monitor*'s writer, George B. Merry, was able to find fourteen questions "being raised by citizens" to give him pause, a remarkable journalistic feat. You'd be hard put to find fourteen questions to ask on whether Vietnam had proved to be one of our more successful ventures in foreign affairs. Mr. Merry also had a few questions of his own. Such as: "What tangible evidence is there that the former dumpsite would be any less expensive to build a stadium on than the area near South Station originally preferred by Mayor White?" One possible bit of evidence was that the estimate on the purchase and preparation of the South Station site alone had been more than twice as much the entire cost of building a stadium on what—as I'm sure you've noted—was no longer a dump in Mr. Merry's eyes but a *former dumpsite.*

And, of course, he had his reservations about me and my character. My background showed that I had been involved in sporting promotions in several different cities, for instance, and there was therefore no assurance that I would stay on to see the financing through. Since I would be ninety-four years old by the time the bonds were retired, you have to admit that he had a darn good point there.

Governor Sargent was heard from later in the day when the press somehow stumbled across him while he was on a walking tour through Roxbury, letting the ghetto-dwellers see how concerned he was about them and, possibly, performing other productive deeds on their behalf. "There have been more games played with the stadium than the Patriots have ever played themselves," he growled.

There certainly had been. Sargent's game was just about to start with an onside kick. "The city told me they were going to submit financial proposals," he muttered, darkly. "I'm still waiting." Two simple sentences. Two flat misstatements. The financial proposals were being submitted by Jack Warner, his own man. And he wasn't still waiting. Jack had phoned the State House the previous afternoon to inform them that he was sending his report right over by special messenger. Maybe nobody tells the Governor about these things. Then again, maybe someone does. Maybe Goveror Sargent believes half the things he says. If he does, he's too gullible to be a Governor.

All good politicians are adept at speaking out of both sides of their mouths. Sargent has a truly amazing talent for surrounding himself with words. He speaks pure Octagonese, which is Pentagonese-plus-three. Listen: "I don't think it's up to the Governor of any state to propose a stadium and insist that it be located in a certain place. Boston wants the stadium, they keep coming in with proposals, but they don't tell us how they're going to pay for it."

In two brief sentences he had put both the burden and the blame on White, expressed his reservations about the site which White had presumably selected (presumably to benefit himself or his friends), and placed himself behind the canard that I had misled them about the financing. Every bit of it through implication and indirection. And every bit of it false.

Asked specifically about the financing, he could only confirm that the new information had cast a very different light on the picture. "I want a stadium probably more than anyone else," he said, dropping in his standard line. "But I'm not going to ask the taxpayers to pay for it."

Yes, the trouble with the whole thing, said the man who had thrown it to the press in the first place, was that there has been too much publicity and too little action. For all he knew, he added, with a keen eye for the headline, the plan might very well be another "paper tiger."

After he had taken a couple of days to digest Warner's report, he resurfaced long enough to pronounce the plan "far from perfect." "I am trying to learn, finally, if everybody really means what they have been saying, and if everybody is really talking about the same plan that's been presented to me."

That's all. The Governor had left himself in a position where he was able to jump in any direction without moving. The Governor's words were, as always, impervious to attack because he hadn't really said anything. I see a great future for that man in American politics. The White House itself is not completely out of the question.

Sooner or later, of course, he was going to have to move off dead center. The moment came, appropriately enough, during the celebration of the birthday of George Washington. In the Great Commonwealth, there has always been the lovely custom of throwing the doors of the State House open on Washington's Birthday for any of the citizens and freemen who have been a-lust all through the year to shake the Governor's hand. The Great Commonwealth was celebrating Washington's Birthday on February 16, beating the rest of the country to that honor by a whole year. The Governor took the occasion to announce that he was going to get to the bottom of the stadium proposition once and for all, by holding private meetings the next day with, consecutively, Dr. Walsh, Jack Warner, me, and Billy Sullivan. I was down for 11:45. Considering that I was such a notorious liar, the Governor greeted me quite generously. With photographers and everything. I could see right away that he liked me. He liked me so much that he asked not one question about the financing. Or, for that matter, about anything else. My friend the Governor simply told me how happy he was that I had made my proposal and urged me to persevere. It was up to me and him, he said gravely, "to pull the chestnuts out of the fire" —how can I ever forget such a colorful phrase?—and save the Patriots for the football fans of the city.

"That's just the way I feel," I told him. "That's why I did it."

Once the meetings were over, the Governor was asked whether he now thought we were all talking about the same plan. "Very much more so than a week ago," he said.

That looked like a breakthrough. Or did it? Well, maybe yes . . . and then again, maybe no . . . and then again, maybe. "This thing has been a comedy of errors for years. This is why I'll take until next week to study all the information given me today before I make an announcement of my position."

All we wanted from him, you understand, was permission to run the extra days.

At the end of the week, he announced that he'd need another week to complete his studies. "We're trying to make the plan work," he said. "The figures," he said, "are difficult to work out." What figures he was talking about were never quite revealed. Whatever plan finally emerged, it was clear, was going to be the Governor's.

The plan, as it emerged, was the very same plan we had started with three weeks earlier. Same plan exactly; same figures exactly.

The announcement was scheduled for noon on Saturday, February 28, and so the office was empty except for Rudie, Nick, and myself. We had prepared two press releases, one of them expressing our delight and the other our regrets. When the bulletin came over the radio that the Governor had approved, Rudie Shaffer looked at me with the closest thing to distaste that I have ever seen on his amiable accountant's features. "Congratulations, Champ," he said. Whereupon I, in an instinctive gesture of triumph and pride, put my fingers to my forehead and went, "Bang."

Joy reigned, it could be said, restrained.

There was no longer the slightest chance, you must understand, of running the extra days before our regular meet started. Nor, since we still didn't know when our harness meet was going to be run, did we have the slightest idea where we could put them afterward. The logical place would be at the tag end of the meet. If we did that, we'd be breaking the spirit of our agreement with Rockingham. The other possibility was to run an isolated twelve-day meet. The likelihood of filling our stables for a twelve-day meet completely surrounded by nothing was, to put it as optimistically as possible, remote.

I'm not going to cop any pleas here. Whatever troubles I had brought down upon my head were richly deserved. I should have known that nobody is more suspect than the selfless benefactor. When a guy like me who has been running around for years calling himself a cheap hustler offers to do something for nothing, people are going to be looking for your angle.

I had told Jack Warner at the beginning, and I kept telling everybody to the end, that under no circumstances was I going to put my head into the political Mixmaster. Quite frankly, I didn't care any more whether they built the stadium or not. My only concern was that if the proposal didn't go through, there would always be the suspicion that I had misled everybody about the financing; in which case I would carry a sign across my chest distressingly reminiscent of the Big A they used to place upon unmarried young ladies who had tasted of unsanctified pleasure. My sign would read: CHEAP HUSTLER & FOURFLUSHER.

Fortunately, I did not want for the opportunity to set the facts straight. Wherever I went to speak, the first of my interrogators was sure to ask, in the sly, conspiratorial manner of a man who wanted me to know that he was no more of a fool than I was, "Well, yeah, but isn't the state really putting up the money?" As patiently as possible, I would explain that if we didn't run the races there wouldn't be any tax money. And that zero tax money wouldn't build any stadium or educate any children or feed any hungry people. "I have merely tried to create a philosophy for raising the money," I would say. "Beyond that, I am not, nor will I permit myself to be, involved. Where they put the stadium, how they build it, I couldn't care less."

That doesn't really seem to be so difficult to understand, does it? And yet the accusation that I was trying to put over a fast one followed me to the end. Even after the stadium was voted down, the *Globe* and the *Christian Science Monitor* maintained their First Amendment rights to be stubbornly, constantly, and fanatically wrong by savaging me all over again for having tried to trick the taxpayers into thinking that we were going to be paying for a stadium which they would be paying for themselves. In a classic example of unconscious prejudice, the *Monitor's* City Hall man wanted to know why the money wasn't being used to build a $20-million vocational high school "that would do so much in training black and Puerto Rican teen-agers." All right, I can understand that the *Monitor* wouldn't go for the idea of building a pre-med school

for black and Puerto Rican teen-agers, but is a school of science completely out of the question?

What $20 million, though? Now that we didn't have the dates, where
was the money going to come from? It's like Toots Shor says: If you're
sober at noon, you're not trying. If you can't bring yourself to understand that you can't hatch any chickens by sitting a hen on a rock, you're
not trying. And if you're not trying it's because you don't want to.

Before it was over, you could have shaken me awake in the middle
of the night and I would have said, "I have merely tried to create a
philosophy . . ."

I did have an angle before it was over. My angle was to prove that
I had no angle. I was in a position where I was going to have to fight
to become a public benefactor, whether they liked it or not.

Whether I liked it or not, all I was going to get for it was abuse.
"Veeck has cast himself as the injured innocent, done in by wily, evil
politicians," said the Worcester *Telegram*. "What nonsense! He is a
smart, engaging, aggressive individual—a match for any politician who
ever lived." Which puts Talleyrand in his place very nicely.

And all I could look forward to when my machinations were done was
extra work for myself and my merry men. My merry men were growing
more mutinous by the day. Every time I saw Rudie, he would look at
me with disbelief and very slowly shake his head.

The Boston City Council has nine members, only eight of whom saw
themselves as the next mayor. Fifteen days remained before the NFL
meeting was to open in Hawaii. That didn't panic them. Nine days
slipped by before the hearings began. They didn't get around to voting
until the NFL meeting was over.

Mrs. Hicks had promised to hold an open hearing in Neponset. By
some failure in communication, undoubtedly unintentional, she scheduled her hearing for the same night the leading civic organizations of
the community were holding a mass meeting of their own to hear Jack
Warner present his case. Mrs. Hicks had badly underestimated the
people she was dealing with. The civic organizations had bright, young
leaders who suspected, although I can't imagine why, that she was
going to pack her hearing with shills. Mrs. Hicks was promptly advised
that the reputable Neponset organizations were not going to lend
themselves to her "horror show" and, further, that the kindest thing she
could do for them would be to leave them alone. The Neponset hearing
was canceled.

The City Council's own horror show degenerated into a two-week, two-way political war on Kevin White. The Governor had ended his proclamation on a ringing note of self-affirmation. "I now await formal city approval of this plan. I want a stadium built and I stand ready to do my part to build it." Loosely translated, that meant the onus was going to be on the Mayor if he couldn't get the formal approval of the City Council. It also meant, as we eventually discovered, that he was going to get it over the Governor's dead body.

The Governor's fine hand showed through when the general manager of the MBTA, one Leo Cusick, came in, out of the blue, to inform the council that nobody had told Warner the Transit Authority was going to build a station at the stadium, as Warner had been claiming.

Warner shot back that both Cusick and his superior, Robert C. Wood, had told him they would, specifically and unequivocally. Warner contacted Wood in London over the weekend and came back with the word that Wood had confirmed their understanding and had promised to testify to that effect when he returned to Boston the following week. Cusick called a press conference a couple of days later to announce that he had contacted Mr. Wood in Copenhagen and could assure them that Mr. Wood would be telling the council on his return that the station was not going to be built.

Wood came back and testified—with some care—that he wouldn't build the station unless it was necessary to build it. "We are a transportation agency," he said. "We will be responsible for adequate transportation to and from the stadium."

A tempest in a teaspoon of no consequence whatsoever except for the confusion that was created in the battle for public opinion. There already was a rapid-transit station only three blocks away. Cusick's story was that they had only agreed to run buses from the station to the stadium. Wood's version was that he had promised to either run the buses or build the station, according to the needs of the situation. When it came right down to it, you could live without either the station or the buses. Fenway Park is just about the same distance from the nearest subway station, and Red Sox fans have been taking that little walk for decades. You walk about as far in some stadiums after you park your car.

But Jack got stubborn about it. The subway station was in his plan, he had been promised that he was going to get it, and there was nothing I could do to convince him that he should let the darn thing drop. But, then again, how could he? To drop it would have seemed like an admission that it had been he who had lied.

As charge and countercharge followed each other across the headlines in succeeding days a cloud was cast over the more essential items of his plan. The Boston *Globe* ran a story under the headline: BOND MEN PESSIMISTIC ON BRA STADIUM PLANS. Any reader who was interested in slogging though the not necessarily intriguing details of a financial story would have found that every man quoted by name was, on the contrary, more than optimistic. Any reader who had the fortitude to make it almost to the end would have come across a key paragraph which read: "None of the experts doubted that $16 million in bonds could be sold. Two persons called that sum 'peanuts.' "

To save what was left of my good name, I found myself propagandizing more and more openly for the passage of the bill, even while I was insisting that I would have no part of anything that smacked of politics. I was not only wining and dining politicians at the track but—heaven help me—I was seeking them out. (The horses weren't running yet, but there were always special shows—like the Book Show, or Automobile Show—going on. When the shows were on, the bar was open, and when the bar was open, the pols were hanging around.) And then came one of those wayward, unpredictable episodes that are so far removed from the mainstream of an event that they can only be looked back upon, with wonder, as a kind of bewildering footnote. A fluke. Into the Paddock Club, in the middle of all this controversy, came a Cleveland attorney named Bill Krause, who was a friend of Nate Dolin's and, therefore, mine. And who was his luncheon companion on this auspicious occasion but that estimable lady herself, Louise Day Hicks. How Krause knew her, I never asked. What their business was, I never knew. I am not a prying man by nature, and I had my own fish to fry. Not for years had I tapped such resources of my undoubted charm; never had I taken such a personal interest in the cuisine. Need I say that she left me with her solemn word that she was solidly behind me and the stadium? Need I say that I thought, in momentary exhilaration, that I had saved the day? Need I say that she marched into the council chambers a couple of days later and helped to kill it?

Why? The councilmen were swapping an old dump for a brand-new municipal stadium, that was all it came down to. It was costing the city nothing. On the contrary, a football franchise is worth millions to a city in cold cash. There was nothing in it for them, though, so they didn't care. As far as they were concerned, it was far better to have no team than to lose an opportunity to play the favorite local game known as "Get the Mayor!"

A classic example of the contempt in which they hold the people, to say nothing of the legislative process itself, came in the midst of the brouhaha about the subway station, when the first five councilmen to arrive in the chamber happened, by the sheerest chance, to be the five members who comprise the Legislative and Home Rule Committee. Three of those members were Mrs. Hicks, Joseph F. Timilty, and Gerry O'Leary, who, also by sheer coincidence, comprised the hard core of the anti-White coalition. All, by no coincidence at all, were ambitious to succeed him. Joseph F. Timilty is not the son of the Joseph Timilty who was once the Police Commissioner of Boston. He's his nephew. The name is good enough. The old Joe Timilty was Joe Kennedy's closest friend and his personal envoy to Boston politics, a role which in itself had made him perhaps the most powerful behind-the-scenes figure in the state. Joseph F. had distinguished himself in the early going by suggesting that the money from the twelve days would be far better used to save the parochial school system. Gerry O'Leary had been a great schoolboy halfback in Boston and he might very well have been an All-American at Holy Cross if he hadn't developed an unfortunate habit of breaking his leg. The chairman of the committee was John L. Saltonstall, who everybody seemed to think was the son of Ex-Governor and- Senator Leverett Saltonstall, although he was, in reality, his cousin. No matter. His name did him no more good in Boston politics than Teddy Kennedy's. Although Saltonstall was cut from a somewhat different bolt of cloth from his three colleagues—he had begun his career as a civil-rights attorney, for one thing—he had dreams of being hit by the same bolt of lightning. John L. Saltonstall (*not* the son of Leverett and no kin whatsoever to John L. Sullivan) thirsted to become mayor of Boston.

Say this for Mrs. Hicks. She was traveling under her own steam and on her own abilities, without resort to either a famous name or a football helmet.

To while away the time while they were waiting for their more lackadaisical colleagues to show up, Saltonstall was prevailed upon to call his committee into session so that he could accept Timilty's motion to substitute South Station for Neponset as the site for the stadium. It carried by a vote of 3–2. Having allowed the vote, which he knew was stacked against White, Saltonstall had piously voted against it.

"Neponset is a bad site," Timilty announced. "It's not centrally located." Neponset was all of two miles south of the center of the business area; on a clear day it takes you about five minutes to get there. They're worried that the twelve days won't raise enough money for a $16 million stadium and so they're moving it to a central location where the land alone, according to the earlier studies of the site, was going to cost them about $30 million.

The whole thing was a charade. The vote was no more than the expression of five councilmen who happened to be in the same room at the same time. The people in the know snickered that although Timilty had made the motion, Mrs. Hicks had been calling the tune. The South Station site had been up before the legislature for a vote during the previous mayoralty campaign, and White had been all for it. He had wanted the stadium, and that was the only site under consideration. Although the situation was altogether different now, Mrs. Hicks was putting herself in a position where she would be able to say, *Aha, you were all for it as a campaign issue, but now that I'm proposing the same thing you suddenly call it a fraud.*

These people don't care. The stadium was worth millions to the city in revenue. And they play their games and thumb their noses.

Out-of-all-fairness note: Do not permit me, in my righteous indignation, to mislead you. The political opposition had a substance which bit deeper than any pure jockeying for position. By which I mean that some of the legislators who stepped out quickly to oppose the Neponset site felt that their ambitions ran parallel to the wishes of the people they represented. The issue which had rent the Democratic party in half can be defined very neatly by telling you that Mayor White was commonly being referred to during those days as Mayor Black. Taken in that context, the issue of preserving a lower middle-class-residential area from an incursion of outsiders (which in this case seemed to be an incursion of Sunday traffic) had a powerful subliminal appeal. The words themselves were enough to touch off other and realer fears. By the time they discovered that the local opposition was as small as it was noisy it was too late for any of those politicians who might have wanted to change their position to backtrack. Stuck as they were with a bad case and minimal support, there was little for them to do except raise the level of their demogoguery.

All the while they were playing their games, the NFL was watching from Hawaii. Calls were going back and forth between Billy Sullivan and his lawyer every night, and the NFL was pushing back its own action day by day. In the end, the football people threw up their hands and appointed a three-man committee to study the situation. No thanks to the pols, Boston still had a football team.

Once it had become clear that the NFL wasn't going to rescue it, the City Council finally got around to the business of voting. It started by voting 5–4 to transfer the site back to Neponset. And then it killed it, 7–2. Three of the public servants apparently preferred to vote against Neponset rather than against any place else. Before they killed it off, though, they all went scrambling around to post some goodies on the record for their constituencies. Thomas I. Atkins was the Negro member of the council. He had been the fourth irreconcilable opponent of the stadium from the beginning, not because of any vendetta with Mayor White but because he loathed the BRA and anything it was involved in, from the previous regime. Mr. Atkins, who was ambitious to become the first black mayor of the city, had presented an alternative proposal containing such highly constructive innovations as reserving a minimum of 8000 seats per game at $1 a ticket for low-income citizens.

In as pathetic a performance as you are ever likely to see, Saltonstall met the issue head on by being both for and against the stadium at every turn. He had opened the hearing that final day by moving that both the city and the state make new studies of both the South Station and Neponset sites, which would have easily taken the thing into 1984. After he had cast his vote with the majority on the conclusive tally, he moved for reconsideration of the vote, carefully explaining for the record that although he had not been able to vote for the plan in its present form, he might be able to vote for it after his proposed studies had been submitted. Needless to say, he was outraged when the motion was defeated again. "By a slick parliamentary maneuver the council was prevented from voting for a stadium plan containing safeguarding amendments necessary to protect the public interest," he cried. He was so angry at his opponents for refusing to give him his study that he had found it necessary to vote their way.

On such a note as that, the Neponset stadium came to an end.

The stadium didn't.

I should have taken E. M. Loew more seriously. Billy Sullivan had been back from Hawaii only a day when the City Council took its vote, and yet the word was already trickling around, and with a tone and persistence that had to be given credence, that the Patriots would be going to Foxboro. To give myself credit where credit is due me, Billy Sullivan told me, personally and in a couple of letters, that he wanted to thank me for coming up with the proposal when I did, because otherwise he would have gone to Hawaii empty-handed and the franchise would undoubtedly have been moved. I can also state without fear of contradiction—and if I am, I'm going to state it anyway—that I gave E. M. Loew, that shrewd and crafty old man, the idea of attaching the stadium to a racing operation.

With no cost for the land, Loew built his stadium—a replica of the stadium we had on the boards—for just about the $10 million Warner had projected. The critics who had been screaming that Warner's figure had been a wild underestimate were strangely silent.

The critics who had been saying that if it was so good why didn't private enterprise go ahead and build it weren't altogether wrong. They weren't altogether right, either. The shrewd and crafty old man set up a Stadium Realty Trust and offered bonds to the public.

Boston lost some part of its football team. The Boston Patriots had become the New England Patriots, and their dateline reads: Foxboro, Mass. Foxboro, you will remember, lies about twenty miles south of Boston.

Neponset still has its dump. Citizens wending their way home on soft summer evenings can view it as they drive past and oh, how their hearts must leap with gratitude as they contemplate its broad, sweeping lines and understand that there, save for the vigilance of their elected officials, might have stood a great, loathsome, unsightly football stadium.

15

The Third Wheel

The night before our grand opening, we threw a press party at the
Logan Motel for the girl jockeys. The television cameras were there.
The out-of-town press was abundantly represented. Every woman
writer in town must have been there. But only one Boston sportswriter
showed. Larry Claflin, the columnist for the *Record American*, came
purely as a social gesture. I knew Larry from the old days when he was
traveling with the ball club. The coverage in the Boston papers was nil.
I was beginning to have the feeling that somebody was trying to tell me
something.

The third wheel in the network, meshing very nicely with the interlocking ownerships and the politicians, is the press.

Much as it pains me to say this, it should be obvious to any student
of civic affairs that nothing is permitted to exist to the detriment of a
major city unless the press is either blind, incompetent, or corrupt. To
put it succinctly, no city could build up such a sweeping tradition of
political corruption unless the press was a partner.

Back in 1954 a scandal of sorts broke around Boston sportswriters
when an investigation by the Providence *Journal* revealed that a large
number of sportswriters and other newspapermen were on the payrolls
of the racetracks in a "public-relations" capacity. Many writers in fact

were on the payrolls of more than one track. Not only that. The same investigation discovered that ten reporters were on the State House payroll. So you had a situation where a rewrite man was writing publicity releases for a State office and submitting them to his own news desk, which then, of course, handed them right back to the rewrite desk. At the time the publisher couldn't see anything wrong with that. Two of the publishers declined to comment on the situation at all. Indeed, the *Journal* went on to reveal that Dave Egan, the leading sports columnist and a brilliant writer, was a bagman of sorts for Rockingham Park. Scandal means that when the word got around town everybody shrugged his shoulders and said, "So what else is new?"

I don't know what a check on the various payrolls would reveal today. What difference does it make? A newspaperman doesn't have to be on a payroll, any more than an amateur has to accept a check. I would doubt very gravely whether any of the writers were aware that they were being listed back in 1954. I would also doubt that their employers anticipated that an out-of-state reporter was going to come prying. They certainly didn't have to worry about the Boston papers. The practice of permitting political reporters to work for governmental agencies had been going on for forty years with the full knowledge and consent of their publisher and editors.

I do know one thing. In due course of time the franchise for handing out the publicity jobs at the State House was given to a former political reporter. For his services as broker, he took only a 50-per-cent kickback. Nothing unreasonable about that. The work, after all, was guaranteed not to tax the talents of the publicity men overmuch, and the expenses attendant to serving as go-between may have been considerable.

What we have demonstrated so far is a tight interlocking relationship between the tracks and the newspapers, and between the politicans and the newspapers. Not to leave the circle unclosed, the same interlocking relationship existed between the tracks and the politicians. Scores of public officials ranging from legislators to tax assessors were on the payrolls for salaries totaling well over $150,000. On top of that, or underneath it, the politicos had always been permitted to "sponsor" worthy constituents for track jobs paying a minimum of $1 million in salaries, and that's the best kind of patronage a politician can have.

And that's just what could be determined by calling the track operators and the politicians themselves. The tip of the iceberg.

Our field of interest here is going to be limited to the relationship between the sportswriters and the track. The full journalistic picture has been sketched in only as a backdrop against which to present the smaller picture. Where the newspapers themselves are so tightly allied to high political officials, where the news desk is so openly on the payrolls of the very public agencies it is supposed to be patrolling, the sports desk, which is after all only the toy department of a newspaper, is not likely to undergo any spiritual crisis before it decides to play the same game with equally eager—or equally vulnerable—sports promoters.

I was told by countless people that you had to play the game. I was informed through friends of friends that, considering the rewards to be had, the sum involved was negligible. I was urged by the wise guys not to be so stiff-necked about it. I mean, I was acting like it was my own money or something. Dave Haber, who was still on the Suffolk payroll, mentioned to Realty Equity that he kept hearing we weren't treating certain segments of the press in the manner to which certain segments of the press had become accustomed, and that once this lamentable oversight was rectified—discreetly, of course—we would see quite a change. I was never approached directly with either a request or a demand for a pay-off, to clear that up, although—as we shall see—it came about as close to that as it's possible to get. Always it was done through indirection and innuendo. Rumor had it, it seemed that the other tracks in the area handled things a little differently, a little more sympathetically.

There were even intimations that we wouldn't have to soil our hands by dealing with the turf writers directly; the practice that had evolved —rumor had it—was to pay a sports editor or someone and let him take care of everybody who needed taking care of. The strange thing about it—or maybe it's not so strange—is that when somebody comes in to challenge a corrupt system, there is an instinctive reaction on the part of everybody who knows about it to rationalize the corruption. To explain it away. The justification was that racing is a pari-mutuel sport. The temptation for the underpaid turf writer to bet is so strong, it seems, that it is only fair for the track to subsidize it.

Well, I won't pay for coverage. I have too much pride in my ability to run a good operation. It's as simple as that. To the writer-on-the-take, alas, it's every bit as simple. Where corruption runs so deep, an odd but perhaps inevitable reversal of values sets in. If everybody is corrupt, nobody is corrupt. It's just the way things are, and since there is always a tendency to accept the way things are as the way they are supposed to be (especially if you are profiting by it), I was looked upon as an outlander who had come into their town with a phony reputation as a guy who knew his way around. I mean, I was a terrible disappointment to them.

Now, I want to be very careful about a couple of things here. I want to be careful, in the first instance, not to present myself as a knight in shining armor. I am more than willing to woo the writers. I'll woo 'em with gifts, given an appropriate occasion, and I'll woo 'em by making their surroundings as comfortable and luxurious as possible, and I'll woo 'em with charm. As Christmas presents—when I still had a few bucks to play with—I sent out huge meat platters to all the newspapermen and radiomen and TV-men in town. Attractively packaged and with about ten pounds of beef tenderloin on top. Those who didn't have families were sent beautiful little television sets. To make the gift as memorable as possible, I used that old gag of sending them out on Thanksgiving, so that ours would be the first gift that was received. When the first day of spring came up dark and overcast, I sent flowers to all their wives along with a card which said: *We just thought this might brighten up the first day of spring a little bit for you.*

I also want to be careful to define both the players and the field of play. When I speak of vulnerable promotions, I am not speaking of the baseball, football, hockey, or basketball teams, all of which are given massive coverage on a daily basis. Where the big, respectable sports are concerned, there is a continuing and almost insatiable public appetite that has to be fed. I am referring to the slightly disreputable sports, like boxing and wrestling and, more recently, the roller derby, which are totally dependent upon an infusion of publicity focusing upon a particular event at a particular time. Boxing promoters have always paid off. Openly and gladly. The sight of boxing writers lined up for the pay-off before and after a fight was a familiar sight back in those pre-TV days when boxing was still a full-time business. If I had found myself promoting fights instead of horseraces, I'm not so sure I'd have thought twice about it. That was the way things were in my own experience. I knew most of the writers who were taking and in one instance I knew, and loved, the writer who had been given the job of passing the money out. You couldn't tell me they weren't good people. You couldn't tell me they were corrupt. I mean, that's the way it's done, right? It's all part of the game, right? If it wasn't worth it to the promoter, he wouldn't be paying, right? And, anyway, it all comes off the top. Right . . . ?

We're all hypocrites, and certainly include me in, that's all I'm saying. And if you don't think so, you're kidding yourself.

Having fallen off my horse and dirtied my armor, I shall now remount and ride on as if nothing had happened. The difference between pari-mutuel racing and those other vulnerable sports is that racing is a continuous operation with a corps of regularly assigned writers. The similarity was that we were considered to be equally—and perhaps even more—disreputable. The operators of the tracks had never been able to shake themselves loose from the attitude that they were operating on the tolerance of the better elements, an attitude which goes back to the initiating of racing in New England, when it had been necessary to pussyfoot past the church.

The Wonderland Factor comes very strongly into play here. As I have said repeatedly, the dogs came first. Wonderland wrote the law, Wonderland had the power, and Wonderland set the policy and the tone. As a basic strategy, it did not seek publicity, it discouraged it. It accepted the fact that it was disreputable. It acted as if it was on the lam. Under those circumstances, the most favorable press it could conceive of was the bare minimum necessary to let the customers know it was in town. Dick Johnston's main job, as publicity director, was to keep Reynolds' name out of the paper, and we know how well he succeeded. Wonderland was willing to pay to keep its existence a secret, on the theory that (1) if you didn't mention it too much, nobody would pay any attention to it, and (2) if anything embarrassing did come up, Wonderland would be in a position to keep it from being written about.

A policy born of discretion had been able to linger on through the years because of the very nature of dog racing. Nobody would have been assigned to cover Wonderland anyway. Dogs are essentially uncoverable. I mean, how do you report a dog race? A horse at least has a jockey. A trainer. An owner who either has impressive bloodlines of his own, or is a scuffler who has been able to beat the bluebloods at their own game. There is an aura of wealth and hedgerows around the clubhouse. There is a history that goes back to antiquity. It is even possible to give a horse a personality if you work hard enough at it and don't let anyone too near the horse. And because there are human beings involved in the running, a horserace has a strategic pattern.

Playing the dogs is like shooting crap in a bowling alley. The announcer says, "There goes Swifty," a mechanical rabbit is let loose on a rail which runs around the inner circumference of the track, and eight dogs come jumping out of their box and into a sharp turn, where they go bumping and skidding and sprawling until they finally straighten out and run a race. If nobody bumps, the favorite is probably going to win. Some dogs just run faster than other dogs.

Although there are no fouls—how do you lodge a foul against a dog?—they do have stewards, and that's a job where it helps to have a college education. Before every race, the stewards inspect the entries. If each of the entries has four feet, more or less, they can feel pretty safe in deciding that it's a dog all right.

Wonderland, with its insignificant overhead, had prospered mightily without publicity. Suffolk Downs, which was constantly in trouble, had dutifully gone along. First out of fear, and then because of an instability brought on by a constantly changing ownership, and finally because with Linsey calling the shots Suffolk Downs was pretty well under wraps.

The only racing entrepreneur who thought publicity could be helpful was Lou Smith, and even with him it came more from a desire to remove the stigma of his calling than to attract people to the track. He went out and built himself an image, and then lived up to it, before the word had been coined, as Uncle Lou, the friend of all mankind. Everybody in Boston knew that Uncle Lou was a philanthropist and humanitarian because Dave Egan, who wrote about Uncle Lou often and glowingly, kept telling them so. Egan's contribution to all the track operators whose payrolls he graced was to depict them as men of World Class decency with an almost excessive instinct for charity.

So there you have the irony of it. The other tracks were paying without any particular desire for or expectation of publicity. I went after it shamelessly. I was always around. I was, as best I could, making news. As a result, I certainly got more personal publicity than any of my predecessors at Suffolk Downs. But the track, as a track, didn't. On a daily basis we received less coverage than the out-of-state tracks. And when it came to the conflicts, some of the turf writers always seemed to be far more interested in the welfare of Rhode Island and New Hampshire.

Sports coverage has to be divided into three distinct sections: the turf writers, the sports editors, and the general sportswriters and columnists.

The turf writers, the men assigned to the track on a daily basis, had been chosen with strict regard for the undercover nature of their work. Sam McCracken had come into the press box originally as the teletype operator for the *Globe*'s old handicapper, Eddie Welch, had inherited the job upon his death, and in due time had been given a teletype operator of his own. On-the-job training, I guess, but in his case he had learned the job well, and I was personally fond of him. Gerry Sullivan had been the teletype operator for Norman Charlton, the *Herald Traveler*'s handicapper, and had taken over the job when Charlton wangled himself a job as a steward. The *Record American* has two handicappers. Bob Waldo is the turf writer. Dave Wilson is the **** 4-star Special ****.

None of them are reporters in the usual sense of the word, that's the important thing. They are handicappers. As an extra duty, they were awarded the job of writing up an account of the day's races, and that's exactly how they treat it. As an extra duty. The way they handle it, from everything I could gather, is to watch just the feature race and tell their readers how it was run, pretty much the same information that could be found in the comments under the *Morning Telegraph* chart of the race which is printed in all their papers.

The handicapping took them almost no time at all. An hour if they were in a hurry to get out of there, two hours if they wanted to dawdle. We maintained an index file of the past peformances of all the horses; when the entries came out, all they had to do was pull the cards. If the entries came in a little late because we were trying to put together the best possible card, their moaning was enough to rend the hardest heart. Their favorite subject was that "quality racing" was the only way to draw more people to the track, and yet you'd have thought we were deliberately holding the entries back to spite them.

Maybe I have been spoiled. I had always found upon coming into a new city that the good writers are always looking for the kind of story that will expand their horizons, and, in the process, make themselves and their jobs more important to their newspapers. The romance of newspaper work had never, alas, entered my turf writers' souls. Anything that threatened to turn them into reporters was viewed as an intolerable imposition. After a big race it was even up to us to supply the quotes from the jockeys. I invited them to cover the luncheons with the horsemen, and not one of them was remotely interested. When Maffeo popped up as the hottest kid rider in the country, the only coverage he got was from the out-of-town writers. Here was a kid who lived in Boston, had broken big right under their noses, and was winning more races than any other jockey in the country. He was an Italian immigrant in a city where there was a large Italian population—yes, even larger than the Irish—and, on top of everything else, he was a colorful, ebullient, cooperative kid. His contract was owned by Dick DeStasio, who knew them all from way back and was doing everything he could to get his boy the recognition that was his due. Maffeo should have been a publicity bonanza for us. Not with our turf writers he wasn't. What they did with him was nothing.

The big disappointment, though, was in their complete indifference to the promotions. For while we didn't advertise most of them, it was always our fond hope to generate the feeling through the reporting of the events that exciting things were happening at old Sufferin' Downs. Since the turf writers weren't reporters, I could hardly blame them for lacking the sharply honed instincts of a reporter. It went beyond that, though. The turf writers viewed the fun and games as, at best, an unnecessary distraction and, at worst, an irritant. Whether you agree with our over-all philosophical approach or not, I don't see how it is possible to deny that the Joe Fan promotion was a good one. When you give a horse away under circumstances where anybody in the place could have won it, that's an excellent human interest story. When the winner turns out to be as appealing as ours did, you'd think it would be almost irresistible. It was reported, where it was reported at all, down at the bottom of their dispatches with the rest of the notes.

I want to be careful not to do anybody a disservice here. It wasn't that, being teletype operators, they didn't know racing. Eli Chiat, who is the chart-caller and sometimes writer for the *Morning Telegraph,* had been the teletypist for the *Record American* at Suffolk at one time too. But the *Telegraph* also had a feature writer at the track, Freddie Galiani in our first year and Nick Sanabria in our second, and they functioned as reporters who moved around the administration office and stable area interviewing people.

In most other cities, the turf writers are precisely that. Reporters. Not handicappers, reporters. When Steve Cady of *The New York Times* came in to cover a big race, he would check in with us in the front office, brief himself on the event, and then proceed to nose around for any conceivable angle that might be turned into a feature story. After he was through with us, he would head right for the stable area. When he came in to cover the Yankee Gold Cup, for instance, he discovered that the Don Meade, Jr., who was listed as a rider in one of the earlier races was not only the son of the man whom many horsemen consider to be the greatest jockey who ever lived but would be riding in his first race. Immediately he asked Nick to set up an interview. He turned out an excellent feature story on him, wholly apart from his report on the big race. Exactly the kind of story we had been trying to interest our turf writers in, with our usual lack of success. Our guys were content to either mention or not mention the riding debut of Don Meade, Jr., in their notes.

Cady isn't unique. The *Washington Post's* Jerry Strine operates the same way. He's not a handicapper, he's a reporter. A good reporter, about the best in the country, because he's possibly more knowledgeable about horses than Cady. The best coverage we got in New England was from the Providence *Journal-Bulletin,* whose track editor, John Aborn, came down frequently and always headed right for the back side to talk to the horsemen. The next best coverage came from about a dozen little weeklies around the Boston suburban area.

The one exception in the Boston press was Herb Ralby, an all-around sportswriter for the *Globe.* Ralby didn't come in that often, but when he did he was almost fanatical about chasing down notes in the jockeys' quarters and among the horsemen. Beyond that, he was always eager to sit down with me and dig into the intricacies of the various lawsuits. He functioned, in short, as a working reporter. So we lost him in the end. Like most of the Boston papers, the *Globe* was on a youth kick, and Ralby, who was approaching that age, was harassed into retiring. Which is a commentary, isn't it? Here you had the hardest worker in the Boston press corps, and they thought he was too old.

As far as the suits or the hearings were concerned, the turf writers didn't even want to hear about them. "Cityside will cover that," they'd say. You were left with the not necessarily conflicting impressions that (1) they were afraid that somebody at the paper would ask for a briefing and they would have to reveal their deficiencies and (2) they understood that other people on the paper might have a vested interest in the tone and texture of the reporting. And yet it was always quite interesting to me, I must say, that in the face of such a passionate disavowal of interest they were always so very conversant with the opinions and attitudes of Wonderland.

The suits were covered by the State House and court reporters, the same guys who normally covered the Attorney General's office. And, surprisingly enough, so were the commission hearings—when they were covered at all. It was perhaps not unnatural that the reporters always seemed to be huddled with the people they had been associated with for so long: the people from the AG's office and from the dog tracks.

On the whole, then, my relationship with the turf writers was the strangest and most unsatisfactory relationship I have ever had with any newspapermen. In the early days I would hustle back to the conference room after the races to lift a few glasses with them. As it became increasingly evident that we weren't achieving anything, that they resented me and everything that I was either doing or not doing, I just stopped going.

Which takes us to the sports editors. Sammy Cohen, the sports editor of the *Record American* is the most valuable man in town for anybody operating a racetrack. Sammy is what is known as a man of principle. When he's close to you he performs. Not just what he's going to do anyway, like a lot of guys. He goes all out. In his way, Sam Cohen is a great editor. He had saved the *American*, which was the afternoon Hearst paper before the merger, by conceiving the idea of replating the back page of the early edition, printing it on green paper, and converting it into a racing sheet—the Green Sheet—consisting entirely of handicappers. He then shipped the racing edition all over New England as well as to the track; all the way to Portland, Maine, and even up to Montreal. As a result, the *American* was able to hang on for years as the only major newspaper in the counry that was kept alive on circulation alone.

He also practically invented Dave Wilson, the premier handicapper in New England. Wilson had come up from Baltimore when racing came to New England, and almost immediately he became the only handicapper in the country to pick Bold Venture to win the Kentucky Derby. For thirty-five years, Wilson has remained the only handicapper who really counts. So much so that there is a lively local debate on whether he bets his own selections or holds out the good ones. (He is *not* the onetime handicapper, I hasten to insert, who once picked eight winners out of eight in the Green Sheet and, according to local lore, had eight straight losers at the track.)

At the same time Sam Cohen was saving the *American*, he was also beefing up the *Record*'s sports page so that it was the most significant part of the paper. From everything I have been told, he picked Dave Egan practically out of the gutter, dubbed him the Colonel, kept him reasonably sober, and fed him the subjects to write about. It is Sam Cohen who is generally given the credit for dreaming up the Uncle Lou image for Lou Smith, and he was most certainly the man who had Egan promote it. Sam has complete control over what goes into the paper, not merely because he's in the position to hand out the assignments but because he also handles the make-up and layouts himself. During the racing season you could count upon an almost weekly tribute to the virtues of Uncle Lou in Egan's column, and in season you could count upon equally moving tributes to the operators of Taunton and Raynham. Not to mention the boxing and wrestling promoters who were, when the occasion arose, well and affectionately mentioned.

It wasn't as a eulogist that Egan made his reputation, though. When it came to wielding the scalpel, he was right in there with the great journalistic surgeons of all time. Sam Cohen had recognized from the first that Egan possessed a rare talent for witty, cutting vilification and he picked the Colonel's targets for him with a virtuosity that made him the most controversial and widely read columnist in the city. The Colonel's feud with Ted Williams, for instance, was carried off so brilliantly that every time Ted threw a tantrum or went off on a hitting tear, half the city ran to see what the Colonel was going to say about him now.

Good writing can cover a multitude of sins, and in Egan's case it did.

When you come right down to it, Sam Cohen is more than just a great editor. He has all the nobler instincts of a promoter and, believe me, it takes one to know one. It has been his custom to advise and influence all the promoters in town, and he has always been particularly generous in taking the promoter of any new enterprise under his wing. Lucky they are to have him. He is, as I have said, a very, very valuable man to have on your side.

Suffolk Downs had been one of the lucky ones in the past, because Sammy was always very close to Joe Linsey. We got nothing from him. We were made to understand that nothing was what we were going to continue to get from him, which kind of made it an even deal. Well, not quite. I wouldn't want you to think that Sammy was bashful when it came to calling Nick for a table in the Paddock Club when his brother-in-law was coming to town. Nor would I want you to think I didn't grit my teeth and give it to him. I was being pure and noble, yes; I wasn't trying to start the Revolution.

The sports editor of the *Herald Traveler* was Cliff Sundberg, who was the only editor who was a hot racing fan himself. Sundberg is the kind of bettor who carries a black book around with him to record his wins and losses. A great patron of the horses and dogs. Unfortunately, I cannot say that he allowed his interest in racing to influence his editorial judgment where we were concerned. Early in the game he sent one of his writers, Bill Liston, to do a feature story on me. And that, pretty much, is where it ended.

A year or so later, one of the paper's feature writers came over to interview me for a series of profiles it was doing on all the sports executives in the city. A profile on Abe Ford, the wrestling promoter, appeared; a profile on Sam Silverman, the fight promoter, appeared; a profile on Dick O'Connell, the general manager of the Red Sox, appeared; a profile on Billy Sullivan appeared. I was supposed to complete the series. Very abruptly, the series was scrapped. Normally, you'd shrug your shoulders and say . . . well, things like that happen. The exigencies and vicissitudes of the business. We'd live. Except that Nick had received a call from an old friend deep in the bosom of the *Traveler*'s organization; an old friend who thought Nick just might be interested in knowing that the word had come down that they weren't supposed to use anything on Veeck. Why, he didn't know. "All I can tell you is that we got the word."

Under ordinary circumstances there wouldn't have been very much we could have done about that either, except to tuck it away in the Verrrrrry Interesting file. As it happened, though, we had an excellent *entrée* into the highest echelons of the corporation. The *Traveler* rented our premises, in conjunction with an independent operator named Jim Donahue, to put on four highly profitable shows; the Boat Show, the Automobile Show, the Trailer and Camping Show, and the New England Industrial Show. Donahue was also somewhat involved in the corporation's desperate but unsuccessful effort to save its television license —which really meant saving the newspaper itself.

Donahue, whom I always found to be a very decent guy, expressed total disbelief that anything as ridiculous as an embargo on little ol' me could possibly exist. To set our minds free on that score he vowed to find out what had really happened.

All that meant, as far as we were concerned, was that he was going to be coming back with some kind of a reasonable and logical explanation. We would still have the privilege of determining whether or not it was also a persuasive one. The only reason for doing the series in the first place, Donahue told us, was that the paper had wanted to build up

Abe Ford—why and for what, deponent knoweth not. It was scrapped, we were told, because Hal Clancy, the editor-in-chief, hated Billy Sullivan from some time in the deep, dead past when Billy hadn't played ball with him on something or other, and when he saw the profile on Sullivan he had blown his stack, pronounced the whole series stupid, and ordered that it be canceled on the spot.

Very persuasive. The only two things that were left unexplained was why a longtime employee was willing to risk his job because he was so anxious to tell Nick a lie, and how it was going to hurt Billy Sullivan, whose profile had already appeared, to cancel the profile on me.

For that matter, it also left unexplained why J. J. Smith, who had taken over the paper's gossip column while we were there, had used the first item Nick gave him and never used another. Harold Banks of the *Record American,* the most widely read gossip columnist in town, used almost everything Nick gave him plus a few stories he stumbled across himself. So they couldn't have been completely bereft of interest. But Hal Banks is his own man. His deal with his newspaper is that it is to keep its hands off his stuff, or he will take it across the street. You can make that kind of deal in a city which has three newspapers where only one can operate profitably.

The reference to Billy Sullivan up there reminded me how unfair it would be to leave the impression that Cliff Sundberg never mentioned me at all. During the final days of the City Council hearings, with the stadium proposal heating up to a vote, Sundberg led off his periodic column of quick notes by paying his respects to me, to wit: "Bill Veeck will come out smelling like a rose even if the stadium proposal goes down the drain. Suffolk's president is a promotional genius, no doubt about it."

Right on target, eh? The Old Conniver. I'd come out smelling, all right. Like all thirty tons. And all I was trying to do was to create a— ahhhh, forget it!

The *Globe* was somewhat different. Different—as in indifferent. Jerry Nason, the sports editor, is primarily a baseball man with a strong personal side interest in track. Track and Field, I mean. People-running. He ran a solid sports page, heavily oriented toward the traditional team sports and heavily weighted toward statistics.

An old-fashioned sports page in many respects. Harold Kaese, another old-line baseball man, could deal with the dispute between the jockeys and the horsemen by compiling a scrupulously researched piece pegged around Maffeo's income. His view of journalism simply did not run to writing a personality study of Maffeo himself. Well, that isn't fair; I don't know that. What it was, I think, was that writers like Kaese were uncomfortable about moving into an area they didn't know anything about. The only time I saw Ray Fitzgerald, another old-line baseball writer, except at sports affairs was when he asked me to appear in the *Globe*'s booth at the Sportsmen's Show. That was the night I spent with Ted Williams. Fitzgerald sat around with Ted and me for a couple of hours so that he could write a column on our conversation about trading ballplayers, and dropped me off later at Ted's hotel. If there was anything he could ever do for me, he said, all I had to do was holler. And he meant it. But there is always an unspoken agreement in this kind of thing, it seems to me, that I know the kind of story he'd be interested in and wouldn't embarrass him by hollering on something that was outside his line. He saw me as a baseball man, and his only interest in me was as a baseball man. But he was the only writer to defend me after I had fled the premises.

The lead columnists were, really, the only bright spot. Bud Collins of the *Globe*, Tim Horgan of the old *Herald Traveler*, and Larry Claflin of the *Record American*. Collins and Horgan could be classified as New Breed sportswriters, with far-ranging interests. The *Globe* had wooed Collins from the *Traveler* by allowing him to write himself a contract that gave him complete freedom to go where he wanted to go and write what he wanted to write. To England for the tennis matches; to Africa for a safari. Having lost Collins, the *Traveler* was so terrified at the possibility of losing Horgan that Tim had complete freedom too.

If Timmy knew the word was out at his paper not to use anything on Veeck, that would have been reason enough for him to come barreling out to do a column on me. If he didn't know about it, nobody there would have dared to tell him.

Both of them were at pains to set themselves apart from the seamier side of Boston sportswriting. Shortly after we sent out the Christmas presents, Bud Collins informed us that in keeping with his policy of never accepting a gift from anybody he might be writing about he had shipped the portable television set on to the Chelsea Naval Hospital. And when Tim Horgan asked me to speak before the Varsity Club at his alma mater, Tufts, it was only on the specific understanding that my acceptance would place him under no obligation to me in any way.

Unhappily, neither of them was race-oriented in the slightest. When they came to the track they were coming, if I may assume no false posture of immodesty, to write about me. Their interest was in the sociology of sports. They are not nuts-and-bolts men. As often as not when one of them did come out to the track, we'd get so caught up in solving the monumental global problems of the day that I'd blow the somewhat more manageable problem of implanting an idea that might get us some publicity.

Larry Claflin was a different breed of cat. Claflin is less cerebral and much more closely attuned to the controversial sports story and the swift, cutting jab. Being more of a streetcorner guy, he was at home on a racetrack. Like his colleague, Freddie Ciampa, he enjoyed grabbing a *Telegraph* and handicapping a few races. Because Larry had traveled with ball clubs, the relationship which sprang up between us could be likened, in some degree, to the camaraderie of the road. He was an all-around sports man, and he saw me as an all-around sports man. He did a couple of columns where we picked the Bowl games together. Things like that.

There was one other great difference between Claflin and his opposite numbers on the other papers. Larry didn't have anything like the ironclad contracts they had, and that meant he probably didn't have the complete freedom they had and most certainly didn't have the security. The *Globe* and the *Traveler* would have gone to almost any lengths to keep Horgan and Collins happy. Down at the *Record American*, the only man who had to be kept happy was Sam Cohen. Under what very well may have been difficult conditions, Larry Claflin gave us more coverage, and more favorable coverage, than any writer in the city.

The night before the running of the $200,000 Yankee Gold Cup, which was to become affectionately known in our front office as "Veeck's Folly," Mary Frances came up from Maryland and we threw a champagne dinner in the Paddock Club. At our table was a very small, very select group of writers and their wives—the writers who had, in my opinion, done everything they could to give us space under conditions where they knew they were not exactly endearing themselves to their editors. They hadn't put their careers on the line by any stretch of the imagination, I don't want to give you that idea. But they hadn't done themselves any good by any stretch of the imagination, either. I had invited them casually and individually, without telling them who else was going to be there. As far as that goes, we had never discussed the situation in those terms. But they could look around and see. They could have whatever pleasure might come from knowing that I re-spected and honored them, and that their wives were there to see it. I don't know whether the message got through, but it did seem to me that it was one of those fine, fine nights where everybody was walking free and easy inside himself.

But, you know, I think I did as much for them by giving them the opportunity for *not doing themselves any good* as they did for me. I had given them the chance to prove to themselves that they were not purchasable, and that's a very great thing indeed.

The venality of the Boston press offended me, something I would have thought to be impossible. Moral indignation is not my style. I'm more of a cynical amusement man. Listen, I'm not going to kid you. The angelic smile you see upon my face is pure acting. What I'm saying is this: The politicians are a pain in the neck because they keep you from doing what you're trying to do. But that's the nature of the beast. You study them as you might study any other species of predatory animal. You marvel at their behavior. If you cannot stand the sight of blood, you turn away. But you would no more assume a stance of moral indignation at anything they might do than you would condemn a wolf pack for swooping down upon a flock of sheep—or castigate the jackals who slip in to pick the bones. The sportswriters disturbed me for reasons which I came to see were very personal, and involving my relationship with my daddy; a relationship which had never been completely resolved, alas, while he was alive. My daddy was a sportswriter himself before William Wrigley plucked him from the Chicago *American*, when I was three years old, to make him president of the Chicago Cubs. I will tell you that my father was as honorable a man as ever lived, and you are entitled to take it as prejudiced testimony. But when I tell you that Judge Landis, that mountain of probity, always said that William Veeck was the most honest and honorable man he knew, you know that it has to be so. My daddy was a man of dignity. Not the false dignity that is a disguise for stuffiness. The true dignity that comes from a man's sense of himself and never questions any other man's right to follow where his sense of himself takes him. My daddy was the kind of dignified man who could build a championship team with the wildest, hardest-drink-ing, most rambunctious crew of ballplayers in the history of the Great Game, a crew which swaggered through the league in the daytime and rollicked through the dives and back alleys of Al Capone's Chicago at night. Hack Wilson, Grover Cleveland Alexander, Rabbit Maranville,

Charlie Grimm, Pat Malone, Rollie Hemsley. The names of blessed memory. A man's private life was his own affair as far as my daddy was concerned, just so long as he reported to the park every day in condition to play and didn't proselytize among the younger players. The players couldn't be blamed if the boss's fifteen-year-old son, coming of age in Prohibition Chicago, went trailing after them. Hack Wilson. Oh Lord, how I idolized that hard-living, wildly generous, freakishly built, beautiful man.

I cannot say that I was a son to gladden his life. My high-school career was so much fun that I had to be sent to Los Alamos Ranch School for the credits to get me into college, whereupon I turned my one year and a half at Kenyon College into one long, floating party. I can't say whether I would have straightened out eventually, either. The party came to an abrupt end at the beginning of my sophomore year when I learned that my father had been stricken by leukemia. I rushed home to find him on his deathbed, heavily drugged. It was too late to make amends.

The world had already turned over by then. Prohibition had ended. The market had crashed. The Depression had clamped down upon the country. I went to work for the Cubs as an office boy at $17 a week.

I am not going to lay myself down upon a couch and regurgitate my life. Dredged guilt is as self-indulgent—and, in the end, as forced—as false humility. I could hardly be unaware that, when viewed from the surface, I would seem to be as different from my daddy as it is possible to get. "How could as wonderful a man as Mr. William Veeck have had such a jerk for a son?" Donie Bush once cried out after I had plagued him unmercifully. *How could I be?* I could have cried back. *How could anybody be? I'm not the wonderful Mr. William Veeck. I'm only me. Crazy Bill. Look . . . at . . . me.* I didn't have to say a word, though, did I? I had him looking at me, all right.

And yet, I have always been dimly aware that I am only William Veeck's crazy son when the cameras are popping. When the lights go off, I'm William Veeck's dutiful boy. Belatedly. My father had always considered himself a newspaperman at bottom. His great ambition was to retire to a small town and run a paper of his own. I know that he never lost the self-educated man's awe for the world of knowledge that can be found between the covers of books. I have a compulsion to read. I have not spent a day of my life since his death without a book on my schedule. I know that I leap at any opportunity to write a sports column or a book review.

I knew my father as the operator of a baseball club. I became the operator of baseball clubs. He built championship teams and set attendance records. I set out to build championship teams and set attendance records. If there was a guiding principle in his relationship with his fellow men it was that nothing was insoluble if a simple sense of fairness was brought to the discussion by both sides. It would be a blatant lie for me to say that I am always honest, always honorable, always dependable. I'm not. If that's your definition of fairness, I don't qualify. Fairness is nothing more than equal opportunity as far as I'm concerned, because opportunity is everything. I will say for myself that I will go a long way to give a man his opportunity, and that once I have given it to him I will never take it away. I am constitutionally incapable of firing anybody, no matter how incapable he may have shown himself to be or how great the provocation. As long as he has the opportunity, I can always hope that a magical change will occur. These are the kind of similarities that can be compiled on a checklist; that make the point without breaking the skin. All they show, really, is that I took the part of his character that I could handle and went off in the opposite direction, where I knew I was outclassed. I have always known whose son I am, though, that's the important thing. Listen to Bill Veeck, the wise old man, talking: Because of the kind of work I have found myself in and a certain natural gregariousness I have a collection of friends and acquaintances which runs the gamut and spans the spectrum. Nowhere, ever, have I heard a son honor his father (and I am using the word in the Biblical sense) because his father was a rich and powerful man. I can tell you, though, and I have seen it over and over again, that their eyes moisten over and their voices crack in saying nothing more than "Well, you know how it was with my father, Bill. He was never much good at making money, but he was such a *good* man."

I know on those dark nights when I find myself suddenly and desperately alone and know the truth of myself that no matter what else I may be I am William Veeck's son. And that's a comforting truth to know.

What does being William Veeck's son have to do with my reaction to the Boston press? Just this. I can see that in whatever town I landed, I always gravitated—could it have been by anything except design?—to the same kind of honorable old sports editor. From Sam Levy in Milwaukee, who was supposed to be so tough and would give you the fairest of shakes if you were open and honest with him, to Warren Brown in Chicago and Gordon Cobbledick in Cleveland. Holy mackerel, if anybody had come into Cobbie's office and so much as *suggested* that it was possible to buy space on his sports page, Cobbie would have throttled him with his bare hands. I loved those honorable old men, and I can see now that the role I played with them was always that of the slightly fresh, somewhat irresponsible, but essentially goodhearted and hard-working young man whom they had to publicly chastise from time to time—out of honesty to themselves—without quite being able to hide the underlying note of affection or, even, the faint smile of indulgence. I can see now how I always manipulated them into the role of a stern but affectionate father who was forgiving me my transgressions.

When you come to the last roll of the dice, a whole string of memories are touched off. When you come to the last roll of the dice, there is unfinished business to be settled.

The venality of some segments of the Boston press disturbed me more than I cared to admit because it disturbed me on so many levels. The single thread that ran through all levels was that I *expected* better from sportswriters. I *expected* more from newspapers.

The whole thing came to a head in the coverage of the $200,000 Yankee Gold Cup. The richest race in history was going to be run in an area where there had never been a race worth more than $50,000. The coverage was . . . well, respectable. That's all. Nothing commensurate with the size or importance of the event. In answer to any suspicion that I might have been getting a little paranoiac about our press coverage by then, I'll quote Steve Cady of *The New York Times*. Knowing that he was going to be covering the race, Cady had been reading the Boston papers all week and he couldn't understand the paucity of publicity. Two days before the race, he checked in to catch the drawing for the post positions. His dispatch that first day reads as follows:

> This being Boston, Veeck's Gold Cup promotion has been having trouble keeping its headline above water in the local pages. Today's major sports headline announced yesterday's 4–3 victory by the Red Sox over Cleveland.
> The biggest [story] headlines the fielding problem of Ken (Hawk) Harrelson, the controversial slugger traded by the Red Sox to the Indians earlier this year. "The Hawk Lays Three-Run Egg," said the *Herald* referring to a misjudged drive that allowed three Boston runners to score.

In the *Globe*, it was " 'I'm the Goat,' Hawk declared," and "Hawk Really Pressing. Finishes Series 1 for 18." Stories about the Gold Cup were relegated to the bottom of the front sports pages.

The Red Sox were playing out in Cleveland, understand. My main concern in setting the date for our big race was that the Red Sox would be on the road. Far from being in a hot pennant race, they were going absolutely nowhere.

When all was said and done, we got more publicity out of town than we got in Boston. And even with that, the out-of-town representation was less than we were expecting. At the last minute, a half-dozen cancellations had come in. Now, you can interpret that either way. You can offer it as evidence that the race simply did not have that strong an appeal, or you can offer it as evidence that other out-of-town writers had been reading the Boston papers and coming to the conclusion that it couldn't be so very much after all.

The best coverage was in the trade paper, the *Morning Telegraph*. Tim Horgan came in for a pre-race column, and Larry Claflin wrote a column which began, "Bill Veeck promised big-league racing when he first arrived in our city a few months ago, and Saturday afternoon at Suffolk Downs Bill is going to show the racing world what he meant."

But Waldo's column on the day of the race was headed: RACING SCENE SHIFTS TO OL' ROCK JULY 4TH. The *Herald Traveler* went very little above its normal coverage, and the *Globe* made do with Sam McCracken's routine columns. After it was over, McCracken gave me a glowing personal review, which was swell for me but did not a thing to swell the attendance for a race that had already been run.

In anticipation of a glorious day, we had already announced a post-race champagne party for the owners, jockeys, writers, and assorted friends. I was standing at the bar, putting on a brave front which consisted mostly of trying to keep my eyes from glazing over, when Dave Wilson came sidling over to ask me, in his unaccustomed role of reporter, for my impressions of the day. An artistic success, I said. Greatest horserace I had ever seen. "In other words, I took a bath." He mentioned the lack of publicity. I observed that, in view of the caliber of the horses in the field, it did not seem that the turf writers who had been harping so relentlessly on the importance of attracting quality racing to

New England had felt impelled to put their mouths where our money was.

"I could have told you it was going to be a flop." He smirked. "You didn't use the right tactics. Maybe you ought to have a little talk with somebody who knows how racing news is handled on the papers around here."

Do you know what the worst thing that can happen to you after you have taken a financial bath is? It's to be smirked at over a fine-stemmed crystal glass filled with your own champagne.

16

Massacre Called Off on Account of Rain

One of the things I was determined to do for the second season was to develop a whole new approach to our advertising. Advertising is meant to do two things. To notify people who are interested, and to grab the attention of people who haven't been. Since we were working on a very short advertising budget, my grand design was to organize the new campaign around a catchy slogan. Something more catchy than "Post time: 1:30," which had been the extent of the previous regime's imagination, and somewhat more intriguing than "Have you seen what's up at Suffolk Downs?" the catchline we had been going with. The agency and I had collaborated on that, and even I didn't like it. The general theme I was working around was *How come you've never been to Suffolk Downs?* The trick was to put it in a way that would be unselfconscious, inviting, and titillating; and, on top of it all, express our disbelief that people could have been depriving themselves of so simple and inexpensive a pleasure. I put a lot of work in on it, and after I had jotted down a couple of dozen lines on a long sheet of paper, I threw them at Nick. As always, we were holding our conference in the various saloons we were hitting after my speaking engagement of the night. Nick would write down the ones that appealed to him on a cocktail napkin and stuff it into his pocket. In the morning, he'd throw the cocktail napkins, all balled up, onto Rudie's desk. "Last night's work," he'd say. "What do you think?" One of the lines he had jotted down for future consideration was, "You're kidding . . . you've never been to Suffolk Downs?"

We ended the night in a little restaurant-bar that was in a big shopping center built into the bottom of a hill. The restaurant was below street level. A creepy joint. One night we made the mistake of sitting at the bar, and the wind kept blowing our glasses away from us. The only thing to say for it was that it was the only place open in those particular environs that late at night. Even with that, the waitress came over, finally, to kick us out. "You're kidding," I said, in genuine surprise that it had become so late so early. And I could see the look in Nick's eyes.

On the way out he said, "I like that line. 'You're kidding.' I think it's what we're looking for. Try it on me again." So we sat down on the curb in front of the restaurant, and it was such a natural that no matter what inflection you put into it, it worked.

It was amazing what that slogan did for us. As often as not, the chairman of the program committee would work it into his introduction. "You're kidding," he'd say. "You've never been to Suffolk Downs? Well, we've brought Suffolk Downs to you. Bill Veeck." For people who would normally have been shy about just walking up and introducing themselves, it was the perfect icebreaker. Especially women. "I just love those commercials, Mr. Veeck," they'd say. "And I'm not kidding."

We printed up a raft of bumper strips with just, "You're kidding . . . you've never . . . ?" and a line drawing of our symbol, a waggish, fun-loving horse leering down upon it. We couldn't print enough of them. They were all over the city, and when Mike brought a batch of them home to Maryland they became the campy thing to have among the college crowd.

We did something else. Now that we had the time to sit back and collect ourselves, we worked out a promotion for every Saturday. Two of them were Special Events, the kind of theatrical extravaganzas that lent themselves naturally to our theater-on-the-turf. The others were pure fun.

My favorite? In perusing the kind of almanac that lists all the state birds and state flowers, I saw to my delight and amazement that the Massachusetts state bird was, of all things, the chickadee. Since I'm a pushover for that kind of trivia myself, there was nothing to do but let the world in on it—that share of it within earshot, at least—by running a Chickadee Handicap for the amusement and edification of our clientele. They might not be big winners at the track, but if they ever became contestants in a quiz show and were asked, "What's the official bird of the Commonwealth of Massachusetts?" they would be armed to the teeth. Instanter, I struck the Commonwealth Handicap, which had been my prime candidate for striking anyway, and renamed it the Chickadee.

You think of Chickadee, and who immediately comes to mind? At least it did to Bud Collins when we tried it on him at lunch one day. He made the right answer.

If you didn't say W. C. Fields, you had better go back and sharpen your weapons. It's impossible even to say "My little chickadee" without impersonating W. C. Fields. Or immediatley adding, "Yes, indeed."

We had a lot of fun. We gave away a lot of prizes.

Two lucky winners got themselves a cageful of chickadees. Actually, we couldn't get any chickadees. It turns out that they are a dirty, pugnacious little bird whom nobody wants around (not too dissimilar in several crucial markings, as any bird-watcher can tell you, from the green-fingered, slippery-tongued Boston politician), so we settled for parakeets, who kind of look more like a chickadee ought to look, anyway.

We presented two hundred life-size posters of W. C. Fields to the same person. We also had posters hung up all around the track and were more than willing for the customers to take them home at the end of the day as souvenirs.

Film clips from many of W. C. Fields's masterful expositions of the art of comedy were presented on our closed-circuit TV throughout the day.

We gave away:

A lifetime supply of fifty (50) certified W. C. Fields skimmers.

One case of W. C. Fields spirits. And because W. C. Fields never stopped at one case, yet another case of W. C. Fields spirits.

Also twenty cases of beer. Just the kiss of the hops . . .

Through great good fortune (ours, not the producer's) Mae West, the co-star of *My Little Chickadee*, the delicate little creature herself, had returned to the silver screen in a moving picture of calamitous proportions named *Myra Breckenridge*. Thus we were in the enviable position of being able to add to the day's festivities (ours, not the winner's) by handing out two (2) tickets to see the Reincarnation of Mae West. A loser may be defined as a guy who goes through life without winning anything except two tickets to *Myra Breckenridge.* Listen, it could have been worse. We could have given him ten.

Speaking of reincarnation, we hired a local actor, renowned far and wide for his remarkable impersonation of W. C. Fields—yes, indeed— to circulate among the crowd and do his stuff. He was also in the winner's circle for the trophy presentation. The announcement went: "Making the presentation in the featured Chickadee Handicap is A. C. Fields, a cousin of W. C. Fields. A. C. Fields is the brother of D. C. Fields; they are the current sparks at Suffolk Downs." Which is pretty bad, I know, but it was never what W. C. Fields said it was the way he said it.

On to the extravaganzas.

The single most famous race in the history of mankind is the chariot race from *Ben Hur,* a race which has stood up against all competition as the greatest moving-picture spectacle of both the small-screen and wide-screen eras. Why, then, I had asked myself upon first coming to Suffolk Downs, should I not rerun the race, in all its pomp and ceremony, in our 1969-type coliseum by the sea?

The problem was that the chariot business had come upon hard times in the past few centuries, what with union salaries and the invention of the Stutz Bearcat. A luxury item. An endangered species. The only living chariot I knew of was in residence at Caesar's Palace in Las Vegas, where it sat in solitary splendor to impress the tourists. Billy Weinberger, the president of Caesar's Palace, is an old friend of mine. Billy was able to tell me that his chariot had been built by the same superb craftsmen who had built the chariots for MGM's *Ben Hur.* He was also able to inform me that it had cost him something around $7500. Much, much too superb for my blood. Nothing looks lousier than a chintzy chariot race. The moviegoing public has become accustomed to take its chariot racing with a cast of thousands, and that meant we were going to need a bare minimum of five chariots. I heaved the heavy sigh reserved for Great Overpriced Ideas, and back it went to simmer on the back burner.

A year passes. It is a warm spring day in May. The threat of the horsemen's boycott has ended, but I still have not made up my mind whether to file suit against the Attorney General on the harness dates. I pick up the paper and see that MGM, beset as it is with financial difficulties, is going to auction off all its props, including, it says—a message from them to me—the chariots from *Ben Hur*.

I called Billy Weinberger again, and he got us off to a flying start by offering to give me his chariot in return for speaking at a charity affair he was running in Las Vegas. Even better, he checked out a friend of his who was going to be at the auction and passed on our instructions that he could go as high as $3000 a chariot and—as you never fail to add in these things, to warn people against doing anybody any favors—"maybe a little bit more."

I'll tell you, Billy's friend did some job. Apparently the chariots were knocked down separately. Charlton Heston, playing the role of a sentimental actor, bought his. Stephen Boyd (who wore the black) lost out for some reason or other (I guess he forgot to add the "maybe a little bit more") and he was kind of bitter at us. As it happens, he had the wrong villain. Some guy kept phoning us long-distance to tell us we had his chariot, the black one with a boar on it. Obviously, a nut. To shut him up, we finally agreed to check the auction number painted on the front of the chariot against our shipping order, and darned if he wasn't right. We arranged the first cross-country chariot exchange on a basis of you send us our chariot and then we'll send you yours. Billy's guy had picked up the other four for us for a total of $7600, just about what it would have cost us to have one made up new.

The fifth chariot I picked up myself. According to the Caesar's Palace press agent—and why should he lie?—theirs was an exact replica of Caesar's chariot; yes, boys and girls, that selfsame chariot which a clutch of silversmiths labored over twenty-four hours a day for three solid months so that Caesar would look like a sport when Cleopatra came sailing into the harbor on that fancy-shmancy barge of hers. The Las Vegas publicity people had a whole documentary worked out for the presentation ceremony. All the usual stuff: cameras, script, newspapermen, Roman goddesses . . . you know how it is. The three goddesses, who had undoubtedly been selected at random from the goddess pool, came equipped with the traditional mini-togas and in the matching pattern of blonde, redhead, and brunette that was *de rigeur* back in classical Rome whenever the goddesses got together to form a trio. Who amongst us can ever forget the wunnerful, wunnerful Cato Sisters? I took hold of the reins, as directed, and, as the cameras whirred, took the lovely ladies on a brisk spin around the fountains that cleanse the air in front of what is customarily referred to as "the plush $60-million resort hotel." Anything which costs over $50 million is entitled to be called plush. The Cato Sisters were entitled to be called either plush or statuesque according to the predilections of the viewer.

There's something about a chariot that brings the emperor out in you. Behind me, I could hear the roar of the Coliseum, the shout of the crowd, the smell of the greasepaint . . . No. By concentrating intently, I was just barely able to make out the voices of three goddesses scream-ing—in faultless blonde, brunette, and redhead—to let them out of there. Nothing I could do about that. I was only holding the reins. The tandem of horses kept charging around and around until somebody of greater authority than a one-legged emperor told them to stop.

I'll tell you all you have to know about a chariot. It's really just a ramp on wheels. You stand there, balancing your weight, and once you get the feel of it you have a sense of power that you can never get sitting on the old buckboard. By the time the date of the race was growing near, my ten-year-old daughter Lisa was staying with me, and we would wander down to the stable at the end of the day, hitch up a single horse to Caesar's chariot, which was in far better shape than the others, and take a delightful little ride into the cooling evening and the setting sun.

The MGM chariots had to be pretty well refurbished—cleaned and greased and painted. Before the final overhauling and tightening two days before the race, the wooden wheels were left to soak overnight in the infield pool, and, things being what they are these days, one of them was stolen. What anybody thought he was going to do with one wooden wheel I couldn't tell you. All I know is that John Tomasello had to jump into the station wagon and drive to New York to pick up a replacement, which, by what was probably sheer luck, fitted perfectly.

All right, we had the chariots. We still needed five teams of horses and some gallant charioteers. Let me tell you something: It isn't easy in these effete times to find horses that are accustomed to racing in chariot harness. After a search of the New England area had proved fruitless we decided that the logical thing to do was to call the copyright owners out in Hollywood. Hollywood referred us to an outfit in Staten Island that does most of the television commercials involving horses and stagecoaches and the like, plus a certain amount of stunt work for the movies. It came in with five teams of horses and worked out the proper harnessing techniques, which apparently require a far more delicate balancing of stresses for chariot racing than for a stagecoach operation.

The charioteers were no problem at all. The two closely connected questions we had asked ourselves were: (1) Whom could we get? (2) How could we get the most publicity out of them?

The local disk jockeys were the gallant group that came immediately to mind. Beyond the play on words, it had always been my experience that disk jockeys are willing to go for a kind of gag where they have to put themselves on the line. Partly, I suppose, because they are young, high-spirited fellows to begin with, but also because they seem to have a highly developed sense of competition, which may have something to do with the rating system. From a purely practical viewpoint, they have to fill so many hours of air time that they welcome the kind of promotion they can talk about for a couple of weeks. From an equally practical viewpoint, we welcomed the prospect of allowing them to fill it by saying "Suffolk Downs" a lot.

Anyway, we sent out the call and came up with ten intrepid volunteers. With only five chariots, we had decided to beef the program up by running two trial heats, with the winners then meeting each other head-to-head for the national Bun Hur championship. The final match race was going to be worth $1000, with $600 going to the winner. The other purses were scaled from $250 to the guys who finished second in the trial heats down to $100 for the ones who finished fifth. To be perfectly honest about it, I got the boys together and suggested that they pool the money and divide it up evenly, which would have come to $240 a man. No chance. Not my tigers. All ten of them wanted a shot at the big end of the purse.

We had scheduled the Ben Hur Handicap for the final week of the ninety-day meet to give our fans something to remember us by. Two nights before the race, we had the disk jockeys come in for a trial run around the track. Just to get the feel of the thing, I told them. That wasn't the only reason, though. The people from the Staten Island outfit, which was run by a guy named John Franzreb, had been warning us from the first that we were out of our heads if we thought a bunch of radio personalities were going to be able to handle a pair of horses that powerful. "I'm just going to tell you," the head guy kept saying, "these horses are going to be all over the track. It will be a miracle if you come out of it without a bad spill." Since the alternative was to have their stunt men do the actual driving while the disk jockeys stood alongside as sort of copilots, I wasn't sure I could accept this as a wholly dispassionate opinion. The disk jockeys didn't want any part of that kind of arrangement, anyway. My tigers were going to do their own chariot-driving.

Just to be on the safe side, though, I had told Franzreb's people to bring five of their own drivers down to stand by, just in case. And just as well. Those horses just took off—whooooooossssshhh—and ran away with the disk jockeys. A couple of the professional drivers told us afterward that the horses had been hyped up. For our own good, you know. To protect us, and to protect their horses. And, of course, they were right. Even with the professionals at the reins, we had to run the race clockwise instead of counterclockwise so they would have a straight run up the stretch after the race was over and on through the quarter-mile chute to get the horses back under control. The disk jockeys came back from the trial run ashen-faced and shaken. A couple of the more intrepid young men were still determined to go it alone, so they put it to a vote, and bravery was a big loser.

The promotion was a lot of fun. As the week of the great day dawned, we sent a telegram to Charlton Heston, the reigning champion, challenging him to defend his title. Heston wired back: "Sorry I can't be there to inaugurate your chariot program but in order to protect my unblemished record I only drive in fixed races."

The races themselves were a huge success. You can tell how well a promotion has gone over by how much it has cost you; i.e., in the percentage of fall-off in your concessions receipts. The heats were run after the second and fourth races, with the grand finale going off after the eighth. The moment the horns sounded forth to announce the entrance of the first charioteers, the concourse completely emptied and the spectators pressed down into the apron. We had worked very hard to create an atmosphere. The chariots paraded around the track to the accompaniment of the music from the *Ben-Hur* sound track. The charioteers, decked out in various forms of Roman costume and headgear, were standing, stiff and erect, as if they felt the eyes of the Emperor himself upon them. Frank Turner, the only Ogden man I became close to, getting into the spirit of things, had hired some girls to pass amidst the crowd, in flowing togas, with huge platters of grapes.

The extra drivers made the race even more exciting because they gave the disk jockeys a chance to crack their long whips as the chariots were careening around the turn, while the real drivers were handling the horses. As far as the competition was concerned, a certain pattern was uncovered. Caesar's chariot with its rubber tires simply went faster than the others, and whoever drew it won. Ken Carter of WRYT drew it for the second time in the final and was an easy winner over Don LaTulippe of WEZE. The fans loved it. The publicity was great. We got a six-column picture spread in *The New York Times,* and three- and four-column cuts all over the country.

The other extravaganza was built upon a historic event in which horses had also played some little part. The 94th anniversary of Custer's Last Stand was hard upon us, and how can any racetrack operator with the best interests of his customers at heart let a 94th anniversary pass unsung? The date itself wasn't too convenient. The actual anniversary date is June 26, which was to fall on a Friday. We could have held it the next day, of course, except that June 27 was the date of our big race of that year, the $75,000 Massachusetts Handicap, which we were presenting on the turf, over 1 1/2 miles, for the first time. (It was won by another import from France, this time with a French jockey. I have a feeling that if I do any traveling, I have some friends in France.) Since we were going all out to win a reputation as the foremost turf track in the country, I wanted to run a $35,000 turf stakes four Saturdays earlier as a kind of full-dress preview. A doubleheader was clearly indicated. The Custer Memorial Stakes could stand as a memorable promotion in itself while also serving as advance promotion for the Mass. Handicap.

Willy-nilly, that established the anniversary date as June 6. We were not going to be stubborn about it, though. Any historian who wanted to be a sorehead about it was perfectly entitled to speak his piece. The Indians were just beginning to become fashionable at that time, and I would have been filled with admiration for any academic willing to take the risk of caviling over the re-enactment of the most celebrated of their victories.

Purely academic was what the whole thing turned out to be. After all my juggling on the dates, I had fastened upon the only day that could have wiped us out. Oh, well, Custer's timing wasn't wholly beyond reproach either.

We put a little teaser in our advertisements. Like this:

> No kidding? Custer gets another chance?
> History may repeat itself. Might not, though.
> Who wins?
> Well, come on out and find out!

A teaser was all it was. There was no chance of doing it right unless we were able to enlist the aid of an Indian tribe which could provide a reasonable amount of authenticity this far from Montana, and so I had spent a full month lunching with the various Sachems of New England. The whole office had been hard at work for three months. Altogether, we spent more time preparing for this one event than was spent on all the other promotions put together. We weren't putting in all that time and effort to take the Indians' victory away from them. Neither were the Indians.

The Improved Order of Redmen of Massachusetts, representing twenty-nine tribes, was going to re-enact the battle of Little Big Horn, playing the parts of Custer's troopers as well as of Crazy Horse's Sioux warriors. The Redmen were so enthusiastic about it that they were constantly on the phone with new ideas. The Saturday before the race they came in for a final runthrough, and we went over the script for perhaps the tenth time. The night before the race they set up their Indian villages around the infield lagoon, complete with tepees and campfires and all the indicated utensils and paraphernalia. Would you believe that one of the tepees was stolen during the night. Again. If you should happen to run across a tepee with a wooden wheel sitting out front . . .

There were going to be a whole day's activities, with war dances and games for the kids during the early part of the program. The logistics alone were impressive. We had bought a batch of pogo sticks from Mike Holovak's sports store, and either bought or borrowed all manner of games and amusements. The Improved Order of Redmen sent us the waist sizes of the tribesmen who were going to play the parts of troopers, and we rented the cavalry uniforms from the Broadway Costume Company. We had a supply of salamanders and blankets for the sending of smoke signals. Salamanders, for those of you who have allowed your Indian lore to grow rusty, are the stovelike implements used in the Florida citrus fields to hold the frost off. We had also laid in a supply of wigs and headbands and—ahhh, civilization—make-up. The wigs had been bought (Jack's Trick Shop) in a lot of a hundred, which would leave us with all that were needed for ourselves and the waitresses. The waitresses eschewed the wigs and showed up with their own brightly colored headbands. Rudie looked uncannily like an Indian in his wig, though. An Indian squaw. To show how much guts I have, I had a full headdress for myself. I still looked like the lascivious barker for a carnival side show.

For the edification of the spectators, we had replicas of all the Seventh Cavalry flags. Courtesy of John Tomasello. The Tomasellos had been called in as usual (they kept the place standing) to coordinate the work that had to be done on the track, and John became so fascinated with the whole project that he volunteered to do the historical research. In addition to the regimental standard of the Seventh Cavalry (which had actually been left back in camp) and the cavalry guidon carried into battle, Custer had his own personal flag, cut in the shape of a fishtailed pennant. It had been designed by his wife: crossed white cavalry swords against a half-blue, half-red background), and he dutifully flew it above his command post and never failed to have it carried into battle. Whatever else you want to say about Custer, he was a good family man.

As the morning of Little Big Horn Revisited dawned, we were ready. Thirty-five horses, some of which the Indians were shipping over and some which we were renting, were to be vanned in from midmorning to early afternoon. We had arranged to corral them across the street in an abandoned driving range. Water and bales of hay were to be shuttled over on a time schedule that had already been worked out.

Forty-five chairs were to be set up on the infield between the flower bed and the tote board, for the Redman's Band of the Wahpatuck Tribe in Wakefield. Forty-five box lunches were to be distributed by the concessionaire as soon as the bandsmen were settled in. Plus sandwiches, milk, and—ugh—Cokes for the kids.

The re-enactment of the battle, which was to take place just before the running of the Custer Memorial Handicap, had been charted out on a minute-by-minute schedule, courtesy Rudie Schaffer. On an average Saturday, the seventh race went off at 4:42. The horses for the eighth race left the stable-area gap, headed for the paddock at 4:45, and began their parade to the post at 5:01. At a given signal at 4:00, the Indians were to leave the driving range and gather in the stable area. At the completion of the seventh race the Indians would proceed to the gap gate, follow the horses for the eighth race down to the paddock area, and continue on behind the clubhouse and into a clump of trees just below the clubhouse turn.

That would leave us with nine minutes to put on the battle.

As the band strikes up the tune of "Garry Owen," the cavalry song you have heard in a thousand movies, the troopers of Seventh Cavalry can be seen circling around the far side of the track. Immediately, an Indian brave goes galloping across the infield to the lagoon, leaps into the waiting canoe, and paddles across to the other side. He jumps onto one of the two pinto horses tied there and rides to the grove of trees to deliver the word to Crazy Horse.

In the village, Sitting Bull rises up, in full regalia, and begins to make his medicine. On the troopers ride, into the jaws of the impending disaster. Into the waiting ambush. At the propitious moment, the Indians come charging out through the opening we have cut in the fence, surround the cavalrymen, decimate their ranks, and to the steadily heightening strains of "Garry Owen," chase the survivors up the track.

The horses for the Custer Memorial Stake are now leaving the paddock to begin the parade to the post. At the completion of the race, while the horses are returning to the unsaddling area, a group of braves are carrying their prisoners back to the village and tying them to the stakes, which may not be historically accurate but serves the dramatic purpose of informing the spectators that the show isn't necessarily over. The Sachem of the Improved Order of Redmen of Massachusetts is in the winner's circle, we announce over the loudspeakers, to make the presentation. And that's the signal for Chief Crazy Horse, accompanied by an honor guard of his braves, to come charging down the stretch holding a yellow-haired scalp aloft on a long spear. As they gallop pass the winner's circle, the spear is dipped just enough so that the Sachem can grab the scalp and place it on top of the trophy before he hands it over to the owner of the horse that has won the Custer Memorial Stakes.

Early on the morning of June 6, it began to rain. It rained and it rained and it rained. And then it poured. An absolute deluge. The amazing thing was how many of the Indians showed up on schedule. They were so disappointed, especially the kids, that I waited as long as I could. At noon, the sun came out. We stepped onto the track, and it was a sea of mud. Right up to the ankles. The infield grass was sodden. The tepees were practically awash. There was nothing to do but call it off and assure them we'd do it next year. It wouldn't have been the same, though. The letdown had been too great. You can only work yourself up to that first fine peak of enthusiasm one time.

We were washed out, that's all. Custer should have been so lucky.

17

The Voracious Animal, Eating Itself Up

I had anticipated that my new career as a racetrack impresario would be the Cleveland Indians revisited. It turned out to be the St. Louis Browns revisited, only worse. During my final year of penance in St. Louis I did a lot of kidding about getting out of town one step ahead of the sheriff. Kidding was all it was, though. In St. Louis I was broke but I wasn't in debt. I never doubted for a moment that I was the master of my own destiny. At Suffolk Downs I was never able to kid myself, after the rug had been pulled out, that I was.

It wasn't any lack of knowledge about racing that did me in. It was a lack of knowledge about the refinements of high conglomerate financing. A conglomerate is a pyramiding of companies. When the pyramid collapsed, we were right there to be buried in the avalanche.

I had insisted upon absolute control of the operation of the racetrack, and I had it. What I hadn't been smart enough to do was define the financial relationship between Suffolk Downs and Realty Equities. This was still the parent company, and we were still a wholly owned subsidiary. As the parent company, once the hard times came, it had the power to drain us dry. When you don't have any money, students, finances become the controlling factor in operations.

I had been told that Morris Karp was a rampaging specimen of financial wizardry on the hoof, and by the time we were ready to open the gates to the customers I could see what a remarkable pay-as-you-go deal he had put together. Not for us. For him. The selling corporation, Eastern Racing, had $12 million in common stock outstanding, plus another $1,250,000 in preferred stock. Realty was paying Dave Haber, Joe Linsey, *et al.* $5 million in cash and/or shares of Realty Equities stock based upon the market price of $30 a share. Whatever unhappiness might have existed on the part of those innocent bystanders, and considering the deteriorating income of Suffolk Downs it was limited, turned to sheer ecstasy when the Realty stock went straight up to 36.

The principal attraction of Suffolk Downs from the point of view of a real-estate operator was that there wasn't an encumbrance of any sort on the plant. Karp's plan, which we fully understood, was that he would immediately mortgage the plant for $6 million; that is, he would take a bank loan on behalf of the track for $6 million, at half a point above the prime rate not to exceed 9 per cent. What that meant as far as our 10-per-cent override on the profits above $1 million was concerned was that we would be paying up to $540,000 in interest the first year and a smaller amount, as the principal was eaten away, for the next ten years. If you're wondering why that didn't bother us, you have forgotten that Nate and I were holding options to buy 30 per cent of the track. I will tell you now that those options were based upon the cash that was being put up, not the whole purchase price. We had a powerful personal stake in that loan. With leverage yet. It put us each in a position to gain 15-per-cent ownership very cheaply. Every payment we made would be decreasing a corporate debt and thereby increasing our equity in the track.

In addition to the interest on the loan, we were carrying Dave Haber on the payroll for $80,000 a year. Okay, that's almost a standard procedure in the purchase of a big company these days. We knew it was going to be part of the nut going in, and we could live with it. Soon enough, though, we discovered that in addition to the $1 million we would be paying the cities of Boston and Revere in real-estate taxes (where are you, Lady Godiva, now that we need you?) we were being hit with a holdover bill of about $275,000 in back taxes. That, we hadn't figured on. That, we didn't intend to live with. Nate Dolin was already renegotiating our contract. Realty agreed that the back taxes would be absorbed somehow in the renegotiation. You know something? That contract was in the process of being renegotiated from the day I arrived at Suffolk Downs till the day I left. Every time a new contract was just about ready to be agreed upon—which wasn't easy, considering Realty's incredibly complicated financial structure—Realty would take another slice out of us and Nate would have to start all over again.

I played no part in it. In the first weeks and months when we were trying to do a hundred things at once, I didn't even have time to think about it. The foremost concern in those hectic days, the concern that overrode everything else, was finding the best possible concessionaire. I was in the middle of it, with Nate, wherever I could be, trying to negotiate the best deal with four different companies. Including Jerry Jacobs of Sportservice, the concessionaire I really wanted. A concession as attractive as this one seldom comes up for grabs, and we were able to work out one of the best contracts on record, 40 cents a head for everybody who came into the track, including the horsemen. We were just about to close the deal when it suddenly developed that the irreducible part of any deal as far as Morris Karp and his attorney were concerned was that they be able to borrow $1,250,000 against an assignment of the concession contract, so that all receipts were sent directly to the bank instead of to us. Does that figure ring any bell for you? It should. The precise amount of money that was due in cash, for the preferred stock.

Let us pause for a moment to contemplate the sheer brilliance of the deal that Morris Karp has worked out for himself. He has paid for the common stock by mortgaging our plant and putting up some of his own stock, and he is now paying for the preferred stock by selling off our future concession receipts. *He has bought the track with nothing except paper—and paper was exactly what it turned out to be—and ended up with a cool million dollars in cash in the bargain.*

If the concession money had been going to pay off the kind of debt that would have increased our equity, I might not have minded quite so much. But it wasn't. It was merely to aquire the preferred stock that some of the shareholders held. As far as the effect on the track was concerned, they had taken away the main source of our operating money. As far as the effect on our override was concerned, they were now going to forget whatever basis had been set up for the first renegotiated contract and renegotiate another contract with Nate on this new basis.

With all that, I still didn't believe that Realty could be in any real financial difficulty. It seemed to me as if it was an example of a financial wizard unable to resist the opportunity of exercising his wizardry. Realty Equities was obviously a solvent outfit. Its stock was at an all-time high. Its theater subsidiary operated 78 moving-picture theaters, and it was building shopping centers, with theaters in all of them. It had a highly profitable subsidiary which invested in small businesses. It had an interest in a savings-and-loans association holding company. Its last statement had shown earnings of almost $1.3 million in a six-month period. A story in the *Wall Street Journal*, based upon an interview with Karp, pegged the estimated profits for the coming year "conservatively" at $4.5 to $5 million.

The fact, however, was that the first faint glimmer of trouble ahead had come as early as January 6, 1969, which by no coincidence at all was my first day on the job. Jerry Deutch, the Realty official we were most accustomed to deal with, had called to ask me to meet him at the First National Bank first thing in the morning. I discovered upon my arrival that I was there to help him arrange a $6-million loan. It gave me a pause because it could only mean that even with such solid collateral they hadn't been able to work out the financing with their own banks, in either New York or Texas. Or even perhaps (as I frankly didn't consider at that stage of the game and don't know for certain even now) they didn't want to show such solid collateral to their regular banks out of fear that it would be grabbed for some other loan that needed shoring up.

It gave me a pause, if you know what I mean, but not really. More accurately, it brought out the opportunist in me. If, in fact, Realty was momentarily strapped for money, I was going to protect myself. "You know," I said. "I'm not a cheap operator. I'm rather expensive, and I think there are a lot of things that should be done for this track. I would think the least we need is a three-quarters-of-a-million loan for improvements on top of whatever else you're negotiating about."

So they threw that on top of the $6 million, and when we got out Jerry said, "Don't worry, everything is fine." If you're operating a business in Boston, sound business practice dictates that Boston is the place to place your loan. *Yeah*, I thought, *but at the last minute?* I say I thought it. More accurately, the thought flitted through my mind. At any rate, I had not the slightest thought of pulling out. The announcement had been made two months earlier. I'd look like an idiot if I suddenly appeared to have changed my mind. I was there. There was nothing to do but make the best of it. And beyond all that, I suppose, this had happened on a day when I was mentally geared to swing back into action. I was eager to leave the money rooms behind and hustle over to the track to take over.

Now, we didn't draw as well as I had expected; let's concede that without qualm or quibble. As a direct result, in terms of the resultant overestimation of our handle, in accordance with our existing contract I overpaid the horsemen about $200,000. Our half of Berkshire Downs had cost us $275,000. Realty had insisted upon saving money by sending in their own insurance man and auditors. Instead of saving us anything, they cost us an extra $150,000. Add to that the back taxes, the payment to Dave Haber, the interest on the debt, and the money we weren't getting from the concessions, and more than $2 million was lopped off our income. With it all, we finished that first year with a net profit of $254,000. Under the circumstances, not so bad. I hadn't come in to grind out a small profit. The name of the game was the 15-per-cent ownership, and in order to win that game I had to increase the value of the track. Far from increasing in worth, the value of the track had been diminished. Well, the only thing to do was to work harder. The Berkshire Downs purchase would begin to pay off the next year with the 24 extra dates. With luck, we might be able to wipe out the entire debt on the concessions and begin the third year with a clean slate.

And then, before the second year got under way, Realty refinanced the $6 million on terms that were so onerous as to make our situation utterly hopeless. Realty did it without consulting me or, in fact, informing me. The loan had been negotiated in December, and I didn't learn about it for months. First, I will describe the deal it made on our behalf, and then I will explain how it had got itself in a situation where—to try to be fair—it had no other choice. What we are involved with here is the nature of conglomerates, the wonder stocks of the late sixties. Their Rise and Their Fall.

Realty Equity negotiated a $7.2 million loan with a Cleveland company, U.S. Realty, and paid off the $6 million to the Boston bank. In order to raise that $1.2 million in cash, it was paying interest of 13.5 per cent on the whole new loan *plus* 1 per cent per annum on all gross receipts from all business activities conducted on the premises of the track. That brought the actual interest rate to 15 per cent. On top of that, the interest was to increase or decrease by the amount the prime rate increased or decreased *not* from 13.5 per cent but from 8.5 per cent with the additional proviso that it could not under any condition drop below 12.5 per cent, although there was no limit whatsoever on the up side. On top of *that*, if the interest wasn't paid when due, it would go up to 16 per cent (which would make it actually 17.5 per cent). On top of *that*, the loan ran for only twenty months, with an option to renew for another six months, in which case the interest rate was to be increased by another 25 per cent of any increase of the prime rate over 8.5 per cent.

And on top of all that, and this is how I found out about it, nothing could be done to, with, or on the premises without the consent of the mortgagee.

I'm still not through. I said that Realty had done all this in order to raise $1.2 million. It wasn't even realizing that. Because the loan was running only twenty-six months, I was paying $186,000 to a Dallas bank for a back-up deal. In other words, the Dallas bank was guaranteeing to take over a portion of the loan when the Cleveland loan became due.

To recapitulate, Realty had paid back the $6 million on which it was paying 9 per cent (or $540,000) to realize less than $1 million. On the new deal the interest would come to a bare minimum of $1,080,000 annually. To break it down to the bottom line, it was paying an extra $540,000 interest for $1 million, a rate of 54 per cent.

A conglomerate is a company which, in the name of diversification, branches out into other fields, swallowing companies whole. Ideally, the conglomerate takes control of companies which are in roughly similar, or supportive fields of endeavor and have been operating profitably on their own. An exchange of stock takes place, and no money changes hands. The existing management, having demonstrated that it knows its business, stays on, the president joins the board of directors of the parent company, and the new company can call upon the expertise and unlimited funds that are now available to it. International Telephone and Telegraph is the textbook example of a brilliantly run conglomerate. Like all conglomerates, it is a voracious animal. But it does not digest its children.

That's the successful conglomerate. The kind which has survived. There are not, however, that many profitable, solidly run companies waiting around and willing to be gobbled up. The other way to build a conglomerate is to absorb companies which are not so successful. In good times, when the money is easy and the economy is booming, anybody who knows how the game is played and has the energy to play at it can become a financial genius.

By the nature of its existence, a conglomerate is an animal on the prowl; it is always hungry. As it swallows new companies, it is in continuous need of money. Where do you go when you are in need of money? To a bank, of course. What does the rampaging conglomerate put up for collateral? With less favorably situated acquisitions than Suffolk Downs, it puts up its stock. It is possible to secure a loan of $1 million by putting up, say, $2 million worth of stock which is selling at 36. It is possible to do almost anything when you are buying on a rising market with paper.

When the money stops flowing, it's a different ball game. And it had already stopped flowing when we came to Suffolk Downs. In retrospect, it would have been difficult to find a worse time in recent history than the period between January 1969 and January 1971, the two years of our stewardship. The deal had been consummated, to all purposes, when I came to Suffolk Downs in mid-November, two weeks after the election of Richard Nixon. I took over the reins in January, almost concurrently with Nixon's entry into the White House. By the time we opened in April, the Federal Reserve Bank was already in the first phase of what was to be a gradual tightening down on the money supply.

As money tightens, investors take their money out of the stock market. Particularly out of highly speculative stocks like Realty Equities. As money tightens, the economy weakens, and the companies that have been operating marginally during the good times are wiped out. Morris Karp had been laying his healing touch upon some sick companies— Hazel Bishop, a talent agency, a construction company—and as they became shakier and in some cases went under, the weakness of the parent company could no longer be hidden from public view.

As money tightens, the banks are no longer throwing money at you; they are looking you over very carefully. They are also looking over the collateral they are holding. And right here is where you have the fatal weakness of conglomerate-building. As your stock goes down, the bank doesn't have the loan covered any more. By the time it hits 20, the bank is already calling for more solid collateral. If you'd had more solid collateral, even back there in the flush times, you probably wouldn't have been putting up the paper. All you can cover it with is money, and the requirements of raising that money in a tight money market weaken the company further, which drives the stock down lower, which brings on another demand from the bank, which . . . well, the voracious animal has now turned inward and is eating off itself.

Until you find yourself in a spot where you are paying 54 per cent interest for $1 million. Back in the days of the Kennedy recession, Bill Zeckendorf, having astonished financial circles by paying 13 per cent for short-term loans, put it very simply: "I'd rather be alive at 13 per cent than dead at prime rates."

Morris Karp quite obviously had needed $1 million to stay alive. In truth, however, the fact that there still is a Realty Equity must give him a legitimate claim to being a wizard.

The stock continued to go down, down, down. When the auditors first refused to complete its financials and then refused to certify its balance sheet, the American Exchange suspended trading and the stock plummeted down to 2. The age of wizardry had come to an end for Morris Karp. Until, at least, somebody dreams up a new road to the castle. As, no doubt, somebody will. In the interim, a lot of geniuses have been shaken out of the weeds.

Caught in the debacle were all those stockholders who had been given Realty stock for their old Eastern Racing stock and had not sold it. And don't think we didn't hear from them. Particularly from one stockholder who had something like 30,000 shares. If you want to hear how unhappy a man can be, talk to a man who suddenly finds himself in possession of $60,000 worth of stock where $1 million used to be. The truth was that his stock wasn't even worth $60,000. Anybody who had tried to dispose of 30,000 shares of Realty stock on the over-the-counter market would have been very fortunate indeed to find a buyer willing to give him much more than $30,000.

All I could tell him was that I was in the same boat. As, in more ways than one, I was. For if I had been in a position to pick up an occasional clue of weakness, I had also been in a position to satisfy myself that the over-all condition of the company was quite secure. The first faint clue had come at the First National Bank in Boston that day. The next clue came when Larry Lane called us in early September, shortly after the commission's appeal on the kids suit had been turned down. It had just come to the commission's attention, we were told, that $30,000 had been taken out of our OUTS account, as it is called in the vernacular of the trade, at the First National Bank back in July. The account is a special account for the money that hasn't been claimed on winning tickets. According to the law, a winning ticket can be cashed at any time during the year of the bet or the entire following calendar year. After that, the money goes over to the Commonwealth. Under the circumstances, we were worried enough about possible retaliation that we checked into the matter very carefully and discovered that Realty had withdrawn the money, without telling us a word about it, and returned it eleven days later. That gave us something new to worry about. If Realty had needed $30,000 for ten days that badly, we felt that it would be an excellent idea to send to New York for its balance sheet. Joel and I have both read a few balance sheets in our time, and Joel is an expert. It showed a balance of something just under $20 million. Fine. Not fine, with a sigh of relief, though. Fine with a shrug. The fact of the matter was that the balance sheet was so profusely decorated with acquisitions and so tangled in footnotes as to be wholly incomprehensible. To say that the investing public has full disclosure because a corporation has to distribute that kind of gobbledygook to its shareholders is sham, fakery, and balderdash.

It wasn't until the desperado figures of the refinancing were spread out in front of me that I was in any position to appreciate that my ship had been shot out from under me. I suppose, looking back, that I could have called a press conference, cried rape, and whisked myself out of town with no more than a slight blemish on my reputation. It never occurred to me to walk away. I mean, how do you walk away from a sinking ship? There were stockholders to protect. There were creditors to protect. And, most important of all, there was my 15 per cent to protect. The only way out of it for everyone concerned, it seemed to me, was to stay on, keep the banners flying, and protect my interests by trying to find a purchaser.

I was sure Realty would be in a mood to sell, if only because there was nothing left to milk. Once again, I had underestimated the resourcefulness of Morris Karp. There was one place, it seemed, where Realty's credit was still good. The First National Bank of Boston. Realty had, after all, paid back the original $6 million within a year. It had repaid the money we had borrowed to buy Berkshire Downs. And so, although it still owed the $400,000 Jerry Deutch had borrowed to take care of me, they were able to pick up another half-million on a short-term note.

We also had our cash flow, the daily receipts that went from the track to the bank. Realty dipped delicately into our general bank account a couple of times and "borrowed" $385,000. The difference between borrowing and taking consists, in its entirety, of a promise that it will be paid back.

It wasn't until I had worked out a deal with a potential buyer, though, that I was able to appreciate the full scope of Morris Karp's genius. The deal couldn't be closed, I discovered, because the stock couldn't be delivered. Broke as we were, insolvent and overextended and mortgaged to the ears, Morris Karp had managed to pull another $4 million out of our barely breathing body by putting up the stock itself as collateral for a weird second mortgage. Including the 30 per cent in which we had an option. *Our* 30 per cent.

Long before that, Realty was somewhat late on the payment of a Boston loan, and the First National Bank had grabbed all our money. All of a sudden, our checks were bouncing all over the place. Creditors were popping up on every corner. Good, solid, dearly beloved creditors who were as essential to our operation as Ma Bell and Pa Gas. To say nothing of an old Dutch uncle known around the racetrack only as the Revere Police Department. Our arrangement with the Revere police called for them to pay the policemen who were assigned to patrol the track and for us to reimburse them. There is something that is very funny about having a check to the Police Department bounce. The first time. The interest payments to U.S. Realty were in arrears too, of course, and their guy, Eddie Ginsberg, was on the horn every day expounding his quaint notion that we should send him the money Realty owed him. "Boy, have you got a wrong number," I'd tell him. "Why don't you call Morris Karp?"

"Because Karp always tells me the money will be in the next mail and it never comes."

He was lucky. In answer to our plea to pay back enough of what it had borrowed from us to allow us to pay our bills, Realty sent us a check for $75,000. I whipped a check of our own right over to the Revere Police Department, and it bounced so high this time that if I had dropped it on the floor it would have set a new record for the steeplechase. So I called New York and they said they'd send me another check for $75,000.

"Look," I said. "Send me $5000. Send me $10,000. Send it in tens and twenties if you have to. Send it a dollar at a time, I don't care. Just send me something that will clear. Holy smokes, if I give these cops one more bad check they're going to raid the joint."

To get their attention, I'm reminding them that if we go down they're going to go right down with us. And all during this same time I'm back and forth with a fellow named Nesbitt at the bank. "Please don't bounce any more checks," I'm pleading. "We've got all the troubles we need over here. If we go bankrupt, you blow your money. I'm trying to get us all out of this thing. Give me a little room."

He was always very sympathetic. They weren't really trying to annoy me, he would assure me. They were only trying to get some money out of the people in New York who kept promising to send something in the next mail, only they never did. Which shows, I suppose, that people who work with millions can be just as silly as people who deal in dimes.

At last, with the telephone and the gas company threatening to cut off our service, Realty sent us a check which cleared. It was as close as that.

18

Envoi

What happens after you have passed through a time when you're in danger of having your telephone and gas turned off is that a feeling of insecurity settles over your operation. Fortunately for me, the people in the office were great. Better, in certain instances, than I deserved. I had, for instance, misjudged the capabilities of our treasurer, Walter Harrison. Harrison is a tall, thin, quiet fellow with the kind of neat good looks that makes a man seem far younger than he is. I had known that he was an able enough fellow. I had taken a certain lack of self-assertiveness as an indication that both his talent and his ambition were limited to books and figures. It wasn't until the end, when the creditors were swarming all over us, that I came to see that this was a guy who really stood up under pressure. All the more impressively because it was so distasteful to him. He had never before been in a position where he had to lie. It went against the grain. After it was too late, I realized that Walter had the strength and the broad grasp of day-to-day operations to have taken a good part of the load off Rudie's shoulders.

We had the kind of general business office you would expect from a company which had a payroll of eight hundred people and was in communication with the public. Bookkeepers, payroll clerks, IBM card operators, mailers. They had been working there for years. Most of them knew more than I did about running a racetrack, and they knew it. In no time at all, however, we succeeded in establishing a feeling of camaraderie that had never been there before. It's a funny thing. When everybody truly believes they're in something together, the petty jealousies and jockeying for position disappear. Few opportunities for throwing a party were left unseized. Not with Evie Johnson around, they weren't. And whenever anybody back there was getting married, they could be sure Ol' Will would come wandering through with a bucket of champagne.

The first year, we had thrown a Christmas party that had been talked about in hushed voices for months. I will draw a merciful veil over the activities (real or imagined) of the others. Suffice it to say that Nick dragged me out and poured me onto the plane while the party was still going strong because he was so stoned himself that he thought it advisable to get us both home. Suffice it to say that I cleverly tippytoed back down the ramp, gave him time to drive home, and then kept calling him every fifteen minutes with new reasons why he should come back and get me.

The next Christmas it was all gloom. We had run the most successful meet in the history of New England, and for the first time in my life I wasn't going to be able to hand out any Christmas bonuses. I can't remember when I was so low. All I wanted to do was to get home and spend the long holiday season with my family. A night later, while I was talking to Rudie, he mentioned casually that Nick and Connie Del Ninno were going to have a party for the whole crew at their house. Just so they could all get together and cheer each other up. "We'll have it at the track," I said grimly. "I'm coming back."

In some ways it was the best Christmas party I've every attended. In some ways it was the worst. What they had decided to do was to thumb their noses at poverty by making it a kind of Christmas scavanger-hunt. For gifts, they scraped up everything that had been left over from any of the promotions, with an occasional item of no expense thrown in here and there to fit a gag to a particular person.

Walter Harrison, for instance, was given a pair of drawers with dollar signs painted all over them, to signify he had the financial shorts. The assistant treasurer, Frank Durante, got three dozen doughnuts. No, not to signify that our financial statement was made up of nothing but zeros. Frank was in charge of buying the doughnuts for the early-morning coffee break. We were so far gone that petty cash had run out, and Frank had been springing for the doughnuts.

The payroll clerk was given a gift certificate entitling him to a copy of *Thirty Tons a Day* on the day of publication, "to keep him well supplied with something to dish out."

John Tomasello got one of the pogo sticks left over from Custer's aborted Stand to help him make his rounds around the track, now that gas was short.

The younger girls in the office were given mistletoe and stuffed toy poodles as tributes to their undoubted beauty, and Nick got an old-fashioned curling iron to beautify and pamper his hair—in the happy event that it should ever grow back.

As the festivities were coming to a close, Santa presented me with the only gift that had cost anything. A $30 piranha. Our old piranha, which I had brought up from Maryland to grace the clubhouse fishtank, had jumped out of the tank in a fit of unfishly exuberance one night and expired of parched fins. The new one was in a water-filled plastic bag so that I could take it home with me.

"Well," I said, "I'm headed back to New York, and I've never known of a piranha that couldn't eat a Karp." It was the best line I could muster on short notice, and to show how kindly everybody was feeling, it got a good laugh.

In addition to the gifts, Santa had a stack of gag telegrams, typed up on real telegram forms. The pay-off in every case came with the reading of the name of the presumed sender.

The first one was to me: CLOSING BIG DEAL INVOLVING TRADE OF FOURTH MORTGAGES ON TWO UNDERWATER PROPERTIES. PREVENTS MY NOT ATTENDING YOUR FESTIVE OCCASION. HAPPY CHANUKAH.
     MORRIS KARP

Walter Harrison's telegram read: SENDING YOU CHECK STOP I MEAN STOP PAYMENT ON CHECK STOP AFFECTIONATELY YOURS.

It was signed by David Golden, the Treasurer of Realty.

I also had a telegram from B. A. Dario: RUNNING TODAY STOP YOUR CHRISTMAS PARTY UNFAIR COMPETITION AS I ONLY HAD 183 DAYS RACING AND DON'T GET BACK INTO ACTION UNTIL NEW YEAR'S DAY.

Nick's telegram came from Ken Harrelson on behalf of his restaurant, the 1800 Club, where we frequently went for lunch and where Nick airily signed the tabs: LOOKING FORWARD TO SEEING YOU AGAIN SOON STOP VIA THE ACCOUNTING DEPARTMENT.

The final telegram was to me, too:

    WE KNOW IT'S BEEN TRYING
    A DIFFICULT YEAR
    WE'RE HOPING AND PRAYING
    A SOLUTION IS NEAR

MAY YOU HAVE FUN
HOLDING THE LINE
AND AFTER YOU'VE WON
WE'LL BREAK OUT THE WINE

THE WHOLE GANG

It was the most difficult moment I have ever gone through in my life, and at the same time the most moving. They were telling me that they understood. They were telling me that whether or not better days came, we'd had a grand time while it lasted. There's a way that success, and only success, can tie people together. There's a way that hard times bring people together, too. Success is bubbly champagne, and champagne is better. But, you know, it just may be that hard times laughed away comes a lot closer to what Christmas is all about. I'm not recommending it. It's bittersweet. There's this about bittersweet, though. It sticks to your mind.

I had to stand there and spread out my hands and say, "I'm sorry. . . . I've never been in this position. For the first time in my life, I don't have anything to give you." It's a terrible blow to your ego, but I had to say it. You can tell yourself it doesn't really matter. And yet, it does. You can tell each other that this is what Christmas is really all about. And still, it wounds you. Through no fault of their own, the cupboard was bare. All I could say was that their loyalty and support had not gone unnoticed. "Just maybe I'll come walking back down the pike one day and illustrate how much I appreciate it."